PENGUIN ANANDA

IN SEARCH OF ONENESS

Moosa Raza, retired from the IAS, is a polyglot and a respected scholar of Islam. He has been principal secretary to the chief minister of Gujarat, chief secretary in Jammu and Kashmir, an adviser to the Governor of Uttar Pradesh and secretary to the Government of India in the Cabinet Secretariat and in the ministry of steel. Currently, he is the chairman of the South Indian Educational Trust (SIET), which runs six educational institutions, and of the Executive Committee of Coastal Energen Pvt. Ltd. In 2010, he was honoured with the Padma Bhushan. He lives with his wife in Chennai.

MOOSA RAZA

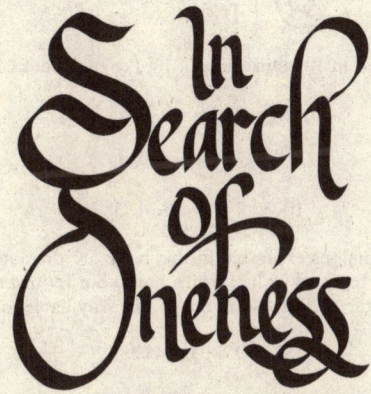

In Search of Oneness

The Bhagavad Gita
and the
Quran through Sufi Eyes

PENGUIN
ANANDA

An imprint of Penguin Random House

PENGUIN ANANDA

USA | Canada | UK | Ireland | Australia
New Zealand | India | South Africa | China | Singapore

Penguin Ananda is part of the Penguin Random House group of companies
whose addresses can be found at global.penguinrandomhouse.com

Published by Penguin Random House India Pvt. Ltd
4th Floor, Capital Tower 1, MG Road,
Gurugram 122 002, Haryana, India

First published in Penguin Ananda by Penguin Books India 2012

ISBN 9780143417835

Typeset in Adobe Garamond by R. Ajith Kumar, New Delhi

Printed at Repro India Limited

'To God belongs the East and the West. To whichever direction you turn, you face the countenance of God. For God is All Embracing and All Knowing . . . Say call "Allah" or call "ar-Rahman", whatever the name you call, to Him belong the most beautiful names.'
—Quran 2:115; 17:110

Contents

Acknowledgements

I would not have been able to complete this book without the assistance of my family: Jafar, Shahla, Gazala, Maliha and my wife, Husnara. Smruthi's help was of great value, especially in the Sanskrit quotes. At Penguin, Kamini was always a pillar of support and Shruti took the book to the final stage.

Introduction

In the aftermath of the destruction of the twin towers in New York in 2001, there was a wave of anti-Muslim feelings all over the world. Its momentum has not abated yet. The pogroms in Gujarat in February–March 2002, subsequent to the earlier event, led to anti-Muslim and anti-Islamic feelings in some sections of the Indian society. There were even discussions about finding a final solution to the 'Muslim problem'. Sometime during 2002, I was approached by Ms Sudhamahi Regunathan, the then vice chancellor of the Jain Vishva Bharati University of Rajasthan, in a rather perturbed state of mind. As a believer in the Jaina concept of Anekantvad, she felt that the misunderstandings that existed between various religions, especially among the elite of India, require to be actively addressed. She wondered if I would be willing to address a group of senior executives of various corporate houses in Delhi and professors from other universities and talk to them about Islam. I gave a series of three lectures on Islam in the auditorium of the National Museum in Delhi. Since the audience consisted almost entirely of non-Muslims, mostly Hindus, my lectures necessarily placed Islam and its founder in the context of India, Hinduism, the Vedas, the Upanishads, the Bhagavad Gītā and the great epics of India. I also touched briefly on the Sufi interpretation of Islam and the role the Sufis played in the religious life of Islam. Sudhamahiji, I am told, later produced a CD based on these lectures.

Since I had quoted profusely from the Bhagavad Gītā and the Sufi texts to explain the basic beliefs, the philosophy and mysticism of Islam, she later wondered whether I would be willing to give a lecture on the Bhagavad Gītā to another set of people. I was quite reluctant to do so as I believed, and continue to believe, that my knowledge of the Gītā is not of a level worth exposing to the scholarly and the erudite. However, she somehow persuaded me and I gave a lecture on the Gītā with the title 'The Bhagavad Gītā and I'. I chose this title to make it clear that I was planning to speak on the Gītā on the basis of my personal encounter with that song and with some of the people who had integrated its teachings in their personal lives. The title helped me escape any criticism of my lack of in-depth knowledge of the great book.

Many friends who heard the lecture later wanted me to expand it, giving more details of the encounters which could not be covered in a one-hour lecture. That was how this book was conceived.

***

It is very unfortunate that though the Hindus and the Muslims in India have been living together for more than a thousand years,[1] knowledge about each other's religious books is often absent and, if present, it is generally superficial. After Al Beruni's book on India, the *Kitab-al-Hind*, and the fourteen chapters he devoted to the Indian religions, hardly any Muslim writer has studied Sanskrit and read the Hindu texts in the original. Similarly, I am yet to come across a Hindu writer who is capable of writing authoritatively on Islam and the Islamic texts—the Quran and the Hadith in particular. European scholars have devoted considerable attention to Islam and its religious texts as well as to Hinduism and its texts. They have produced well-researched and erudite works for at least over a hundred years. Sometimes, of course, their gaze is orientalist, in the sense that Edward Said meant it. Even so, of late, I have noticed this attitude changing. My effort here is to clear the misunderstandings around the two great books of Indian religions—the Bhagavad Gītā and the Quran. My deep study of these books and related literature has shown me that instead of typifying Samuel Huntington's classic clash of civilizations, they are so close to each other, both in spirit and in language, that they promote a sense of unity rather than of separation.

The famous Dr Hans Kung, professor of ecumenical theology and president of the Global Ethic Foundation, writes:

No peace among nations
without peace among the religions.
No peace among the religions
without dialogue between the religions.
No dialogue between the religions
without investigation of the foundations of the
religions.[2]

The establishment of global peace demands an understanding and a civilized dialogue among religions, especially among the great religions of the world.

This book is a small attempt to understand the foundations of these two great religions—their followers constitute one-third of the world's population—which have been investigated by the savants of both. It would be too much to claim that there are no differences between the religions. Islam is distinct from the other religions, with its own beliefs, rituals and customs and so are Hinduism and Christianity. For that matter, so are Confucianism, Taoism, Judaism, Zoroastrianism and the other religions of the world. However, a civilized and rational approach to all these religions throws up the fact that they all have a common denominator. It therefore behoves us to recognize the dignity of difference, as Jonathan Sachs would have it, and move towards that underlying denominator.

The word 'tolerance' has been much abused in the last few decades. Everybody preaches that we must tolerate Islam, Hinduism, Christianity, Judaism and so on. The word 'tolerance' implies that there is something unpleasant which requires to be tolerated, with forbearance and patience. In the present context, when tensions mark the relationship between various religions, this word has become outmoded. What is required is not tolerance but respect for each other, born out of understanding and appreciation. This is a much higher level of understanding than mere tolerance. Hindus and Muslims of India especially must recognize, understand, appreciate and respect the religious texts of each other.

One is reminded of what Ghalib said in one of his Persian verses, more than a century and a half ago.

Sar az hijab-e-táyyun agar berun aayad
Cheh jalwaha keh b'har kish mitawan kardan.
If man were to come out of the self-limiting veil that covers his eyes, what glorious revelations he will see in every faith.

This book therefore seeks to inculcate that feeling of respect for each other's beliefs and thoughts which the sages, rishis and Sufis have tried to over centuries.

***

The Bhagavad Gītā, one of the significant religious texts of the Indian subcontinent, has been read, paraphrased, expounded on and translated many times by Islamic scholars, beginning with Al Beruni, whose paraphrases of the Gītā sound almost like a commentary on the Quran, to Abdur Rahman Chishti's commentary on the Gītā. Chishti claims the text to be Krishna explaining to Arjuna, by analogy, the secrets of *tawhid*—the oneness of God. 'To God belongs the East and the West. To whichever direction you turn, you face the countenance of God. For God is All Embracing and All Knowing,'[3] says the Quran. 'Call "Allah" or call "ar-Rahman", whatever the name you call, to Him belong the most beautiful names.'[4] Much earlier, the Rig Veda had said 'ekam sat, vipra bahuda vadanti'—truth is one and the wise call it by many names.[5]

There have been many translations of the Gītā in Urdu, mostly in prose. I have even read a paraphrased version of the book in Arabic. However, my coming across Dil Mohammad's translation in verse was an altogether different experience. It was obvious that he had translated the Gītā into Urdu verse not because he was trying to convey a message. It was not a tour de force. Dil Mohammad was obviously deeply impressed by the message of the Gītā and touched by the lessons taught to Arjuna by Krishna. The simple words—a mixture of Urdu and Hindi—used by Dil Mohammad and a rhythmic flow he maintained in the rhyming verses impressed me no end. I read out passages from his translation to a number of my friends who were equally impressed and subsequently bought copies of their own to read.

So, apart from citing Sanskrit and English passages, I shall be using Dil's Urdu translation extensively, for it is a translation done with the heart, not with the mind. Perhaps some of my readers who know Urdu would be encouraged to read the Gītā, if the passages cited in this long essay touch their hearts.

Learning to Believe

As the road wound its way down the dry and dusty plains of the district, I leaned back in the old Chevrolet, thankful that I could enjoy the comfort of air conditioning, rather than suffer the brunt of the summer heat in my own open jeep. Air conditioning was a luxury in the 1970s and only a few got to enjoy it.

We had just left Navsari, a small town in the north of the district of Bulsar (now Valsad), in Gujarat and had travelled a few miles down the highway towards Bulsar town, the district headquarters. As a signpost marking the distance to the next village flashed past, the khadi-clad, rather diminutive-looking gentleman sitting next to me in the car leaned over and softly whispered in my ear, 'Collector saheb, will you please stop the car when you see the signpost for Chikhli? I have to get off there.'

I assumed that my companion perhaps wished to use the washroom, so I told him that a few miles further on from the Chikhli signpost, there was a dak bungalow of the public works department where he could wash his hands.

'No, no. I do not need to go to a dak bungalow. I have to get off at the Chikhli turning because, three miles to the east, there is a small village where my friend and fellow freedom fighter lives. You know Maganlalbhai. He lost his old father recently and I want to offer him my condolences,' he said.

'Then you take my jeep to go to the village, sir,' I suggested.

'No, no,' he protested. 'I am going on a private visit. I cannot use an official car.'

The time was just over two decades after India's independence. I was then serving as district magistrate in Gujarat. The gentleman with me was Babubhai Patel, then cabinet minister for the public works department, later to become chief minister of Gujarat. The third occupant of the car was the Governor of Gujarat, Shriman Narayan, who had served as a secretary to Mahatma Gandhi in his ashram at Wardha.

We were on our way back after a function held to felicitate the octogenarian Mitthuben Petit. She was from an affluent Parsi family of Bombay (now Mumbai), but when she came under the influence of Mahatma Gandhi, she abandoned her comfortable life, decided never to get married and, giving up all her material possessions, became his follower. She lived in the Sabarmati Ashram, performing many of the menial chores required to maintain it. The Mahatma was a hard taskmaster. He insisted that the inmates of the ashram should perform all chores, however lowly, themselves.

At his behest, she even left him to serve the poor, the downtrodden and the oppressed, especially the tribals and the landless labourers known as dublas. She set up an ashram in Navsari even before Independence and spent her wealth on their health and education. After Independence, the government helped her in her social activities by honouring her with visits of its ministers and other dignitaries rather than with any concrete financial assistance.

The previous evening, I had travelled to Navsari in my open jeep—for that was the only vehicle provided to district magistrates by a frugal state government—from my headquarters in Bulsar and called on Mitthuben to inform her that Governor Shriman Narayan and his wife Madalsaben had decided to visit the town on the occasion of her birthday.

The Governor and his wife arrived, accompanied by Babubhai

Patel as minister-in-waiting. Babubhai was a simple man, wore only a khadi kurta and dhoti, was a strict vegetarian and always spoke in soft and measured tones. He had been to jail with Gandhiji during the freedom struggle, a singular honour in the post-Gandhian era.

After the felicitation function, the Governor and his entourage were all set to visit Bulsar for another official engagement and, at his behest, I travelled with him in his air-conditioned car. Only Governors enjoyed this luxury in those days and I had welcomed his invitation to join him and escape the hot winds of summer. I sat in the middle, with the Governor on one side and Babubhai on the other, Madalsaben having stayed back to spend some time with Mitthuben and to meet with the inmates of the ashram.

Now, as we travelled back towards Bulsar in the car, His Excellency who had overheard part of the conversation with keen curiosity interjected, 'In that case Babubhai, since you are going to visit a freedom fighter to condole the death of his father, we will accompany you.'

'I am sorry, sir,' said Babubhai. 'That will not only disturb the whole village, it will also certainly embarrass me. I would not like the villagers to feel that I am trying to overawe them by bringing a Governor with a convoy of cars on a condolence visit.'

In the end, the car was stopped. Babubhai got off on the simmering highway and walked to the distant village in the burning sun, his khadi bag slung over his shoulder. He refused any kind of escort.

I have told this story of Babubhai many a time to diverse audiences. Babubhai established a role model, which influenced a whole generation of junior politicians and civil servants in Gujarat—a model of integrity, non-use of public property for personal purposes and scrupulously observing the rules of propriety.

As I watched him trudge up the village road, back straight, his simple dhoti and kurta stark white in the bright sun, words from the Bhagavad Gītā came to my mind:

> *yad yad ācarati śreṣṭhas tat tad evetaro janaḥ*
> *sa yat pramāṇaṁ kurute lokas tad anuvartate*[1]
> Whatever a great man does is followed by others; people go by the example he sets.

It therefore casts a great responsibility on those who are leaders of a society and of a community. Such people, whom the common people hold in great regard and respect, have to set an example of morality, integrity and probity, both in public and in private in this world, where we are all living in glass bowls like goldfish, for nothing passes unnoticed.

Why was I, a Muslim civil servant, reminded of the Gītā as I watched Babubhai walking away on the village road? Some may wonder—what does this man know of the Bhagavad Gītā? In fact, I have asked myself how I came to the Gītā.

I was born into an orthodox Muslim family. My parents were simple folk, who rose early in the morning, performed their ablutions, prostrated themselves on the prayer mat and got engaged in their daily chores. They did not concern themselves ever with questions like the meaning of life, of existence, of the problems of good and evil, and such other scholarly issues. They did not go into the minutiae of Islamic law but lived their lives according to its dictates. They lived a simple life, gave to charity whenever and whatever they could spare, and brought up their children to be hardworking students and good, decent citizens. My mother, Aasiya Begum, especially encouraged me to read books. She herself knew hundreds of Urdu couplets by heart and readily produced an apt one for every occasion. Often, I saw her deny herself dinner to feed a hungry beggar woman knocking on the door at an untimely hour.

By the time I finished high school, I had read most classics in English and Urdu—from Walter Scott and Alexandre Dumas on the one hand to Shakespeare, Wordsworth, Keats and others on the other. I had also read *Dastan-e-Amir Hamza, Qisas-al-Anbiya, Gul-e-Bakavali, Chahar Dervish, Hatim Tai* and so on. But my knowledge of the Quran was limited to learning the necessary suras or chapters by rote in Arabic and reciting them in my prayers five times a day. Since I had taken Arabic as my second language in high school, I could understand the basic meaning of these suras unlike my parents and most other fellow practitioners of Islam.

In high school I was introduced to astronomy and physics by my teachers. I read Sir James Jean's *Mysterious Universe, The Universe around Us* and his provocative *Physics and Philosophy* as well as Sir Arthur Eddington's *Expanding Universe* and George Gamow's book on Einstein's theory of relativity, *One Two Three, Infinity*. I also read Alfred North Whitehead, Bertrand Russel's *Essays on Rationalism*, Kant's *Critique of Pure Reason*, Schopenhauer, etc. Some of them were the precursors of Stephen Hawking and Richard Dawkins. 'A little philosophy inclineth man's mind to atheism,' wrote Francis Bacon in his essays, 'but depth in philosophy bringeth men's mind about religion.' Bacon, of course, meant science when he used the word 'philosophy', for in his day the word 'science' was not current in the sense in which it is used today. Shakespeare, a contemporary of Bacon, too used the word 'philosophy' in the same sense when he made Hamlet say, 'There are more things between heaven and earth, Horatio, than are dreamt of in your philosophy.' So my little philosophy was certainly inclining me to doubt and I did not have the depth to bring my mind 'about religion'. I was yet to realize the things that were there between heaven and earth which were not dreamt of by science.

By the time I reached the first year of college, I was starting to ask inconvenient questions. My little learning was leading me to start questioning my own basic beliefs. Who am I? Who created this huge universe? If the universe came into existence as a result of a Big Bang and is a self-regulating mechanism, what is the position of God in this whole scheme of things? If God is powerful enough to create this universe and everything in it, why did He create such an imperfect universe? If God is all good, why does He suffer evil in this world?

Over time, such questions led my immature mind to doubt the basic premises of religion altogether. I became an agnostic by the end of that first year. I gave up going to the mosque, fasting and other ritual observances. I did not remain a mere passive doubter. Whenever I saw friends returning from the mosque after their prayers, I would buttonhole them, like the Ancient Mariner, and remonstrate with them for wasting their time in such infructuous pursuits, instead of applying themselves to the acquisition of useful knowledge. I used to argue passionately with friends and strangers in defence of my rationalism and even wrote poems to propagate my newly acquired agnosticism. I can now recall only a couplet of a long Urdu poem that I wrote at the time:

Besood hai dua ko utthaye na koyee haath,
Ek neelgun fareb hai yeh, aasmaan naheen.
It is fruitless. Let no one lift up his hands skywards in prayer.
It's only a blue illusion, not the Heavens.

Whenever I saw my mother perform her ritual ablutions before her daily prayers, I would be amused; and whenever I found her reciting the Quran very devotedly in the early dawn, without understanding a word of it, I would be irritated.

I realized later that my loss of faith and my active exhibition of it was only an outward manifestation of an inner struggle. If there is no God, is it necessary to invent one as Voltaire asked? Or are His sanctums mere refuges to our despair, as Ghalib laments?

Dayr-o-haram aayinae takraar-e-tamanna
Wamandagiye shauq tarashe hai panahain.
The temple and the mosque are but mirrors of insistent desire. It is the helplessness of longing that has carved out these refuges.

Ghalib, the nineteeth-century poet, is considered the greatest Urdu poet of India. His poetry reflects a baffling mix of both mysticism and materialism. Many of his poems questioned the basic tenets of religion.

One summer holiday, in my first year in college, I learnt that my primary school teacher, a simple soul like my father, and a kind and considerate guru, had suffered a heart attack and had been admitted to the Government General Hospital. Khalilur Rahman Saheb, or Moulvi Saheb, as we used to call him, had lost his wife a couple of years earlier and none of his children were in the city to take care of him. They had all migrated to far-off places or were too busy with their own affairs to spare time for him.

Along with a couple of friends who were his erstwhile students, I went to call on him in the hospital. He was lying on a steel bed, all forlorn, in one corner of the general ward. All kinds of tubes and wires were attached to his body and he was being medicated intravenously. There was no nurse or doctor anywhere nearby. Standing by his bedside we recalled the lessons in geography and history that we had learnt from him. He was a rather short man and had to get up on a small stool to reach the top of the blackboard when he drew the map of India, especially the higher reaches of the Hindu Kush, the Karakoram Ranges and the

Khyber Pass through which invaders had infiltrated into India. Like my father, Moulvi Saheb was a devout Muslim, who came to school, dressed in a well-worn long cotton coat, a sherwani, loose pajamas, a pair of old Hyderabadi shoes and a frayed black cap. Once he returned home after his teaching chores, he never stirred out except to shop in the nearby bazaar. It was perhaps such folk Rumi had in mind when he wrote in his *Mathnavi*:

> *Beshtar ashaab-e jannat ablah and*
> *Ta z'sharre failsoofi mi rahand*[2]
> Most of those that inhabit Paradise are simple folk, who have
> kept away from the mischief of philosophy.

Moulvi Saheb opened his eyes on hearing our whispers and responded to our greetings in a feeble but cheerful voice. With a smile on his face and a bright gleam in his eyes, he thanked us for the visit, inquired after our health and joked with us. I asked him (rather inconsiderately as it strikes me now, but I was a callow young man then), 'How is it that in your condition, with no family member around, and no nurse and doctor, you retain this cheerful disposition, this sense of humour, this gleam in your eyes? Don't you feel lonely and abandoned?'

All along as we had been talking, he had spoken in very low tones and we had to strain to catch his words over the beeping noise the monitor was making. But his voice suddenly gained strength as he replied, 'Why should I feel lonely and abandoned? My Lord is always with me. Whenever I am alone, He is close to me. He comes whenever I call Him and sits with me on the bed.'

That answer was like a slap in the face of my agnosticism. It shook me; the confidence, the assurance and the strength of his faith in his unseen God. And as I came out of the hospital I said to myself, 'What if, instead of that old man, I was lying in that hospital bed abandoned by relatives and friends to the mercies of a callous government hospital? He has God sitting by his bedside all the time. I would have no one with me, for I do not have a God!'

That was a turning point in my spiritual life, which first took me to the Quran, then to the Gītā, the Bible, the Upanishads, the Dhammapada, Confucius, Sankara and Ramanuja, Marcus Aurelius, and finally to all the Sufi masters, especially Rumi, Ramakrishna, Ibn al Arabi, Kabir and Bayazid.

My study of the Quran was actually initiated by a senior Bengali friend who was posted in Madras (now Chennai) during my days in school and early college. I had studied Arabic under an Indian teacher who had taught Arabic to Arabs in the holy city of Medina, where his parents had moved when he was a child. Growing up and studying in the city, he had become a schoolteacher there. When his parents passed away and he felt lonely in Medina, he returned to Madras and took up teaching Arabic.

Because of the interest he took in me, I grew to appreciate the beauty of Arabic, its grammatical structure, its edifice of a vast vocabulary built on its trilateral root structure, its sonorous rhythm called the *rajz* and so on. This Arabic teacher taught me the language, but not the Quran. It was during my agnostic period that my Bengali friend introduced me to Ameer Ali's *Spirit of Islam* and *The History of the Saracens*, Guillaume's *Legacy of Islam*, Picthall's translation of the Quran, Muhammad Asad's *Road to Mecca*, which had just then been published and other commentaries on the Quran. With the translations in hand and the knowledge of Arabic, I read the Quran time and again, cover to cover. The early suras revealed in Mecca impressed me the most and continue to do so to this day. I have myself written several essays on some of the chapters of the Quran and the meaning the Quran conveys to one when read as a whole.

My daughter Gazala, while going through the manuscript of

this present book, asked me why I moved from the Quran to the Gītā and what prompted my move to the holy books of other faiths. Readers of this book would notice that I have not moved from the Quran to the Gītā or to any other book at all. In fact, it was the Quran, with its repeated emphasis on the unity of God, unity of mankind, universality of faith and the revelation of God's message to mankind from the very creation of Adam, that impelled me to move back and forth from one holy book to another. In one passage of the Quran, this is made quite clear:

> The same religion has He established for you that He had enjoined on Noah, the very same that we have revealed unto you, and that which we enjoined on Abraham and Moses and Jesus commanding you establish this religion and do not differentiate therein.[3]

At another place, God says:

> And this is in the books of the earliest revelations, the books of Abraham and Moses.[4]

So it was implanted in my mind by the very book which my parents read, my teachers taught and my friends initiated me into, that faith in God was enjoined in all the holy books of mankind and so my search led me to the Old Testament, the New Testament, the Upanishads, the Bhagavad Gītā, the Dhammapada, the I-Ching and the ecstatic writings of the Sufis.

Not content with what was written in the holy books, I sought out people who had internalized the message and translated the revelations in their day-to-day lives.

Early in my search, I encountered many an obstacle—some of my own making and some placed in my path by writers, philosophers, rationalists, logicians and others who professed to follow the Gītā, the Gospel and the Quran but in reality were following their own desires, ambitions and lusts.

There is a famous ancient text known as the *Yogavāsishta*.[5] The author, sage Vasishta, was a rationalist.

He says:

Truth should be discovered by one's own endeavour through rational interpretation of our own experience, deepened and extended by our own aspirations and efforts.

The text then goes on to say:

A devotee of reason should value the works of even ordinary persons, provided they are rational and advance knowledge, and should discard those even of sages, if they are not such. A reasonable statement, even of a child, should be accepted, while the unreasonable ones should be discarded like a piece of straw, even though they are made by the Creator Himself.[6]

In another passage which sounds absolutely contemporary, *Yogavāsishta* says:

All the various views arising at different times and in different countries however lead to the same Supreme Truth, like the many different paths leading travellers from different directions to the same city. It is the ignorance of the Absolute Truth and misunderstanding of the different views that cause their followers to quarrel with one another and bitter animosity. They consider their own particular dogmas to be the best, as every traveller may think, though wrongly, his own path to be the only or the best path.[7]

So while Vasishta advocates the use of reason to discover the truth for oneself, al-Gazali in the twelfth century set out to discover the truth for himself through reason and logic, but ended up losing his faculty of speech in the process. In a remarkable autobiography, *Awakening from Darkness*, al-Ghazali writes of the spiritual crisis he faced while occupying a very high position as a professor in the Nizamiyya University of Baghdad. He had to exile himself from his family, his sovereign and his home for eleven years and wander all over the Middle East in search of God. Ultimately, he realized the Absolute, not through reason or logic, but by passing through the selfsame seven stages that the *Yogavāsishta* mentions.

I too decided to go in search of God and unity, called tawhid in Arabic. My search, of course, started with my own religion and my own book—the Quran.

It is also about what I found at the end of this search—that since the time of Adam, God has never stopped communicating with His creation. He has sent messages to us through various messengers and many languages and this message remains the same: 'Believe in Me and Me alone.' That message has sometimes been distorted over the passage of time. We have added myths and our own interpretations to it but its core remains the same. Whether it is the Quran or the Gītā, the Avesta or the Torah, at their heart they hold a message from the same Supreme Being.

Speaking to God

Rumi relates this story in his *Mathnavi*:

> Once, Moses saw a shepherd on the road who kept crying out, 'O God, O Lord where do I find you that I might serve? Sew your moccasins, and comb your hair, wash your clothes for you, and pick your lice, bring milk for you, kiss your little hands, rub your feet and at bedtime sweep your place to sleep! May my goats all be your sacrifice!' 'Who is that you are talking to?' asked Moses. 'To the one who has fashioned us,' said the shepherd. 'And made earth and heavens come to light.'[1]

This story struck me deeply when I read the *Mathnavi* because of my own yearning for a personal relationship with God. I wanted to speak to God the way the shepherd did—as a friend. I needed a window through which I could speak to him.

Rumi said about religion:

> A room with no windows is Hell. To open up windows is the primary function of religion.[2]

I started my search for a relationship with God from my own religious book first. This search took me through many windows, books and commentaries on the Quran from the classical to the modern.

13

The Quran is the Revelation which Prophet Muhammad received from Allah over a period of twenty-three years, from 610 to 632 CE. It was originally taken down by his companions on whatever material was on hand, including parchment and shoulder bones of camels, and later collected and compiled by his immediate successors within a short period of his demise. Muslims believe the Quran to be the last revelation of God to mankind and that it completes and authenticates all revelations sent to mankind before Prophet Muhammad. From the very beginning, the companions of the Prophet, his successors, and later scholars wrote commentaries on the Quran. Each of them interpreted the Quran in the light of his own knowledge and his view of life and times. Commentaries continue to be written on the Quran even to this day, both by Muslim and non-Muslim scholars. I have written my own personal interpretation of the Quran elsewhere.

The references in the Quran to the revelations given to other seers before Prophet Muhammad led me to study the Dhammapada of Buddha, the Analects of Confucius, the I-Ching of Lao-Tze, the Old and New Testaments and nearer home the Bhagavad Gītā and the Upanishads. While I did read the scriptures of these ancient religions, it was the Bhagavad Gītā that fascinated me most.

The Bhagavad Gītā forms part of the famous Indian epic the Mahabharata, which describes the battle between the Kauravas and Pandavas; cousins by relationship. The Kauravas have usurped the rightful patrimony of the Pandavas, through cunning and deceit, and have been hounding them from pillar to post. Arjuna is the commander of the Pandava army—he is a warrior par excellence.

The action described in the Gītā takes place on the battlefield of Kurukshetra at the beginning of the war. Krishna, as Arjuna's charioteer, drives him into the open space between the two armies. Surveying the two armies consisting of brothers, cousins and kinsmen, and overwhelmed at the imminent death of so many brave warriors, Arjuna drops his bow, the Gandiva, and refuses to fight. 'Of what use is a kingdom gained at the loss of so many kith and kin, cousins, and teachers?' he asks. Krishna exhorts him to take up arms, perform his duty to establish dharma—Truth and Righteousness.

Krishna then teaches him about the reality of life and death, the immortality of the soul, indestructibility of the self, non-attachment and the nature of Supreme Reality which is eternal, uncreated, the beginning and the end, and which comprehends all. This discourse of Krishna, addressed to Arjuna, forms the eighteen chapters which are the Bhagavad Gītā. The Bhagavad Gītā, which means the 'Song Celestial', is dated by some scholars to the fifth century BCE.

Many Gītās

Everyone who has read the Gītā and commented upon it has brought his own personal viewpoint to bear on the interpretation, just as the commentators have done with the Quran. Even the translations of the Gītā in English, Hindi, Gujarati, Tamil and Urdu do not agree with each other in all respects.

Sankaracharya's (788–820 CE)[3] commentary on the Gītā, *Gītā Bhāsya*, is one of the earliest. A monistic commentary, which interpreted the Gītā in terms of advaita (non-dualism), in which the liberated person in right knowledge ends all activity and realizes that the Highest Reality is one without a second, the end of all distinctions between subject, object and the ātman, i.e., the self.

As Ghalib would put it, Sankara could very well have asked:

Asl-e shahood-o shaahid-o mash-hood eik hai
Ya Rab a phir mushaahida hai kis hisaab mien
The witness, the witnessed and witnessing is one in essence.
Then to what account is all this seeing, witnessing and
observing?

Sankara died young, at the age of thirty-two. But during his
short life, he practically restored Brahminism, which in the ninth
century stood for Hinduism, and gave it a philosophy and an
ideology which has not been equalled since then. It would not be
an exaggeration to claim that India has not produced an original
philosopher of Sankara's calibre since then. The philosophy of
Vedanta has not only continued to influence Indian thought
down the centuries but has inspired, directly or indirectly, many
Muslim Sufis, both in India and abroad.

For Sankara, the whole essence of the Gītā was gathered in
verse 66 of Chapter 18 where Krishna asks Arjuna to abandon all
religions and irreligions alike—*sarva dharmān parityajya*—repose
in and seek refuge in God alone, for He is the only Reality. The
entire realm of duality, including the object and the act of devotion
is itself illusory.

sarva-dharmān parityajya mām ekam śaranam vraja
aham tvām sarva-pāpebhyo mokṣayiṣyāmi mā śucaḥ[4]
Abandon all varieties of religion and just surrender unto
Me. I shall deliver you from all sinful reaction. Do not fear.

For Sankara, devotion and bhakti were merely the first stepping
stones on the path of spiritual eminence. Full salvation was
achievable only through actionless meditation.

Bhaskara (ninth–tenth century CE) in his commentary
acknowledged one Reality, Brahman, but posited that its energies

(sakti) constitute a real world consisting of souls and matter, etc. He disputed Sankara's monistic interpretations.

Ramanuja (1017–1137 CE),[5] a proponent of *visistādvaita* (which qualifies the non-dualism or the non-duality of Reality that is internally differentiated), emphasized the devotional element in the Gītā. He believed that the world is real, that the true self is not Divine, but when liberated, it is identical in knowledge to all the other selves. He constantly attacked Sankara for his monistic belief and interpreted the Bhagavad Gītā as an exemplary devotional bhakti text. Ramanuja tried to resolve the paradox of Divine Supremacy and Divine Accessibility. For Ramanuja, ultimate bliss could only be gained through intense devotion to God, by following the bhakti-mārga (way of devotion) rather than jnāna-mārga (way of knowledge), posited by Sankara.

Vallabha,[6] a pure non-dualist (*suddhādvaita*), also wrote a commentary in which he emphasized that the true self when liberated is the Supreme Brahman and that bhakti is the most important means of obtaining liberation.

The most famous dualist, Madhava[7] wrote two works on the Gītā asserting an eternal and complete distinction between the Supreme, the many souls, and matter and its many divisions. Madhava lived almost two centuries after Sankara. In utter contrast to Sankara, he held that God, human souls and matter are all eternally distinct. Salvation is not the final merging of the individual soul in the Brahman—union with God—but drawing close to Him and dwelling with Him eternally, contemplating His glory. In his teachings, Madhava was at the opposite end to Sankara's pure monism, and close to the belief held by many Muslim mystics.

Abdur Rahman Chishti,[8] who was a staunch believer in Ibn al Arabi's monism, interpreted the Gītā in the same vein as Sankara. For him, when the individual soul reached its acme of perfection, it ceased to exist, it is annihilated and only God remains. 'Muhyial Din is no more,' cried Abdul Qadir Gilani, the great Sufi of Baghdad, 'I am God!' Abdur Rahman interpreted the Gītā in the same vein.

In recent times, Bal Gangadhar Tilak (1856–1920) wrote a lengthy commentary, *Srimad Bhagavadgita Rahasya*, emphasizing action—a life of work founded upon knowledge and centred on devotion. His commentary reflected his personal concerns with the freedom movement against the British Raj and the need to motivate believers to act rather than to remain passive spectators of the exploitation of the Indian masses.

Gandhi translated the Gītā into Gujarati and in his commentary emphasized the need for the true follower of Truth to act without selfish concern for personal well-being. His interpretation of the Gītā stands in stark contrast to Tilak's interpretation, for he finds the Gītā a lesson in non-violence.

Aurobindo (1871–1950), in his *The Message of Gita*, saw the song as propounding an Integral Yoga, and stated that the Divine is beyond all issues of dualism and non-dualism.

Similarly, other translators and commentators such as Swami Vivekandanda and Dr Radhakrishnan talked of the religion taught by the Gītā—a universal religion in which there is one Absolute who is called by many names (*ekam sat, viprā bahudā vadanti*). Recent devotional commentaries of Swami Bhaktivedanta and Swami Chinmāyānanda have reflected their deep involvement with the Krishna Consciousness or Upanishadic philosophy.

All these explanations and commentaries overwhelmed me. Some of them were highly abstruse and involved concepts beyond my nascent comprehension while others reflected more the personal proclivities of the commentator along with his concerns with contemporary issues. In fact, much of what I have written above is knowledge of the Gītā gained over a lifetime of reading, not of my young days alone. And the comments I have made on the commentaries may be, in the eyes of the scholars of Gītā, utterly misplaced. I can only plead my limited understanding as an excuse. I have found some of the esoteric commentaries on the Quran equally abstruse, for example, Ibn al Arabi's and Zamaksharri's.

However, for me, whose knowledge of Sanskrit is limited, the most attractive translation, because it is the most easily comprehensible, is the one in Urdu by Khwaja Dil Mohammad, who was born in Lahore, Pakistan, in 1884 and died there in 1961. He was a teacher of mathematics who fell in love with the Gītā. He was also a member of the Lahore municipality and we are told that a road is named after him there. This translation is called *Dil Ki Gita* (Gītā of the heart) which is a pun on his name as well. It is in rhymed Urdu couplets. I found it easy-flowing and it reproduces the meaning and spirit of the Gītā in the most easily comprehensible language for me. It is interesting that it was Dil Mohammad who induced me to delve into the bhakti aspect of the Gītā. I found myself in the august company, in this regard, of Mahatma Gandhi who was 'induced' to read the Gītā by two Englishmen and reached its core through reading Edwin Arnold's translation.

While reading this translation for the first time in my early fifties, I reflected on my schoolteacher on his hospital bed, when he had found his Lord sitting with him in his darkest hour and I found in the Gītā:

īśvaraḥ sarva-bhūtānāṁhṛd-deśe arjuna tiṣṭhati
bhrāmāyān sarva-bhūtāni yantrārūḍhni māyayā[9]
Isvara (God) dwells in the hearts of all beings, O Arjuna, and by His māyā causes all beings to revolve as if mounted on a machine (like on a merry-go-round) or like puppets on a string.

God dwells in the heart of man, claims the Gītā. The Quran affirms that He is nearer than the jugular vein. But man rarely realizes this proximity for he is blinded by the veil of māyā, illusion. Is this māyā self-created which blinds man to the presence of God in his heart and closer than the jugular vein, or is this māyā too, a creation of God?

So what is māyā? The word māyā has been interpreted variously by commentators down the ages. For some, it is a magic illusion. For others it denotes the phantom character of the phenomenal world. Space, time and causality are all unreal to the Absolute Being, conjured up by the individual consciousness, by the Self, for its own delusion.

Sankara maintained that the whole phenomenal world is unreal (*avastu*). As a magician (*māyāvi*) causes to issue from his person a phantom or wraith which has no real existence and by which the magician himself is entirely unaffected, so God creates from Himself a universe which is an utter phantom which in no way affects His Absolute existence. In this concept, God is a Transcendent Reality and the world is an illusion created by God. At the same time, the universe, illusion as it is, is a fact of consciousness so real for its creatures.

Ramakrishna Paramahamsa comments on this: 'Poison within the teeth of a snake causes no harm to it. But that poison injected into others causes death to them. Similarly māyā that is Iswara causes Him no harm. Rather it is an adorable attribute of His. And this māyā keeps all beings in bondage.'

Ibn al Arabi,[10] one of the greatest mystics of Islam, has given perhaps the most lucid and most comprehensible definition of māyā, as used in the Gītā, but independently of the Gītā. Ibn al Arabi arrived at his own definition of creation and the Creative Imagination, which he calls khayal.

He claimed that what he wrote had no ideological bias or preconceived objective. As he says:

> In what I have written I have never had a set purpose, as other writers. Flashes of divine inspiration overwhelmed me, so that I could only put them from my mind by committing to paper what they revealed to me. If my works evince any form of composition, it was unintentional. Some works I wrote at the Command of God sent to me in sleep or through mystical revelation.[11]

Ibn al Arabi is the proponent of the mystic inspiration of *Wahdat al-Wujud*—Oneness of Being. His conception of the relationship between the Cosmos and God is that the Cosmos is not and cannot be other than God, not that it is God or that God is the Cosmos, that is, God is identifiable with and yet not merely equal to the Cosmos. This idea emerges from a Hadith Qudsi, a sacred utterance of the Prophet through whom God spoke, 'I was a hidden treasure, and longed to be known, so I created the Cosmos.'

The differentiation that thus arises between God and the Cosmos is a result of the divine self-consciousness, the link between the Creator and the created, between the knower and the known; it is the very principle of creation. Everything that is caused to exist derives its essence from divine knowledge. Although the created may be non-existent in themselves in the ordinary manner of speaking, nevertheless they are of the Reality, because they are recognized by the Creator. That is perhaps the most comprehensible explanation of māyā and the closest one can get to its understanding.

I was fortunate enough to visit Ibn al Arabi's magnificent mausoleum in Damascus. It happened to be a Thursday and there was a large group of pilgrims visiting the tomb of the great shaikh. He lay buried in an inspiring mausoleum built by Sultan Selim of the Ottoman Empire in the sixteenth century with a beautiful mosque close by. Parts of the entrance and the mihrab[12] reminded me of the architecture of the famous mosque of Cordova which preceded it by more than five centuries. I witnessed the procession of pilgrims that comes to pay respect to the great departed soul even after the passage of eight centuries.

Withdrawing from the speculations on māyā and the Creative Imagination, when I looked into the Quran, I found this passage:

wa nahnu aqrabu ilayhi min hablil wareed[13]
For we are nearer to him than his jugular vein.

Though God is nearer to us than our jugular vein, we are not conscious of that presence because of the darkness of our *nafs*, the obscuring self that comes in between as a veil. All one had to do was to remove that veil.

This was a much simpler concept to understand. This was not a distant, transcendent God, but someone to whom I could relate personally. But it still raised the question—if the Lord dwells in the heart of all beings and is closer to man than his jugular vein, how then do I see him with my carnal eyes? Can the creator of māyā and the Creative Imagination be visualized?

Remembering God

Where is He to be found? And how is He to be found? Mystics and saints of every religion and clime called upon him, silently or aloud. The Quran exhorted the Muslims: 'Remember God often with much remembrance'[14] and 'O men, call to mind the grace of God.'[15]

Sufis have claimed that Prophet Muhammad taught *dhikr*—Remembrance—to Abu Bakr in the cave where they had both taken refuge from their enemies when emigrating from Mecca to Medina. This was a way of silently summoning God's help. This was the silent dhikr (*dhikr khafi*). Later he is said to have taught Ali to remember God aloud (*dhikr jali*).

Summoning of God into human consciousness through dhikr—Remembrance of God—is another form of sādhanā. Gītā refers to the chanting of the holy names (nāmā), japa yajna (Gītā: 10:25) and the devotee is advised to engage his mind in thinking of the God-man, '*mat manāḥ bhava*' (Gītā: 9:34). The chanting of the holy name is practised in Chinese Buddhism where it is known as the *nianfu* and in Japan as the *nembutsu*. Often, this chanting becomes a repetition of the holy name in a routine way, without the presence of the mind.

But God should be remembered with both the tongue and the heart. Often while the tongue may continue to utter the name of God mechanically, the heart (i.e., the mind) may be wandering elsewhere.

A man is said to have told the famous Sufi Uthman al-Hiri, 'I recollect with the tongue but my heart does not become friends with the recollection.' The Sufi replied, 'Be grateful that one of your limbs obeys and one of your parts is led aright: maybe later your heart too will come into accord.'

From the individual dhikr meant to summon God into one's consciousness, the Sufis proceeded to collective Remembrance—the *sama*, culminating in Rumi's whirling dance and the qawwali recitations of the Indian subcontinent. But how does dhikr help? Rumi gave me a hint in his *Mathnavi*:

Cries and groans are a powerful means
And the All-Merciful is a mighty nurse.

The nurse and the mother keep excusing themselves.
Till their child begins to cry
In you too God has created infant need
When they cry out, their milk is brought to them
God said 'call on God' continue crying
So that the milk of His love may boil up.[16]

Dhikr, remembrance of God both in privacy and in gathering is not the only way of evoking God-consciousness in your heart.

Another way is to observe the myriad manifestations of God in the universe, in the natural phenomena that surrounds us and into our own deep selves until the truth is made clear to us.

The Quran told me to look at the clouds and how they were created, at the earth and how it was spread out, at the mountains and how they were rooted in the earth, at the heavens and how they were raised, for the signs of God.

The Quran also told me that the presence of God is to be found in the creation of the heavens and the earth, in the alternation of the night and the day; in the sailing of the ships through the oceans for the profit of mankind; in the rain which Allah sends down from the skies and the life which He gives therewith to an earth that is dead; in beasts of all kinds that He scatters across the earth; in the change of the winds, and the clouds which they trail like their captives between the sky and the earth.[17]

And the Gītā tells me:

yad āditya-gatam tejo jagad bhāsayate 'khilam
yac candramasi yac cāgnau tat tejo viddhi māmakam[18]
The splendour seated in the sun, illumining the whole Universe, and that in the moon and fire, is from Me.

Again the Gītā says:

> *bhūmir āpo'nalo vāyuḥ khaṁ mano buddhir eva ca*
> *ahaṅkāra itīyaṁ me bhinnā prakṛtir aṣṭadhā*[19]
> The earth, water, fire, air, ether; the heart and mind (of man)
> and the Ego—these are the eightfold divisions of my nature.

The Gītā affirms:

> *aham ātmā guḍākeśa sarva-bhūtāśaya-sthitaḥ*
> *aham ādiś ca madhyaṁ ca bhūtānām anta eva ca*[20]
> I am the soul residing in the heart of every creature. I am the
> beginning, the middle and the end of all things.

In a magnificent passage of the Yasna, the holy book of the Parsi
religion, Zarathustra, the prophet of Iran, asks a series of rhetorical
questions of God, Ahura Mazda:

> This I ask Thee, Lord, answer me truly: Who is the first
> father of Righteousness through generation and birth? Who
> appointed their paths to the sun and stars? Who but thou is
> it through whom the moon waxes and wanes? This would I
> know, O Wise One, and other things besides.
>
> This I ask Thee, Lord, answer me truly: Who set the earth
> below and the sky (above) so that it does not fall? Who is
> the creator of water and the plants? Who yoked swift steeds
> to wind and clouds? Who, O Wise One, is the Creator of
> the Good Mind?
>
> This I ask Thee, Lord, answer me truly: What goodly
> craftsman made light and darkness? What goodly craftsman
> sleep and wakefulness? Who made morning, noon and night
> to make the wise man mindful of his task?

This I ask thee, Lord, answer me truly: Who created
Right-mindedness venerable with the Dominion? Who made
the son dutiful in his soul towards his father? Recognizing
Thee by these signs, as the Creator of all things through Thy
Holy Spirit, I go to help Thee.[21]

The concept of the presence of God in every natural phenomenon
was echoed in all Sufi thought until Sufism became a highly
esoteric discipline.

In the fourteenth century, Sayyad Raja, the father of the famous
saint of Gulbarga, Gisu Daraz, wrote:

That being pure and absolute in every place, age, moment,
In each direction, every alley, every view manifest I saw.

Rābi'a Basri, the earliest mystic of Islam who lived in Basra, Iraq,
in the early eighth century, made her life a living paean to the love
of Allah. She found His presence in every manifestation and she
saw it proclaiming His Unity:

O God, whenever I listen to the voice of anything you
have made
The rustling of the trees
The trickling of water
The cries of birds
The flickering of shadow
The roar of wind
The song of thunder, I hear it saying:
'God is one! Nothing can be compared to God.'

Rābi'a is here echoing the Quran when it says *yusabbihur ra'du*[22]
(and the thunder sings his praises).

If the Lord dwells in the heart of all beings and you can see Him everywhere, in the burning sun, in the bright moon, in the earth, water and sky and in the voice of thunder, then how does He come and sit with a heart patient on his deathbed? It was all very well to see God in all the natural phenomena. But will He come to me when I call Him?

During my agnostic days, I called upon Him to show me if He exists. Some lurking faith in a corner of my doubting heart made me call upon Him in times of distress. But I got no answer. I never saw Him come and sit by me. Perhaps, I thought, I would find him if I resume my regular ritual prayers which I had abandoned. After my experience with my schoolteacher, I resumed my prayers—I started going to the mosque and performing the rituals. I called on Him several times. But I never got a response. The Quran assured me of His claim, 'I answer the call of the caller when he calls on Me.'[23] The Gītā told me that He was in my heart always, so why did He not come when I called?

Perhaps the very names and attributes which the scriptures gave Him blocked the presence which they were meant to evoke. They were so awe-inspiring that imagination strove in vain to comprehend the Reality behind them. He was so disembodied that imagination refused to figure him. The poet Iqbal in a desperate moment cried out:

> *Kabhi ay haqeeqate muntazar, nazar aa libaase majaaz mein*
> *Keh hazaron sajde tadap rahe hain meri jabeene niaaz mein*
> O long-awaited Reality, appear Thou sometime in a material garb for a thousand obeisances are writhing in my expectant brow.

The Bhagavad Gītā describes God as:

The Unborn, the Imperishable,[24] the Manifest (sat), and

the Invisible and Unmanifest (asat),[25] He is the Supreme
Almighty, without beginning, called neither sat nor asat,[26]
yet He is the Beginning, the Middle and the End of all
things.[27] He is the father of the World, the Mother, Essence
and Goal, of all knowledge,[28] there is nothing whatsoever
higher than Him.[29]

While He is beyond even the concepts of Manifest and
Unmanifest,[30] He yet pervades the Universe, all beings dwell
in Him, yet He does not dwell in them.[31]

He is the light in the sun and the moon.[32] He is the
fragrance of the earth, radiance of the flame; the life force
in all beings.[33] He is the strength of the strong, He is the
Desire of all living creatures,[34] He is the Way, the Sustainer,
the Lord, the Witness, the Dwelling, the Refuge, the Friend
and yet the Source and Destroyer (of life), the Abode and
the Eternal Seed.[35]

It is He who causes heat, withholds and sends forth rain,[36]
and bestows all the qualities on beings—mind, knowledge,
vision, patience, truth, self-restraint, repose, pleasure, pain,
birth, death, fear and courage. He also bestows innocence,
evenness of mind, contentment, austerity, beneficence, glory
and shame.[37] Whatever is pre-eminent, glorious or strong, all
this issues as a part of His power.[38] The good, the passionate
and the lustful are all from Him. They are in Him, yet He
is not in them.[39]

Fools disregard Him when He takes refuge in humanity.
They fail to recognize His higher nature. It is only the truly
wise, the sages who delve deep into themselves who recognize
His true nature and knowing Him as the Eternal Source of all
being, worship Him single-mindedly.[40] They are those who
remain steadfast in their devotions, engaged in constantly
praising Him, prostrate themselves before Him with their

hearts and minds[41] and, knowing Him as the One in many, worship Him in manifold ways.[42]

The transcendence of God creates a feeling of awe in the human mind. God, with all the qualities and aspects ascribed to Him in the Bhagavad Gītā is an overwhelmingly awe-inspiring concept. How does one relate to the awe-inspiring attributes that the Gītā endows him with?

So I looked into the Quran to find Allah. Perhaps Allah would be more comprehensible to my limited understanding, I thought in my naivety. I found Allah to be as awe-inspiring as the Brahman of Bhagavad Gītā.

Allah appears as the sovereign judge, because He is the omnipotent creator of man.[43] He is the King of life and death.[44] He is the Most High.[45] He is One.[46] There is no divinity save Him.[47] He is the Real, the Truth.[48] He is the Lord of the East and West.[49] He is Alone, Eternal, unbegotten, unbegetting and without an equal[50] and there is none like unto Him. At the same time, He is also the benefactor (rahman), merciful (rahim), forgiving (ghafur), and ever-forgiving (ghaffar).

Allah is One and Unique, the Living, the Self-subsisting,[51] the Sublime,[52] the High and the Great,[53] the Sage,[54] Light and Light on Light,[55] the Omnipotent,[56] Creator of the World,[57] who does not cease to create.[58] He is also the Hearing, the clean-sighted, the Omniscient, the Witness,[59] the Bountiful,[60] the Surety.[61] No leaf falls, but He knows it; there is no seed in the darkness of the earth, no green shoot or dry, but it is inscribed in the perspicuous Book;[62] no female conceives or brings forth without His knowledge.[63] He is the creator of every act, whatever it be.[64] He is at the same, the First and the Last, the Manifest (zahir) and the Hidden (batin).[65]

The Gītā and the Quran while asserting the transcendence of God also repeatedly emphasize the divine presence in all creation and ask the devotees to look for him in the things he has created. But there were others who denied this. Among them were St Augustine and Blaise Pascal.

St Augustine, the famous Christian mystic (354–430 CE), believed that the study of the natural world would not give us any information about God, for He was to be found only within the human self. He wrote:

> Late have I loved you, Beauty so ancient and so new, late have I loved you! Behold you were within and I was without, and there I sought you, plunging unformed as I was into the fair things that you have formed and made. You were with me, and I was not with you. I was kept from you by the things that would not have been, were they not in you.[66]

Blaise Pascal, the seventeenth-century French philosopher, on the other hand observed agnostically:

> If there is a God, He is infinitely incomprehensible, since, having neither parts nor limits, He has no affinity to us. We are then incapable of knowing either what He is or if He is. This being so, who will dare to undertake the decision of the question? Not we, who have no affinity to Him.[67]

To me, a mere weak creature, Allah appeared too strong, too far, too high and too distant to be familiar with. The discouragement of philosophers such as Augustine and Pascal made the distance even greater. I was in search of a God with whom I could talk and chat, and tell my troubles and travails to, a God who would be my personal friend and confidant. In short, I wanted the God of the shepherd who was rebuked by Moses.

God in the Gītā and in the Quran is both transcendent and immanent. God as He is in Himself is an impersonal Absolute—the Brahman of Gītā and Allah of Quran. But God in relationship to humanity is a personal deity—the Isvara of the Gītā and the Rahman and Rahim of the Quran.

At the beginning of Chapter 12 of Gītā, Arjuna asks:

evam satata-yuktā ye bhaktās tvām paryupāsate
ye cāpy akṣaram avyaktam teṣām ke yoga-vittamāh[68]
Those devotees who, ever steadfast, worship you thus, and those again who worship the Imperishable, the Unmanifest—which of these are better versed in yoga?

In other words, Arjuna wants to know whether the devotee should worship the Transcendent, the Absolute, or the personal God. The answer given by the Gītā is that both forms of worship lead to the same result. But to concentrate and focus on the Absolute and the Unmanifest is more difficult.

The Gītā says:

kleśo'dhikataras teṣām avyaktāsakta-cetasām
avyaktā hi gatir duḥkham dehavadbhir avāpyate[69]
Greater is the trouble of those whose minds are fixed on the Unmanifested because the unseen goal is to gain for those who are embodied.

It is difficult for a finite mind to comprehend and encompass the Infinite, and that is why the poet Iqbal cried out:

Kabhi ay haqeeqate muntazar, nazar aa libas-e majazm
O long-awaited Reality, appear sometime in a manifest form!

For centuries, mankind, which started the worship of God through sacrifices, oblations and havans ended up worshipping idols in search of the 'manifest form'. Mankind went in search of this manifest God in temples, synagogues, churches and dargahs.

In search of such a manifest God, I too went from place to place. Many friends told me that I would not find God by myself. I needed to join a group of seekers who travel forty days at a time annually and go from village to village, halting in old dilapidated mosques and sit reciting the Quran among the simple village folks after each congregational prayer. I joined one such group in my local mosque. I prayed with them, ate with them and travelled with them. I learnt how to correctly perform the ritual ablutions, how to wear my trousers above my ankles, how to sit in prayer, and while eating how to clean my plate and not to waste even a grain of rice on my fingers and so on.

Having spent a year in these *chilla*s, I was no wiser about God than when I started. Then someone said you cannot find the God you seek in the company of such ritual-oriented companions, you need a Sufi master as a guide. I inquired about where to find such a living master, who could point me in the right direction. In Delhi, someone said there was a Sufi saint in Panipat who was held in great esteem by his disciples spread all over India and abroad. I went with a friend to Panipat to meet this saint in his hospice. I saw a number of cars parked at the gate. There were several devotees, some even wearing Western suits and sherwanis. The saint was sitting cross-legged on a soft velvet-covered mattress surrounded by his many adoring and respectful disciples. Dressed in a long white shirt and cotton trousers, with a turban on his head, he exuded an aura of power and authority. Disciples were coming and going from the audience hall. Many just bowed and kissed his hands and left. Some just sat there on the cotton carpet perhaps waiting for a private audience. He received me quite graciously, inquired about my long journey and asked whether I was comfortably housed. Then he asked me where I hailed from. I said I came from Madras.

'Oh, I have many disciples in Madras. Do you know so-and-so, the hardware merchant? He and his family have been my disciples for thirty years.'

When I professed my ignorance, he named another magnate from Madras who owned several shoe factories. 'He and all his friends are my disciples since the last many years. I stay with him whenever I visit Madras.'

I came away from Panipat, having heard of the many rich disciples of the saint hailing from across the subcontinent and even from the USA and the UK but without getting a pointer to God's abode. And I recalled what Khwaja Moinuddin Chishti of Ajmer had described as one of the characteristics of a traveller on the Sufi path: He alone will recognize God who remains aloof from crowds and does not think of himself a seer.[70]

One night, it is said, Caliph Harun al Rashid summoned Fazl the Barmecide, who was one of his favourite courtiers.

'Take me to a man this night who will reveal me to myself', he bade him. 'My heart is grown weary of pomp and pride.'

Fazl brought Harun to the door of the house of Sufyan Oyaina, who was well known for his piety and devotions in Baghdad. They knocked on his door.

'Who is it?' Sufyan asked.

'The Commander of the Faithful,' Fazl replied.

'Why did he trouble himself so?' Sufyan said. 'I ought to have been informed, then I could have come myself to him.'

'This is not the man I am seeking,' Harun commented. 'He fawns upon me like the rest.'

Once I was visiting a friend in Bombay who took me to meet another Sufi master, this time hailing from Gangoh in Uttar Pradesh. He had come on one of his periodic visits to Bombay to meet his disciples and give them his blessings and spiritual guidance.

We climbed two flights of steps to reach the apartment where he was staying. At first glance he gave an impression of spirituality and had a content and untroubled look. Though he was well into his seventies with a white beard, well-trimmed and clean-shaven upper lip, he had not a wrinkle on his face. He looked so young in body and face that one could easily mistake his white beard for a fake.

'You have gained much spiritual blessings by coming to meet me,' he said. 'Every stride you took to reach me, every step you climbed, was a step that brought you closer to God. For the saints of God are His representatives on earth.'

Unfortunately, I did not feel the same way. Do all saints openly make such claims, I wondered, and came away spiritually dissatisfied.

As I climbed down the staircase, I recalled a verse of Hafez:

Hazar nuktae bareektar ze moo een jast
Na har ki sar be tarashad Qalandari danad.
There are a thousand nuances in this, more subtle than a hair. Not everyone who shaves his head becomes a Sufi.

I regretted that I was born too late in India to meet Sharfuddin Maneri.[71]

Sharfuddin writes about a true saint, a spiritual guide thus:

Until such a man has swept the dust from the doorway of some pagan and considers himself as being absolutely devoid of attribution, so that no trace of self-esteem could be found in him, the time for you to kiss him has not yet arrived! If even a trace of self-esteem takes hold of the skirt of your heart, it means you are still just beginning! It is the consensus of the people of the Way that everyone who sees something more in himself than was in the Pharaoh is foolish. They have said, 'It is easy to belittle oneself in the eyes of other people! The real man is he who can appear small in his self-esteem!'[72]

Iqbal lamented that the taverns of spirituality in India have been lying closed for three hundred years. India has not produced a Sufi of the calibre of even Makhdum Saheb in that period.

I wished I had met the saint of Algeria about whom Dr Marcel Carret had written—a frail man of frugal habits, (eating no more than a few dried dates, one or two bananas, a litre of milk and some tea) sitting cross-legged on a rug in a rabat, a monastery, feeding hundreds of people daily and attending to their spiritual welfare without preaching, influencing people solely with his way of life and force of spirit.

'The first thing that struck me was his likeness to the usual representation of Christ,' writes Dr Carret, a French Catholic medical practitioner who had been called in to venture a prognosis. 'His clothes, so nearly if not exactly the same as those which Jesus must have worn, the fine lawn head cloth which framed his face, his whole attitude—everything conspired to reinforce the likeness. It occurred to me that that must have been the appearance of Christ when he received his disciples at the time when he was staying with Martha and Mary.'[73]

In a long association with his French doctor, Shaikh Ahmad al-Alawi never made a claim to spiritual power or special proximity to God. Yet, when he was on his deathbed, the doctor almost became his disciple and remained a devotee for life.

Where was such a person to be found in India? Like Rumi did, I searched for God and a guide to Him in vain.

Many before me, great men and small, scholars, saints, Sufis and even thieves and dacoits had gone in search of God and their own Self! Nietzsche was one of them. His great classic *Thus Spake Zarathustra* has inspired generations of achievers—some good and many evil (including Hitler). Writing about Nietzsche, Iqbal called him a madman:

Agar hota woh majzube firangi iss zamane mein
Tho Iqbal usko samjhata mukaame kibriya kya hai
Had that mad European lived in these times, Iqbal would
have explained to him the station of Divine Supremacy.

Iqbal calls Nietzsche an intellectual failure, a failed genius whose endeavours remained unproductive for want of expert external guidance in his spiritual life. 'And the irony of fate is that this man,' says Iqbal, 'who appeared to his friends "as if he had come from a country where no man lived" was fully conscious of his great spiritual need.'

'I confront alone,' Nietzsche says, 'an immense problem; it is as if I am lost in a forest, a primeval one. I need help. I need disciples; I need a *master*. It would be so sweet to obey.' And again, 'Why do I not find among living men who see higher than I do and have to look down on me? Is it only that I have made a poor search? And I have so great a longing for such!'

There is a certain amount of arrogance in Nietzsche's confession. He was searching for a guide who was higher than him intellectually and spiritually. Since he himself was 'looking down' on the potential guides, he found none. But my failure was not due to any such feeling of spiritual or intellectual arrogance. I looked for a guide among all walks of life. I found glimmers of guidance here and there. But none living seemed to be of the calibre of the guides of yesteryear.

Among the guides of the past, Rumi was one who had sought and found God. Sometimes Rumi found a personal God and sometimes He was a transcendent Absolute.

Rumi wrote:

Cross and Christians, end to end, I examined
He was not on the Cross
I went to the Hindu temple, to the ancient pagoda.
In none of them was there any sign
To the uplands of Herat, I went,
And to Kandahar, I looked.
He was not on the heights or in the lowlands.
Resolutely I went to the summit of the mountain of Qaf.
I went to the Kaaba of Mecca
He was not there
I asked about him from Avicenna,
He was beyond the range of the philosophers
I looked into my own heart
In that, his place, I saw Him
He was nowhere else!

Rumi was luckier than St Augustine. I looked into my heart, but my heart was still empty. Though I had started praying, going to the mosque at early dawn and late evenings, my quest still remained unfulfilled.

What I was searching for was not only a personal God—the God of Rumi's shepherd or of my own ailing teacher—a God whose presence is palpable, felt in the soul, in the innermost recesses of my being. I was also searching for religion itself—a religion which could reconcile me with myself.

'Religion which is essentially a mode of actual living, is the only serious way of handling Reality,' wrote Sir Mohammad Iqbal, poet, philosopher and mystic. But is religion to be found in going to the mosque at early dawn and performing the prescribed rituals?

In his now famous series of lectures delivered in Madras in 1931, Iqbal goes on to say:

And religion which in its higher manifestation is neither dogma, nor priesthood, nor ritual, can alone ethically prepare the modern man for the burden of the great responsibility which the advancement of modern science necessarily involves, and restore to him that attitude of faith which makes capable of winning a personality here and retaining it hereafter. It is only by rising to a fresh vision of his origin and future, his whence and whither, that man will eventually triumph over a society motivated by an inhuman competition and a civilization which has lost its spiritual unity by its inner conflict of religious and political values.

High-sounding words no doubt—words whose import I understood much later in life when I had acquired a religion and my faith in God. But when I read them for the first time, in the first edition of Iqbal's lectures picked up from the vendor on the footpath, I hardly understood the implications of Iqbal's words. In my perplexity, I still needed a guide to show me the path.

One day I decided to call on Abdul Ali, my old schoolteacher who had taught me in the primary classes. My early schooling had been in my ancestral village where my teacher taught me to recite the Quran by rote, and my maternal grandfather excited my interest in classical Persian poetry and Urdu literature. So when I shifted to Madras with my parents at the age of ten, while I knew a little Urdu and less Persian, I did not have the faintest acquaintance with

English. My father took me to this teacher, his classmate in school and an old friend. Apart from being a teacher, Abdul Ali Saheb was a hakim of repute, a doctor of Unani medicine.

'This boy knows no English, beyond the alphabet. He has joined your school in the first form [sixth standard in today's parlance]. God knows how he is going to make out. Please look after him,' my father told Abdul Ali while handing me over to him.

'Don't worry, ka,' the teacher assured him. He had the habit of appending a 'ka' at the end of most sentences, sometimes with a question mark in his tone, and sometimes as a forceful assertion with an exclamation mark.

After my morning prayers in the local mosque, I would repair to Abdul Ali Saheb's house. His house was located in the old Muslim locality of Madras, bordering Royapettah and Triplicane. It was built in the traditional style—the front portion, mardana, was exclusively reserved for men and the back portion, zenana, for the family. There was a single connecting door used only by the teacher. The front portion of the house consisted of a wide hall, where we students sat on reed mats, and a couple of rooms. The hall and the two rooms were lined with wooden almirahs, crammed with books on all subjects. The lower veranda which was open to the courtyard had equipment like mortars and pestles, vessels for boiling and distilling, stoves, etc., where he made his own Unani medicines. During the three years that I studied with him, no student ever crossed the threshold into the zenana. So I never saw his wife or daughter though his son occasionally joined us.

Until I outgrew the primary section, I studied with him—mainly English. By the end of the first year I had picked up enough of the language to start reading books. One morning, he pulled out a book from his shelf and gave it to me.

'Read that book tonight,' he said to me. 'I will discuss it with you tomorrow, ka.' There was an interrogatory note in that last 'ka'.

It was *Treasure Island* by R.L. Stevenson. He had chosen the one book that he knew would hook me to English classics. I sat through the night reading in the light of a kerosene lamp all about the dark English coastal village, the gloomy inn haunted by drunken blind pirates, the English county doctors and squires, armed ships sailing the tropical high seas in search of islands with hidden treasures, one-eyed wooden-legged villains with talking parrots perched on their shoulders and so on. With Abdul Ali Saheb I would read one English book a day. He also introduced me to history—Indian, English and Islamic—and to religion.

Many years after I left him, when I found myself in the bewildering limbo between faith and doubt, I thought I should visit him in search of moral sustenance.

He was still living in the same house, wearing the same cotton sherwani and loose pajamas and the same old maroon Turkish fez with the black tassel. He had grown older and his beard had more of the grey. He was sitting alone in the front room, on the mattress, resting against the wall on a bolster and grinding some herbs using a stone mortar and pestle. Though he looked frailer and subdued, he still exuded the aura of a teacher with authority.

He greeted me with great warmth and inquired after my studies and family.

'I have come to you with a personal problem,' I said and explained to him the spiritual crisis I was facing. He listened patiently and remained silent for quite a while.

'Are you with *wudu*?' he asked then, meaning in a state of ritual purity.

'No, I am not,' I replied.

'Then go into the washroom and perform your wudu, and come and pray two *rakat*s with me,' he ordered.

After we had gone through this ritual, we sat down and he

said, 'The search for God starts with prayer. But searching for God in a vacuum leads one nowhere. While rituals and prayers are an essential part of the search for God, it is a delusion to believe that a mechanical indulgence in ritual prayer, without observance of all the other commandments of the Quran will lead you to God. Ritual prayer, fasting, pilgrimage are all only starting points. Regular indulgence in prayer may not immediately lead to a realization of God. But the actual realization of God, in your own soul, is through the route of righteousness.' Then he quoted the verse of the Quran which defines righteousness:

> Righteousness does not consist in turning your faces towards the east and the west, true righteousness consists in believing in Allah and the Last Day (i.e., the day when all men will be judged), the angels, the Book and the Prophets, and in giving of your wealth for love of Him (without any selfish motives), to one's kinsmen, orphans, the poor and the (stranded) wayfarer, and to those who ask for help and in freeing of slaves from their bondage, and in establishing prayer and the zakat (the annual tax for charity), (True righteousness consists) in fulfilling your promises when you make them, and in remaining steadfast in adversity and affliction, and in times of distress and calamity. Such are the truthful ones, such are the God-fearing.[74]

Allah here emphasizes serving the poor, the destitute, the debtors, the slaves—in short all those who are the distressed members of society, irrespective of caste, creed and religion.

Abdul Ali Saheb was now in full stride. He said, 'You have to seek God, not in the mosques and dargahs alone. You have to see the face of Allah in the face of the beggar and the destitute.' Then he quoted a well-known Hadith Qudsi:

Allah will say, 'O son of Adam, I fell ill and you visited me not.' He will say, 'O Lord, and how should I visit you when you are the Lord of worlds?' Allah will say, 'Did you not know that my servant so-and-so had fallen ill, and you visited him not? Did you not know that had you visited him you would have found me with him? O son of Adam, I asked you for food and you fed me not.' He will say, 'O Lord, how should I feed you, who are the Lord of the worlds?' Allah will say, 'Did you not know that my servant so-and-so asked you for food, and you fed him not? Did you not know that had you fed him you would surely have found that with me? O son of Adam, I asked you to give me to drink and you gave me not to drink.' He will say, 'How should I give you to drink when you are the Lord of the worlds?' Allah will say, 'My servant asked you to give him to drink and you gave him not to drink. Had you given him to drink you would have surely found that with me.'[75]

'So, keep up your regular prayers, but start working for the poor and the destitute, and you will find Allah there,' said Abdul Ali.

'I am only a student, still in junior college. I do not have the money or means to serve the poor. So how would I be able to serve the poor and the needy?' I asked.

My old teacher smiled. Shifting his position on the mattress, he faced me.

'Faith is not merely paying lip service to a belief in God. One reaches iman through amal-salih—faith through good deeds. There is a Hadith of the Prophet, I think it is in Bukhari, and if you go into that room and bring out the right volume, I will show it to you. The Hadith says: "Iman (faith) has seventy branches, the highest of which is that nothing deserves to be worshipped except

Allah and the lowest of which is removing from the thoroughfare that which may cause injury to the user."

'So every kind of service to humanity only goes to strengthen your faith. "He that loves not his brother whom he has seen, how can he love God whom he has not seen?" asked Jesus. You will find that in John's Gospel. It is not necessary to be rich or powerful to do good deeds. Every one of us has been blessed by God with the capacity to do good. Those who have wealth can help the poor by feeding them and clothing them. Those who have power and authority can use it to ameliorate the poverty of people through social justice. You have knowledge. You are a good student. You are good in English, Mathematics and Science. So, there are many poor students who fail in their final school examinations. Go and tutor them,' he said. 'If even one of them succeeds in life as a result of your effort, God will find you.'

Later, I found confirmation of this in C.F. Andrews, a Protestant clergyman and close personal friend of both Mahatma Gandhi (it is reported that he alone among Gandhi's friends called him by his first name, Mohan) and Rabindranath Tagore (who played a crucial role in Gandhi's life). It was he who persuaded Gandhi to return to India from South Africa to take up the leadership of the freedom movement. In his boyhood, he was a fervent believer in the Second Coming of Christ. His father, who believed in the literal truth of the Book of Revelations, had convinced Andrews that the Second Coming was imminent. It was just round the corner.

But as he grew older, this conviction fell away and Andrews faced a moral crisis. In his own words, 'Outwardly I was leading a strictly religious life, in the bosom of our family, going regularly with my father and mother to the church; but inwardly a conflict was going on deep down in the sub-conscious part of my being, and for a long time this remained unresolved.'

Andrews went through this spiritual crisis, which saints like Augustine and al-Ghazali had faced centuries earlier. He continued to pray intensely asking for God's help. Then, suddenly, at the age of nineteen as he prayed by his bed before retiring, his fervent prayers were answered and his faith was restored. The effect of this conversion, which brought him immense joy, was also to send him among the poor. He had found his calling.

He writes:

> An inner compulsion seemed to drive me towards it; and all through my life the impulse to surrender all for Christ's sake and to find him among those who are in need has been present with me so strongly that sooner or later everything has had to give way before it . . . for the happiest moments I have known have always been those when I have been able to find my active work, not in university centres, or among the rich, or even among the middle classes, but among the suffering poor.

That is how I gathered together a group of my friends from the college and started an association to collect funds from some of the well-to-do pillars of the community and paid the fees of the very poor students who had failed in their final examinations and whose parents could not afford the fee of fifteen rupees which would have enabled them to reappear in the supplementary examinations. For want of just fifteen rupees, their education remained incomplete and their careers were ruined. We took a room in the Big Mosque compound and tutored them in subjects in which they were weak. Many of them passed the examinations, went on to further studies and prospered in life.

Many years later, I found a similar maxim about giving in the Bhagavad Gītā:

dātavyam iti yad dānaṁ dīyate 'nupakāriṇe
deśe kāle ca pātre ca tad dānaṁ sāttvikaṁ smṛtam[76]
That gift which is made to a deserving person, who can make
no return, given at a proper place and time with the belief
that 'this must be given', is called sattvik or good.

The Gītā has given a true and precise definition of a gift, a *daan*.
First of all, it should be given to a person who really deserves it.
Such a deserving person should obviously not be a person who has
the capacity in turn to return such a gift, in which case an element
of expected reciprocity creeps into the act of giving. Secondly, it
should be given when the deserving person really needs it—for
a gift given when the need for it has really passed is not of much
use to the recipient. Thirdly, it should be given at a proper place.
Perhaps, Krishna had in mind the need for giving charity either
secretly without too much publicity, or maybe he had in mind
the distribution of daan, institutionally. Fourthly, the gift should
be given as an obligation on the giver, the belief that it is a duty,
it must be given. There should be no element of any expectation
linked to the gift—neither to gain the respect, love or affection
of the recipient, nor of any material gain and nor of earning
name and fame as a generous man. Only if a gift fulfils all these
conditions does it deserve to be called sattvik, true and good.

The Quran carried this concept of a voluntary gift into an
obligatory tax for the poor.[77] It is called zakat and is meant for
the poor, the destitute, those whose hearts are to be reconciled, to
free those in bondage and those in debt, for helping the stranded
wayfarer and to serve God's purposes. The Gītā too had stipulated
that the gift should be given in the belief that it is a duty, that is,
it must be given. The Quran also stipulates that the zakat should
be given at a fixed rate on all your assets, your wealth, both visible
and otherwise. And by defining the methodology of this 'giving',

'both secretly and openly',[78] the Quran has left it to the conscience of the giver—to ensure that charity is to be given for the sake of God, not to earn name, fame, prestige and power!

The Shell of Prayer

Abdul Ali told me to seek God in service to humanity. The Quran told me that God was closer to me than my jugular vein, and that He answers my call when I call Him.

Rumi writes:

One night a certain man called out 'Allah!' until his lips grew sweet from the mention of His name. 'Tell me, O babbler,' said the Devil, 'where is the response "I am here" to all this calling on God's name? Not a single whisper has come from the throne; how much longer will you call out "Allah" in vain?'

Broken-hearted, the man lay down to sleep. In a dream he saw Khidr (the Eternal Guide) who spoke to him saying, 'You have stopped praising God; why have you changed your mind about calling on Him?'

The man replied, 'There was no "I am here" in reply, and so I was afraid I had been turned away from the door.'

'Not at all,' said Khidr, 'God says, 'That "Allah" of yours is my "I am here." The ardour with which you pray is my message to you. All your striving to draw near to me is my way of releasing your bonds and drawing you to me. Your love and fear are the net to entrap my favour. Every "O Lord" of yours is answered with many an "I am here."'[1]

And what does the Gītā say about how to approach God? Does the way to God lie only through the temple and the mosque? Through ritual prayers and sacrifices? Through fasting and mortification? Through meditation, breath control and sama (collective chanting of the names of God), as the rishis and Sufis tell me?

Krishna told Arjuna to devote his heart to God, to worship Him alone, to sacrifice to Him alone and to bow down before Him alone. This is the way to reach Him:

> *brahmany ādhāya karmāṇi saṅgaṁ tyaktvā karoti yaḥ*
> *lipyate na sa pāpena padma-patram ivāmbhasā*[2]
> He who acts, having given up attachments, fulfilling all works in Brahma, is not defiled by sin, just like a lotus leaf in water.

All acts are to be dedicated to and fulfilled in God and are to be performed for His sake alone. The Gītā and the Quran both emphatically preach this message.

Aurobindo Ghose commenting on this verse of the Gītā remarks:

> When works are thus reposed in Brahman, the personality of the instrumental doer ceases; through the acts, he does nothing; for he has given up not only the fruits of his works, but the works themselves, and the doing of them to the Lord. The Divine then takes the burden of works from him; the Supreme becomes the doer and the act and the result.[3]

The Quran asserts that piety does not lie in turning one's face to the east or to the west but in faith, submission and charity, for the love of God alone. In a famous Hadith Qudsi, found in Bukhari (the most authentic collection of the sayings and acts of Prophet Muhammad), we read:

My servant draws not near unto me except through the duties I have cast on him. When I love him, I am his hearing with which he hears, his seeing with which he sees, his hand with which he strikes and his foot with which he walks.

Aurobindo's explanation that the Supreme becomes the doer, the act and the result speaks in the same language.

Does a total surrender to God bring Him any nearer to you and you nearer to Him? Even if I dedicate all my acts to God (in all the implications this surrender involves), can I experience God as my ailing schoolteacher did?

The Sufis who went beyond ritual alone in their rapport with God tell us of various ways of approaching God—through following the divine law scrupulously, through constant prayer and fasting, through dhikr, through sama, through music and dance as the whirling dervishes practise, through breath control and so on and so forth. The ulema insist that the ritual prayer performed five times a day—one of the five pillars of Islam—is the only way of reaching God-consciousness. They quote many a Hadith in support of this claim.

Ritual prayer today, outside the Arab world, has become a mere repetition of the Arabic chapters of the Quran with appropriate prescribed genuflexions and obeisances. In the mosques of the Indian subcontinent, Malaysia, Central Asia, Indonesia, China, etc., where the bulk of the world's Muslim population lives, the imam who leads the prayer recites the Quran in Arabic and the worshippers listen in devout silence, most of them without understanding a word of it.

In the days of al-Ghazali, the twelfth century, when the Muslim empire covered a large part of the globe and Arabic language more or less enjoyed the same popularity as English does today, the Arabic Quran was understood by most worshippers. The devout among them listened attentively and understood, just as those in the Arabic-speaking world do today. Yet, al-Ghazali, even while describing the importance of ritual prayer, exhorted the worshipper to go to the inner meaning of the daily prayers. Citing the Quranic injunction against approaching the ritual prayer in a state of intoxication, he says, 'O you who believe, do not approach the ritual prayer while you are intoxicated, but wait until *you can comprehend what you are saying.*'[4] al-Ghazali's explanation of this Quranic text is interesting. He observes, 'Some say that *intoxicated* means inebriated by many anxieties, while others say it means drunk on the love of this world. The meaning is obviously a caution against worldly attachment, since the words "until you know what you are saying" explain the underlying reason that many are those who pray without having drunk wine yet do not know what they are saying in their prayers.'[5]

To approach God, ritual alone is not sufficient, said Rumi. In *Fihi ma fihi*, Rumi was asked, 'Is there any way to approach God other than the ritual prayers?' Rumi said, 'The answer is more prayer. But prayer is not confined to outward form alone. That is just the "shell" of prayer. Ritual prayers have a beginning and an end, and anything that has a beginning and an end is a "shell" . . . Everything that can be expressed in words and speech and has a beginning and an end is a "form", a "shell". Its soul however is unrestricted and infinite, and has neither beginning nor end.'[6]

In a famous Hadith, Prophet Muhammad joined the elements of faith and action with a strong bond which he called *ehsaan*. 'Ehsaan is to perform your worship as though you are seeing God. If that is not possible, you should at least be conscious that God is seeing you,'[7] he said. 'Ehsaan is the divine spirit that infuses the mere shell of ritual prayers and gives it meaning. Ehsaan is to see God when you are worshipping Him.'

Reading this, I asked myself—if ritual prayer is a mere 'shell' as Rumi said and if without the element of ehsaan, prayer will continue to remain a mere ritual, what is the purpose of performing the ritual prayer at all? Then I recalled Mr Abdul Qadir and his wife who seamlessly combined faith, prayer, fasting and service to humanity.

Mr Abdul Qadir was a civil servant of the old school. I met him in 1960 when I went to appear before the Public Service Commission to be interviewed for the civil services. Subsequently, whenever I came to Delhi from the National Academy of Administration in Mussoorie, he insisted I stay with him in the government bungalow on Akbar Road. He was then serving as the director general of training and employment in the Government of India. In those days, in the aftermath of Independence, the council of ministers under Jawaharlal Nehru was still small and compact and the bureaucracy had not reached bloated levels like in the late 1990s. So, even officials of the status of joint secretaries, who do not even merit a decent flat today, could get the sprawling, colonial-style bungalows in Lutyens's Delhi, spread over several acres, with a large number of outhouses and servants' quarters. His house was always full of guests from all over India, and his outhouses were fully occupied by the homeless and the needy.

Abdul Qadir Saheb, and his wife, Ayesha Begum, were devout Muslims who performed all the prescribed prayers, observed the obligatory fast on the thirty days of Ramadan and fasted on every Thursday and Friday. Even while attending to his official duties, he would not miss a single prayer and he kept a prayer mat in his office room for this purpose.

He had gathered a host of the poor and homeless—poor students, tailors, sweepers and others—in the outhouses and I suspect a good part of his salary went into their upkeep. Many a time, I had joined him in his backyard for the predawn prayers along with the occupants of the servants' quarters. And often I had woken up in the middle of the night to go to the washroom and found him and his wife engaged in the post-midnight *tahajjud* prayers.

During one of my visits to Delhi, I asked him about the efficacy of the ritual prayers which he so assiduously performed.

'Ritual prayer is the heart of Islam,' he told me. 'As you know there are five Pillars of Islam—arkan-e-Islam. The very first is the declaration of faith in God. In the ritual prayer, the very first word you utter five times a day is an affirmation of that faith and your belief in God's mercy and compassion. Prayer links all the five Pillars together, for the Quran repeatedly emphasizes the link between faith, prayer, fasting and charity. By praying together and reciting the Quran in every prayer and invoking the blessings of Allah on the Prophet, a Muslim links himself to God, to the Prophet and to the community.'

He looked at me intently to see whether I had grasped the purport of his words.

'You may recall,' continued Abdul Qadir Saheb, 'that the greatest collection of the traditions of the Prophet, may peace be upon him, the al-Bukhari Sharif, devotes two hundred pages to ritual prayer. The other great collection, that of Muslim, devotes four hundred pages to the same subject.'

He then quoted the famous Hadith of Ehsaan:

Good conduct is to worship God as if you saw Him; for even if you do not see Him, He sees you. Regular performance of the prayers, five times a day and regular fasting are the two strong barriers that keep a man from approaching evil, a golden shield to protect you from evil deeds and thoughts. If a sweeper wore a garment of gold brocade, it would constantly prevent him from even approaching filth—for that would soil his rich and clean garments. Similarly, the man who performs ritual prayers has put on the rich garment of a God-fearing nature—*taqwa*. The garment of *taqwa* is nobler for the heart than is the gold brocade for the body. The man who wears it cannot approach any act that soils the heart.

Many years later, I read the exact simile in Fakhruddin Razi's *Mifthah al Ghayb*.

Abdul Qadir Saheb had worked in the Hyderabad Civil Service in the early 1940s. After the merger of the Hyderabad state with India, he had been co-opted into the Indian Administrative Service. He had spent all his life in simple piety, prayers, fasting, recital of the Quran both in the morning and in the evening and attending to his official duties in all sincerity. He exemplified the ideal of both the Gītā and the Quran—a man who did his duty both religious and secular—without expecting any material or spiritual rewards. Prayer and fasting for him were ends in themselves, means to purify himself. He had no time to read Bukhari, Muslim or Razi. So, I am still left wondering where he got the knowledge of those books.

Once I recall seeing him sitting in the lawn conversing with a gentleman in a sherwani and black cap. Seeing me from afar he invited me to join in the conversation.

'This gentleman has come from the old city to invite me to a function to celebrate the Prophet's birthday. If you are free, why don't you come with me?' he asked.

'Most certainly, uncle,' I replied. 'But won't you introduce the gentleman to me?'

Before Abdul Qadir Saheb opened his mouth, the gentleman himself volunteered.

'My name is Ravish Siddiqui and I edit an Urdu magazine.'

I had of course heard of Ravish Siddiqui. He was a rather

well-known Urdu poet and was quite famous in the 1960s in Urdu circles. In fact, several of his poetry collections were then current and some of his poems were even prescribed as text for Urdu undergraduate courses.

'Oh, you are the well-known Urdu poet. I have read some of your poems,' I said.

Ravish Saheb's face lit up to be so recognized, but the next moment it was downcast. For Abdul Qadir Saheb, ignorant of poets and poetry, asked, 'Ah, so you write poetry too, do you?' This was said in all simplicity, not intending to hurt the poet. I had never heard him say a harsh word to anyone, never pass an adverse comment and always ready to extend a helping hand to anyone who approached him.

When he was about to retire, I happened to be in Delhi on an official visit. I found Ayesha Begum engaged in packing up the few pieces of personal belongings that he possessed. The denizens of the outhouses were lending a hand with lugubrious faces at the impending departure of their benefactor.

'Where do you plan to settle down?' I asked.

'We haven't yet decided,' said Ayesha Begum. I was rather surprised as there was hardly a month left to his retirement. 'You see, with the meagre salary we got and with several obligations to fulfil, we could not save anything. All our life, we had government accommodation and so we found no motivation to save and build a house of our own.' I knew that amongst those obligations were the demands of the poor relatives and the hordes of the destitute and indigent that lived in the compound.[8]

Noticing the wistfulness in his wife's tone, Abdul Qadir Saheb intervened, 'We have always trusted in God. He has always provided for us. So, why should I lose faith in Him at the tail end of my service? He will provide me with a hut somewhere. I will retire there and spend the rest of my life in prayer.'

Abdul Qadir Sahib's trust in God reminded me of the story of Ibn Khafif, a Sufi saint, a disciple of Junayd. En route to a pilgrimage through the desert, Ibn Khafif took his bucket to a well where he saw a deer drinking. As he dropped his bucket into the well, he saw with a shock that the water level had sunk too low to dip his bucket. He raised his eyes to heaven and exclaimed, 'Surely, O Lord I am more important than this animal.'

A heavenly voice replied, 'The deer got the water because it relied on God totally.' Ibn Khafif realized he had relied on the bucket. He discarded it, asked for forgiveness and travelled on. The heavenly voice once again reminded him. 'We were only testing you. Go back. You will now be able to take water with your bare hands.' Later, his master Junayd told him, 'Had you trusted God and not showed your impatience, water would have bubbled at your feet' (Farid al-Din Attar, *Tadhkirat al-Auliya*).

A month later Abdul Qadir Sahib visited Surat where I was serving as the collector and district magistrate. It was a farewell visit. I did not have the courage to ask him again where he was going to settle. But he himself volunteered the information.

'It may be a coincidence, but the very day you left for Surat, I received an offer from the International Labour Organization, Geneva. They have offered me the post of an adviser to the Government of Afghanistan at a salary which is ten times more than what I am getting here. I have accepted the offer. I shall be going to Kabul, straight from Delhi.' His tone reflected his gratitude to God for having helped him so providentially.

My next meeting with Syed Abdul Qadir Saheb was in Hyderabad at his house in Banjara Hills, after his return from Afghanistan, France and the USA. He had served for more than a decade with the United Nations (UN) after retirement from the Government of India, in many important positions and was getting a substantial tax-free UN pension. I found him as the same humble self, in the same self-deprecatory mood. 'God has been very kind to me. My son has completed his engineering education from Srinagar and is in a good job in the US. My daughter, who had passed through a traumatic period, has become a doctor and has now settled down with her two children in our neighbourhood. And God has now given me the wherewithal to help many people.'

Abdul Qadir Saheb and his wife are no more. They died peacefully at a ripe old age, serene in their demeanour up to the last. They remain alive in my memory as embodiments of the virtue of *tawakkul*—utter, unconditional trust in Allah's providence.

In his *Jala' al-Khawatir* (*The Removal of Cares*), a collection of forty-five discourses, the Sufi saint Abdul Qadir Gilani says:

A certain righteous man was asked, 'Have you seen your Lord?' He replied, 'If I had not seen Him, I would be at my wits end.' If someone should say 'How can you see Him?' I would say, 'When creatures have departed from the servant's heart and nothing is left in it apart from the Lord of Truth (Almighty and Glorious is He). He will let him see and draw him as close as He will. He will let him see inwardly (*batin*), as He lets others see Him outwardly (*zahir*). He will let him see as He showed Himself to our Prophet Muhammad (Allah bless him and give him peace) on the Night of Ascension (*mi'raj*) just as He shows Himself to this servant, draws him near and talks to him in his sleep. Sometimes, his heart will tell him in a moment of wakefulness to close the eyes of his physical being, so he sees Him with his inner eyes, just as he is accustomed to seeing things on the outside (*zahir*). He gives him a different inner content (*ma'na*) so he can see Him with it; he sees His nearness, he sees His attributes, he sees His miracles, His grace and beneficence and kindness towards him; he sees His bountiful goodness and His protecting wing.[9]

In another discourse the Shaikh said:

There are some among His servants who are ready to trade the Garden of Paradise and all that it contains in exchange for a glimpse of Him. When He recognizes the genuine sincerity (*niyyat*) in this respect, and that they are truly prepared to make the deal for a single glance, He allows them to enjoy their glances permanently. He lets them enjoy their nearness permanently.[10]

It is not easy to achieve ehsaan, to see God when you are praying, for as the Gītā says, God's vision is not vouchsafed to everyone.

nāhaṁ prakāśaḥ sarvasya yoga-māyā-samāvṛtaḥ
mūḍho 'yaṁ nābhijānāti loko māṁ ajam avyayam[11]
Veiled by my mystic illusion (yogamāyā) I am not manifest to all. This deluded world knows not Me, The Unborn and Eternal.

No one sees His Reality—his unmanifest essence, *avyakta*, which is transcendent, imperishable and supreme.

Arjuna, however, is not satisfied with the claim that, while He is hidden from the carnal eyes of the world, He could be discerned in every aspect of the phenomenal world. Krishna explains to Arjuna that God is sealed in the heart of all beings like the very innermost self of man, that He is the radiant sun, that He is the moon, that He is the sacred lore, that He is the very mind and consciousness of mankind, that He is the highest mountain, the deepest ocean, that He is the beginning and end of all creation, and life and death and that He is Time itself.

> *aham ātmā guḍākeśa sarva-bhūtāśaya-sthitaḥ*
> *aham ādiś ca madhyaṁ ca bhūtānām anta eva ca*[12]
> I am the Self, O Gudakesa, seated in the hearts of all creatures. I am the beginning, the middle and the end of all beings.

> *mṛtyuḥ sarva-haraś cāham udbhavaś ca bhaviṣyatām*
> *kīrtiḥ śrīr vāk ca nārīṇāṁ smṛtir medhā dhṛtiḥ kṣamā*[13]
> I am all-devouring death, and I am the generator of all things yet to be. Among women I am fame, fortune, speech, memory, intelligence, faithfulness and patience.

But Arjuna is still not satisfied with looking at these manifestations, for after all they are only yogamāyā, not God.

'It is impossible to know God in things,' says one of the greatest mystics of Islam, Ibn al Arabi, in his *al-Futūḥāt al-Makkiah*. 'It is impossible to know God in things save through the manifestation of things and through the disappearance of their status. The eyes of the ordinary man stop at the status of things, whereas those who have the illumination of revelation see nothing in things but God. Among them are those who see God in things, and there are others who see things and God in them . . . The greatest illumination in this domain is when the vision of God is the very vision of the world.'[14]

Arjuna is not satisfied with seeing God in things. Arjuna believes himself to be among those who have the illumination of revelation and insists on seeing the essence of God in all His glory. He accepts whatever Krishna has said about God, but still insists on seeing His hidden form, not his manifestation alone.

Arjuna is not like other ordinary men. He has heard patiently the philosophy of the Divine Self, and the Self in Man. But he is a kshatriya, a warrior though momentarily confused by contradictory emotions that have assailed his conscience. He is not fully satisfied by all the explanations so profoundly propounded by his charioteer, an inspired teacher—he wants to face Reality in all its nakedness. Arjuna challenges Krishna to show him the face of God.

Iqbal paraphrases the challenge thus:

That man alone is real who dares—
Dares to see God face to face!
What is 'Ascension' (mi'raj)? Only a search
 for a witness
who may confirm thy reality.
A witness whose confirmation alone
makes thee eternal
No one can stand unshaken in His Presence
And he who can, verily, he is pure gold.[15]

Krishna knows that Arjuna will not be able to see that naked Reality with his carnal eyes and stand the sight of God in all His hidden glory manifested.

na tu mām śakyase draṣṭum anenaiva sva-cakṣuṣā
divyaṁ dadāmi te cakṣuḥ paśya me yogam aiśvaram[16]
But you cannot see Me with your present eyes. Therefore
I give you divine eyes by which you can behold My mystic
opulence.

And with this divine sight Arjuna sees a vision of God, a partial vision.

And what happens to Arjuna when Reality manifests itself, not in its glory entire but in one aspect alone? One recalls the parallel event recounted in the Quran. When Prophet Moses went up to Mount Sinai and heard the voice of God and entered into a discourse with Him, his curiosity got the better of him and he cried, '*arni*'—'Reveal Yourself to me, I want to see you.' But God knowing that the mortal eye, the human brain, is not capable of taking in the whole of Divinity replied, '*lan tarani*' (You cannot see Me). But like Arjuna, Moses too insisted on seeing God. And when God manifested himself, what happened? As the Quran says:

> *falammatajalla rabbuhu liljabali ja'aalahu dakk wakharra*
> *moosasa'aiqan falamma afaqa qala subhanakatubtu ilayaka*
> *waana awwalu al mu'mineen*[17]
> When his Lord manifested Himself to the mountain,
> crumbling it to dust, Moses fell down in a faint. When he
> recovered, he said 'Glory be to thee! I repent unto you, for
> I am the first to believe.'

So the vision of God with carnal eyes is not possible. Only the 'spiritual' vision can 'see' Him, so to say.

Ruzbihan Baqli, one of the passionate mystic saints of Islam, writes of the errors in which even Sufis fall, in pursuit of the vision of God. He says:

> Another of their errors is that a group of them claim to have
> spiritual visions with the physical eye. That is not possible
> in the world, and there is a Prophetic tradition about this.
> There are some who do not distinguish ocular unveiling
> from spiritual unveiling and they imagine that whatever they
> see has itself been seen with the physical eye, but because of
> their extreme immaturity they cannot recognize what has

occurred. A report has come from Prophet (*pbuh*) that Iblis (Satan) sits on a throne between Heaven and Earth, and he shows himself to a group of ordinary people in order to delude them, and he has an effect on all of them. If they provide any sign of that experience, it is not from God, for God is without sign.[18]

Hence, the 'vision' or 'seeing' appears to be only a descriptive term for a spiritual revelation that is not sufficiently describable by words and often misleading.

And the one glimpse of God that Arjuna saw was brighter than the light of a thousand burning suns, simultaneously manifest. Arjuna, like Moses, was frightened out of his wits and stood trembling at seeing the mighty vision and overwhelmed with fear. He stammered and bowed down before the might of God.

The Persian mystic and poet, Nur ad-Din Abd ar-Rahman Jami, in his *Lawaih* (*Flashes of Light*) cautioned seekers to be careful in their desire to see God face-to-face:

'O fairest rose, with rosebud mouth,' I sighed
'Why, like coquettes, thy face forever hide?'
He smiled, 'Unlike the beauties of the earth
Even when veiled I still may be described.
Thy face uncovered would be all too bright
Without a veil none could endure the sight.
What eye is strong enough to gaze upon
The dazzling splendor of the fount of light?
When the sun's banner blazes in the sky
Its light gives pain by its intensity,
But when 'tis tempered by a veil of cloud
That light is soft and pleasant to the eye.'[19]

Allah also vouchsafed his vision to Prophet Muhammad on the night of *Mi'raj*, the ascension. The vision was so ineffable that even the Quran refers to it in language mysterious and mystifying:

> He came forth and stood poised, being on the higher horizon. Then he drew near and hovered above, two bow lengths away, or even nearer. Then he revealed to His servant whatever he revealed. His eye did not waver, nor did it stray and he certainly saw some of the greatest signs of His Lord.[20]

Commentators are still disputing whether Muhammad saw God with his physical eyes or his spiritual eye.

Arjuna saw with his spiritual eye the whole universe with its many parts and divisions drawn into one Unity and he also saw that God has no beginning and no end, envisaging the whole of creation in Himself. One is reminded of the Quran:

> For Him is what is in Heaven and what is in earth and nothing is beyond the bounds of His knowledge.[21]

But Arjuna, frightened out of his wits, asks in despair, 'Who are you, so fierce in form? I cannot comprehend you.'[22]

And the reply he gets echoes from every page of history:

> *kālo 'smi loka-kṣaya-kṛt pravṛddho lokān samāhartum iha pravṛttaḥ*
> *ṛte 'pi tvāṁ na bhaviṣyanti sarve ye 'vasthitāḥ pratyanīkeṣu yodhāḥ*[23]
> Time am I, destroyer of the worlds, and I have come to engage all people. With the exception of you, all the soldiers here on both sides will be slain.

It is in the scheme of things that Time destroys all that the world contains, whether human beings intervene or not. Relentlessly and inexorably, Time destroys everything—galaxies, stars, planets, empires, kings, armies and even the puny creatures that inhabit the face of this earth. They all turn to dust eventually, hardly leaving behind even a memory of their existence.

In the Gītā, God reveals himself in one aspect—the aspect of world-destroying Time. Ovid, the Roman poet (43–18 BCE) remarked, '*Tempus edax rerum*' (Time is the devourer of all things).

Time has many aspects and has been studied by philosophers, scientists, mystics and historians, since centuries. While by definition God is beyond Time and Space, since He created both, as far as human understanding goes, God has always functioned in time.

This particular aspect of world-destroying Time had always intrigued me. There is one chapter in the Quran where God swears by Time and affirms that Man is in utter loss. And when God reveals himself to Arjuna he does so in his aspect of Time that destroys everything. Is the march of Time so inexorable that nothing escapes its ravages? Are there any exceptions? I recalled a lesson I learnt from one of my teachers.

A Glimpse of Eternity

'I saw eternity the other night.'

— John Donne

While I was engaged in my search for God, I studied Arabic prose and poetry with Dr Abdur Rahim Farooqui, who was the head of the department of Arabic and Persian in the Government Arts College, Madras. He was a rather reclusive man, and while walking through the corridor one used to catch a passing glimpse of him sitting in a reclining chair in his gloomy den. Since there was no escape from the summer heat, he would keep the window facing the corridor open, but let down a reed blind.

It was through the interstices of this reed curtain that one could get a peek of the gloomy interior and Dr Farooqui immersed in a heavy tome, with his pince-nez precariously balanced on the bridge of his nose, peering nearsightedly at the small print of the Arabic book. One could see that even in the privacy of his dark room, he would not take off his sherwani. The only concession he made to the summer of Madras was to remove his Turkish cap with its black tassel and hang it on a peg on the wall. Rarely did students visit him in his room. He did not encourage such intrusions as they distracted him from his study. And the forbidding aura of his privacy dampened the desire of even the most audaciously curious student. When the bell rang, he would put on his cap, button up his sherwani and walk sedately to the classroom. He appeared so malnourished that the sherwani sat loosely on his spare frame and thin arms.

One day, impelled by my curiosity and drawn by his reputation as a great scholar in the science and interpretation of the Quran, I ventured to knock on his door. He looked up from his deep absorption, perhaps with a bit of annoyance. 'Come in,' he said, in a rather low voice. I opened the door and while entering, I inadvertently banged it shut. It was a careless gesture on my part. He was a bit startled at the noise.

'And what brings you here?' he asked in a gentle voice without looking up from the closely printed Arabic tome which he was reading.

'I have come to request you to explain the meaning of a chapter of the Quran,' I ventured with some trepidation. For a moment, his quizzical glance rose to meet my eyes. 'Then sit down,' he said, removing his old-fashioned wire-rimmed glasses and placing them on a side table.

I saw that the two rickety chairs provided by the government to the heads of departments for visitors were both occupied by piles of books. As I was looking around for a place to park myself, I found that Dr Farooqui himself had got up and was engaged in clearing a chair for my convenience. I joined him in the task and once I sat down, he went back to his chair.

'And which part of the Quran do you need to have explained?' he asked. I did not note any annoyance in his tone. I had half expected that.

'The chapter named "Time",' I suggested. That is one of the shortest chapters of the Quran and I chose it because of its brevity.

'Ah, an interesting choice,' he said. 'What is your name? I don't recall it.' He glanced at me, questioningly. Once I told him my name, his next question was, 'What is your father's name? What does he do?' Then he asked 'What does your grandfather do?'

'He is no more,' I said. I skirted the question as I had no idea how my grandfather had earned his living.

'May God rest his soul in peace. What was his name?'

I told him.

'And where is he buried?'

'In Bangalore,' I replied.

That is what my father had told me. I had never visited my grandfather's grave.

'And your great-grandfather? Where is he buried?'

'I don't know but my father says, in Bangalore.'

'And your great-great-grandfather? What was his name and where is he buried?'

I had no answer to that and I confessed to my ignorance. I was wondering where all this catechism on my ancestors was leading to, and what it had to do with the Quranic chapter.

'How often do you visit the graves of your ancestors in Bangalore?'

This was an embarrassing question, to which I could not respond, without incriminating myself. I felt guilty at my neglect. He noticed my guilty silence.

'You are the direct descendant of your ancestors. But you do not even remember their names. Obviously, you do not much care to remember them and nor have they done anything remarkable to be remembered by their direct descendant. You do not visit their graves and nor do you even know the cemetery where they lie buried. So, if you, their direct descendant, do not remember them, who else would be interested in remembering them? Do you think anyone else in Madras or Bangalore is in the least concerned about your ancestors or whether they ever walked this earth?'

'No,' I said. 'But how does my forgetting my ancestors explain the chapter of Time?'

He perhaps perceived a note of impatience in my tone. He smiled sardonically. 'If you recall, the chapter of Time, one of the shortest chapters of the Quran, goes like this:

Wal'asri inna al insaana lafee khusrilla allatheena amanoowa
aa'miloo assalihati watawasawbilhaqqi watawasaw bissabr[1]
I swear by Time. Verily Man is in utter loss. Except those that have faith and perform good deeds. And mutually establish the Truth and help each other to persevere in it.

'God here swears by Time which is a great destroyer of the world and which obliterates everything in its path, including even the memory of your own ancestors. Since Time, the all-destroying time, is a mighty manifestation of God, the oath he swears is an awesome oath.

'There is a Hadith Qudsi, a sacred saying of the Prophet, in which Allah said, "Sons of Adam inveigh against Time, and I am Time, in my hand is the night and day."

'God is Time and the passage of night and day decreed by Him leaves nothing in its wake, with the exception of people who perform four acts—people who are firm in their faith in God, who perform good deeds, who help each other in upholding the truth and who help each other in persevering in that effort. These are the people who continue to remain alive in the memory of people long after time has destroyed their physical remains,' explained Dr Farooqui.

'I understand faith,' I said. 'Please explain what good deeds are. How do good deeds help in overcoming the ravages of Time?'

He smiled at the temerity of my claim to understand faith. Perhaps he knew that wiser men than me had struggled to understand and achieve faith with limited success. But he refrained from commenting on it.

'Some people claim to know good deeds even better than faith,' he said. 'What good deeds are has been defined elsewhere in many verses of the Quran. Among the several words used for a good deed are "aml salih" and "birr". Birr is a comprehensive word—it encompasses faith in God, in the authenticity of all the Prophets of God whom He has sent to guide the world from time to time, in charity for the love of God towards your kith and kin, the poor and the destitute, in freeing those in bondage, in establishing the institutions of prayer and poor-tax, in facing all calamities and disasters with courage and fortitude. That is what the Quran says. Besides these and other good deeds, is also the exhortation to avoid indulging in evil deeds. Avoidance of an evil deed is also a good deed. Good deeds are not merely to refrain from being evil and wicked, good deeds do not merely mean helping others, being charitable and tolerant of others' foibles and weaknesses. Good deeds involve even the littlest act that you perform to preserve God's creation and safeguard it. The Prophet prohibited the killing of even the ant and the bee. The Quran says that even the trees and the vines bow down to God in worship. So destroying them callously and indiscriminately is an act of sacrilege. For instance, when you came in you banged the door of the room. God had taken years to nourish and nurture in the forest that teak tree of which that door is made. Many men have toiled in the sun and the rain to cut it and transport it. Many carpenters were engaged to plane it, shape it and bring it to the shop. It behoves us to ensure that that door lasts as many decades and centuries as needed. If we treat it gently, it can last many years. But if we bang it every time we come in and go out, it won't last even a few years. That is one way of showing that we appreciate God's work and the labour of our fellow men. There is a Hadith Qudsi quoted by Tabarsi where God says: "I created more than three hundred and ten virtuous qualities. Whoever brings one of these qualities while acknowledging 'There is no god but Allah', shall enter Paradise." Perhaps one of the qualities is to respect all His creations.'

For a few moments, I felt abashed at the gentle rebuke in Farooqui Saheb's words. But he continued: 'Shaikh Sadi tells the story of a pious man who fell in love with a courtesan. Giving up his piety, he lusted after her. But the courtesan spurned all his advances. In desperation, he went to a magician and asked for an amulet that would break her resistance and influence the courtesan to receive his advances. The magician told him to come after a week, but to refrain from performing even a single good deed during the week. The distraught lover agreed, and abstained from all good deeds during the week.

When he returned, the magician gave him an amulet and said, "It has taken me a week to prepare this very powerful amulet and you will gain access to her instantly." However, when the lover went to the courtesan's house, with the amulet, he was thrown out ignominiously. Furious, the man returned to the magician and demanded an explanation.

"Tell me honestly, and recall. Did you do any good deed during the week?" asked the sorcerer.

"How could I?" said the lustful sinner. "I hardly stirred out of my house. But yes, as I was coming to your house I saw a stone in the middle of the road. I only pushed it aside to prevent wayfarers stumbling on it."

"And that is why my magic did not work. For that single good deed, God saves you from committing the sin of fornication. My sorcery failed."'

I recalled my schoolteacher Abdul Ali quoting a Hadith from Bukhari to this effect.

The professor resumed: 'When I went to Heidelberg in Germany to study many decades ago, I made do with two shirts, two trousers and a single jacket for two years. I wore those clothes so carefully, without rinsing them harshly and drying them gently, that even at the end of two years not a single button had broken. Not that I could not afford to buy a couple of more shirts. But the Quran taught me to conserve. "Eat and drink. But waste not. God does not love the wastrel."[2] And so let us not hasten what in any case Time, that is God as the Hadith Qudsi says, will obliterate with a few exceptions. This world is in any case evanescent and will vanish at its appointed hour. What will remain when everything vanishes will be God, and God alone.'

Qushayri, one of the earliest annalists of Sufism, wrote a manual of Sufism. Since the tenth century, this has become a source book on the technical terminology of Sufism, and has given us the lives and sayings of the early mystics of Islam. His *Risala*, which simply means *The Treatise*, has a passage on 'waqt'—a moment or time. Qushayri quotes:

They say the moment is a sword; that is, just as the sword is cutting, so the moment is what the Real brings to pass and completes. It is said the sword is gentle to the touch, but its edge cuts. Whoever handles it gently is unharmed. Whoever treats it roughly is cut. Similarly, for the moment, whoever submits to its decree is saved, and whoever opposes it is thrown over and destroyed. When the moment favours someone, the moment for him is just a moment. When the moment opposes someone, the moment for him is loathing.[3]

Dr Farooqui in his discourse covered the concept of historic Time in its macro, timeless aspect, as well as its temporal, micro aspect. But finally, whether you treat time—the moment, gently or harshly, you too, like everything else, and everyone else will perish and be obliterated. To repeat the verse of the Quran:

Everything on earth perishes, except the face of Thy Lord, in all its grandeur and glory.[4]

The imperishable is the face of the Lord alone, and I recalled what Krishna says in the Gītā to Arjuna:

paras tasmāt tu bhāvo'nyo'vyakto'vyaktāt sanātanaḥ
yaḥ sa sarveṣu bhūteṣu naśyatsu na vinaśyati
avyakto'kṣara ity uktas tam āhuḥ paramām gatim
yam prāpya na nivartante tad dhāma paramam mama[5]
But above this visible manifest is an unseen, which, when all created things perish, does not perish. This is called the Unmanifested, the Imperishable. This, men speak of as the highest way; they who attain it never return.

The Supreme Self in man too does not perish, for it is a spark, the spirit of God in man—the divine command, *amr*, in the human body.

To reach that state of mind where one can realize the divine in the human, one has to first clear the heart of all impurities, all 'creatures' as Abdul Qadir Gilani said, or one has to reach a state of *sthitaprajna* (equipoise) as the Gītā says. This word has many-layered meanings—secure understanding, steady wisdom, steadfast knowledge. A person who has reached the state of sthitaprajna is not moved by mundane emotions. Elsewhere the Gītā calls such a person *yogayukta*. Prophet Muhammad called such a person *haleem*, and in a famous saying, he exclaimed, '*Kaad al-haleemu an yakoonu nabiyya!*'—a haleem approaches the state of a prophet!

A Superior Man

How does the Gītā describe such a person? The last eighteen stanzas of the second adhyāya (chapter) will ever remain engraved in the reader's heart. They contain the essence of dharma. They embody the highest knowledge. 'The principles enunciated in them are immutable,' said Mahatma Gandhi.

So says the Gītā:

> *prajahāti yadā kāmān sarvān pārtha mano-gatān*
> *ātmany evātmanā tuṣṭaḥ sthita—prajñas tadocyate*[6]
> When a man abandons all desires of the heart and when his spirit is content in itself, then is he called sthitaprajna, stable in wisdom.

The Gītā expounds by saying:

> He whose mind is untroubled in the midst of sorrows and is free from eager desire amid pleasures, he from whom passion, fear and rage have passed away—he is called a sage of settled intelligence. He who is without attachment, who does not rejoice when he obtains good, nor laments when he obtains evil, is firmly fixed in perfect knowledge. One who is able to withdraw his senses from sense objects, as the tortoise draws its limbs within the shell, is to be understood as truly situated in knowledge. While contemplating the objects of the senses, a person develops attachment for them, and from such attachment lust develops, and from lust anger arises.[7]

Two of the most damaging emotions a sthitaprajna or a haleem has to keep under control are lust and anger, says the Gītā:

From anger, delusion arises, and from delusion bewilderment
of memory. When memory is bewildered, intelligence is lost,
and when intelligence is lost, one falls down again into the
material pool.[8]

Control of anger has been emphasized by every religion, every
saint, sage, and every mystic.

> *rāga-dveṣa-vimuktais tu viṣayān indriyaiś caran*
> *ātma-vaśyair vidheyātmā prasādam adhigacchati*[9]
> One who can control his senses by practising the regulated
> principles of freedom can obtain the complete mercy of the
> Lord and thus become free from all attachment and aversion.

This is the divine state of *brahmsthiti*, and having achieved this
state, one is never again bewildered. In that state, even at the hour
of death a man gets into the *brahmanirvāna*, oneness with God.

Sri Ramakrishna commenting on these verses gives very telling
analogies. He compares the senses to venomous snakes:

> People who live in localities infested with venomous creatures
> should always be alert and mindful of danger. Even so,
> people intent on spiritual growth should guard themselves
> against indulgent senses tainted with lust and greed.
> Poisonous snakes fatally hurt people. But the snake charmer
> handles them as if they are creatures of no consequence.
> More than that, he has quite a few of them coil, creep
> and writhe about his body. The senses likewise are
> undependable and treacherous too, in the case of the
> ordinary man. But they are ever tame and subservient to
> the knower of Ātman.[10]

Sri Ramakrishna was born before scientists made even the poison of the deadly cobra, krait and viper into an antivenom serum. Otherwise he might have commented on how even your anger, lust and greed, if controlled, sublimated and channelized, could be made to serve a socially useful purpose.

al-Ghazali insisted that anger and lust, the aggressive and sexual instincts in man, placed there for self-defence and procreation, are natural constituents of the human psyche. And since they are an ineradicable part of the human nature, they can only be tempered and restrained. They cannot be completely eradicated. Nor should they be. These instincts are not in themselves evil but, as al-Ghazali says, anger can be compared to a wild animal and lust to a pack animal.[11]

R.C. Zaehner, in his *Mysticism Sacred and Profane*, says:

It is probably these two faculties Jung had in mind when he discusses the 'shadow' since these qualities which principally contribute to loss of self-control, a condition, as Jung points out, when one is no longer 'oneself', when one 'forgets oneself' or is 'beside oneself'—what the Gītā calls 'bewilderment', 'loss of memory' and 'destruction of wisdom'. The remedy is to recognize it for what it is and once recognized, be subjected to reason or, in Jung's words, the conscious mind.[12]

Gautama Buddha taught the four noble truths to attain nirvāna, salvation, *nijat*. All sufferings (*dukha*), he said, arise from an intensity of desire from craving:

And this, O monks, is the truth of the Arising of Suffering. It is just thirst or craving (tanha) which gives rise to repeated existence, which is bound up with impassioned appetite, and which seeks fresh pleasure now here and now there, namely thirst for sensual pleasure, thirst for existence, thirst for non-existence.[13] Where does this craving come into being and settle itself? Wherever there is what seems lovable and gratifying, there it comes into being and settles.[14]

It is in human nature to crave for all sensual pleasures—sexual, gustatory, olfactory, tactile or whatever. We crave wealth, power, position, authority, name and fame. We admire our bodies and crave to keep them immaculate and beautiful. We even crave knowledge and righteousness; and our craving in the form of curiosity, eagerness to know leads us to sell our souls, like Goethe's *Faust*:

Inflamed by greed, incensed by hate, confused by delusion, overcome by them, obsessed in mind, a man chooses for his own application, for other's affliction, for the affliction of both, and experiences pain and grief.[15]

All religions seek to create a person who has eradicated greed, hate, aggression and violence from his mind, and has controlled lust and greed and put them to right use.

The *Yogavāsishta* calls such a person jivanmukta. Vasishta describes the jivanmukta as the happiest person on earth. He is neither delighted in prosperity nor dejected in distress. Outwardly discharging all the duties of life, he is free within. He is free from the bonds of caste and creed and is polite and friendly to all. He has nothing to attain, nothing to give up. Even in the midst of worldly activities, he is always in solitude and above life's turmoil. Having seen him, having heard about him, having met him, and having remembered him, all beings feel delighted. He has no longer any struggle for livelihood. The guardian angels of the world protect and support him, as they do the entire cosmos. The jivanmukta grows more and more powerful, intelligent and lustrous every day, in the same way as trees grow more and more beautiful in spring. He enjoys life, he is a great man of action and he is capable of the greatest renunciation.[16]

The great Urdu poet Mir Taqi Mir put it succinctly in a quatrain:

Miliye uss shaks se jo adam howey
Naaz ussko kamal par bahut kam howey
ho garme sukhan tho gird aawey ek khalkh
Khamosh rahey tho eik aalam howey
Seek that man who is utterly human; who takes no pride in his achievements. A concourse surrounds him when he opens his lips; and when he falls silent, he is a world in himself.

Confucius (551–497 BCE) or Kung fu-tzu, the great Chinese philosopher, calls such a person who is in control of all his senses a Superior Man (chun-tzu) and he describes the character, cast of thought and gestures of the Superior Man in contrast to the inferior man. The Superior Man is concerned with justice, the inferior man with profit. The Superior Man is quiet and serene, the inferior man always full of anxiety. The Superior Man is congenial though never stooping to vulgarity; the inferior man is vulgar without being congenial. The Superior Man is dignified without arrogance; the inferior man is arrogant without dignity. The Superior Man is steadfast in distress; the inferior man in distress loses all control of himself. The Superior Man goes searching for himself; the inferior man goes searching for others. The Superior Man strives upwards; the inferior man strives downwards. The Superior Man is independent, he can endure long misfortune as well as long prosperity, and he lives free from fear. He suffers from his own inability, not from others' failure to understand him. He avoids all competition. He is slow in words and quick in action. Such is the ideal man as perceived by Confucius.

In one of his famous Four Books, Confucius also explains the Doctrine of Mean, what the Prophet of Islam later called *hilm* and Gītā calls sthitaprajna. The Doctrine of Mean lies in the harmony of emotions that keeps the soul in a state of equilibrium. Such harmony links a person to the cosmic processes of life and creativity. To quote Confucius again:

> While there are no stirrings of pleasure, anger, sorrow or joy, the mind may be said to be in a state of equilibrium. When these emotions have been stirred, and set in their due degree, there ensues what may be called the state of harmony. The equilibrium is the great root of all under Heaven, and this harmony is the universal path of all under Heaven. Let the states of equilibrium and harmony exist in perfection, and a happy order will prevail throughout Heaven and Earth, and all things will flourish.

Confucius has described both a man who is at peace with himself and with the world. Heaven and Earth too can be at peace if humans control their excesses of pleasure and pain, sorrow and joy, anger and greed, lust and passion. Even the cosmic processes of life do get influenced by the individual and collective passions of mankind.

Shaikh Fadhlalla Haeri in the *Prophetic Traditions in Islam* talks of a similar Superior Man:

> The closest description of the man of taqwa is scrupulousness; he combines kindness with knowledge, words with deeds and rarely commits a wrong, his heart is humble, he is content in himself, he eats little food ... his desires have

been extinguished and his anger stilled. Good is expected of him and he himself is protected from evil . . . He forgives those who cause him harm and gives to him who withholds; he re-establishes relations with those who have broken with him. He is far from their corruption but gentle in his speech to them. He is absent from their bad actions and present for their kind actions. He accepts goodness from them and turns away from evil; he is dignified in the face of calamity and patient when faced with their plotting. He is thankful when things go right.[17]

The qualities of sthitaprajna enumerated by the Gītā, of jivanmukta by Vasishta, of chun-tzu by Confucius, of Superior Man by Haeri are epitomized in one Arabic word, *halim*, which the Prophet has used. The word is derived from the Arabic root *hilm* which is described by Pellat in the *Encyclopedia of Islam* (2nd ed.) as a complex and delicate notion which includes a certain number of qualities of character or moral attitudes ranging from serene justice and moderation to forbearance and leniency with self-mastery and dignity of bearing. Hilm consists of controlling oneself and not allowing any violent emotion, sorrow, happiness, or anger to burst out. It is the state of the soul which preserves its calm and does not easily allow itself to be carried away by anger. The basic element of hilm is self-mastery, dignity, detachment, patience, leniency and understanding. Ignác Goldziher, the German orientalist who has studied Islamic attitudes notes that 'hilm consists in not giving way to anger, sometimes going beyond simple moderation to become identical with forbearance'—where one strong man willingly suffers insults and refrains from avenging them. This form of hilm in the scorning of insults cloaks a considerable moral force, since indifference can, if possessed through a certain nobility of character, administer a more profitable lesson than a physical penalty to the guilty man. Hilm is an aristocratic virtue. The Quran calls some of the Prophets such as Abraham, Isaac, Shuayb, halim—long-suffering, patient, gifted with tolerance, slow to punish.

The Quran, describing such persons says:

Wáibadu arrahmanialladhina yamshoona ʹala al-ardi hawnanwa-idhakhatabahumu aljahiloona qaloosalama[18]
The true servants of the Beneficent are those who walk on the earth modestly and who, when addressed by the *jahil*, the rude barbarian, answer 'peace'.

This is a quality of hilm. One of the names of Allah, the thirty-third, is halim.

The Gītā also describes the qualities of a halim:

amānitvam adambhitvam ahiṁsā kṣāntir ārjavam
ācāryopāsanaṁ śaucaṁ sthairyam ātma-vinigrahaḥ[19]
Humility, modesty, non-violence, tolerance, simplicity, service to the teacher, purity (of body and mind), perseverance and self-control.

The Gītā, the Quran and the prophetic traditions describe the man of equipoise, equilibrium, and equanimity in almost the same language. Respect for age and service to the teacher, one who not only teaches you in the gurukul or madrasa, but from whose precepts and practice you have gained some knowledge. He is well-deserving of your respect, regard and consideration. A halim will accord all respect and regard to age, vulnerability and wisdom irrespective of the status, caste, creed or religion.

Rumi tells the story of Hazrat Ali, the beloved cousin and a later successor of Prophet Muhammad:

> Once Ali was hurrying to the mosque to join the dawn prayers (which have to be performed and completed before sunrise) being led by the Prophet himself in the Sacred Mosque. On the way he saw an old venerable Jew walking slowly in the same direction. Out of respect for his age Ali desisted from overtaking him and going ahead. He was delayed in reaching the mosque as the old man was walking slowly. The Prophet was just about to start the short prayer when God ordered him to delay it for a few moments, so that Ali did not miss it.

Rumi concludes this tale:

> When a saint like Ali showed so much respect for a poor old Jew, not even of the same faith, and God himself appreciated the gesture, consider how He will view any honor and veneration shown to elderly saints of known piety and that includes all one's teachers and gurus.

So, reading these descriptions of the man of steady wisdom, and secure understanding, sthitaprajna and steady in knowledge, chun-tzu, muttaqi, I went in search of such halims. I found them not in abundance but here and there. Some turned out to be my teachers in school and college, some I found amongst my colleagues and some in ashrams and mosques. Not one of them possessed all the qualities enumerated by the Gītā or Islamic ethics. But each had adopted some quality or the other of sthitaprajna and risen above the average man.

In college, my professor of English was Professor Ramaswamy.

He died recently at the ripe old age of ninety-four. I met him just a year before his death for the last time. I had been in touch with him from time to time since leaving college more than fifty years ago. He was a great scholar of the Gītā and had assisted President Radhakrishnan in his translation of the book.

Prof. Ramaswamy was a simple man, a strict vegetarian, who would bring to the college his food from home with a bottle of water. While being very orthodox in his religious beliefs, he followed the conventions of the time and always dressed in a three-piece woollen suit and a formal tie even in the high temperature and humidity of Madras. The government never provided air conditioners to mere professors in those days. (Nor does it do so now!) It was reported that he had been deputed by the government to China and had lived there for some time in the late 1940s/early 1950s, as an editor for a wing of the United Nations. He had managed to survive in an omnivorous country with his spartan habits and dietary restrictions. He said, 'I found no difficulty because I needed very little food. I could easily survive on the vegetables and fruits that were available in plenty.'

He quoted the Gītā to me, about three kinds of men. In the fourteenth chapter, the Gītā describes the different human natures—the good and pure, the passionate and the gross— sattvik, rajasik and tamasik. The sattvik man does not act sinfully; he is enlightened and lives in happiness of body and soul. The rajasik man is full of desires, ambitions and tries to fulfil them by aggressive actions. The tamasik man lives in darkness and ignorance. He is ruled by desires of the body—lust, hunger, gluttony, anger and greed. Human nature is a mix of all these three qualities and they are in constant strife in a man's self; sometimes one dominates, sometimes the other. These three types of natures are inclined towards three types of food respectively.

The food that increases longevity (ayu), purity (sattva), strength (balam), health (arogya), joy, cheer, and that which is tasty (asya), nutritious, substantial and pleasant (hrdyah), is dear to the sattvik. Food that is bitter, sour, salty, very hot, spicy, dry and that which causes pain and disease is dear to the rajasik. Food that is stale, insipid, putrid and unfit is dear to the tamasik.

Prof. Ramaswamy told me that he lived mainly on boiled vegetables, boiled rice and fruits during his time abroad and did not suffer even from a minor illness during that period. This was sattvik food.

Just as a man is inclined to like the food his nature dictates, in turn the food he eats also affects his nature. If you eat tamasik food, your nature will also become tamasik, so believed Prof. Ramaswamy. If you do not get sattvik food, it is better to fast.

The Quran enjoins eating of clean (tayyab) and permissible (halal) foods, and prohibits certain foods as they are non-permissible (haram). Pork, carrion, blood and intoxicating drinks are strictly prohibited. Food obtained through illegal and improper means too becomes haram. While the Quran names certain specific foods as halal and haram, God tells mankind, in the Quran:

> Eat of the good things we have provided for your sustenance but not to excess so that my wrath may not descend on you.[20]

La tataghau—do not gorge—is a categorical prohibition against excess in eating. Prophet Muhammad lived in a country that was mostly desert and the people of the desert are inclined to lead spartan lives because luxuries are not available. So the Prophet had no wish to live in any less spartan a fashion than his people. His main meal was usually a boiled gruel known as sawiq, with dates and milk, his only other meal of the day being dates and water. He frequently went hungry and developed the practice of binding a flat stone against his belly to assuage his discomfort. 'All clean food has been made lawful to you,' says the Quran. Clean food is the sattvik food that the Gītā recommends.

But one must remember that what is sattvik in one clime and at one time may not remain so in another clime and another time. So, beyond the specified foods prohibited by name, the Quran leaves it to mankind's common sense and sound judgement to determine what food is clean, and what is unclean.

While commenting on the classification of the three kinds of food that the Gītā mentions, Gandhi applies his own criteria:

If we cling to this classification, we shall not come to the right conclusion. Sri Krishna has first explained the qualities of the sattvik man and then his taste, etc. . . . There must have been a reason in that age for making such a classification, for there must have been persons even then who would eat a handful of chilies at a time. In the present age, there is no need for eating snighta (fatty) foods. If we start eating ghee our food would be not sattvik, but rajasik, such as a demon would love.[21]

The definition of sattvik, rajasik and tamasik food would differ from age to age, clime to clime, culture to culture and region to region. Pork and wine would be tamasik for a Muslim, while beef would be tamasik for a Hindu, even in small quantities. But for a European or Russian, all three in moderate quantities may be sattvik. Hence, the wider definition of the Gītā that all food that is healthy, enables a longer life and palatable is sattvik. That is what the Quran also advocates in the word tayyab, clean and pure, for Muslims.

It is reported of Confucius that while he had no objection to his rice being of the finest quality and nor to his meat being finely minced, he was careful to eat only in moderation. He would not eat rice affected by the weather, i.e., stale or spoiled or turned, and nor would he eat fish that was unsound or flesh that was tainted. He would not eat anything discoloured, smelly, under or overcooked or not in season. (This is the description of the tayyab food of Quran and sattvik food of Gītā.) However much meat there might be, he did not allow what he took to overpower the flavour of rice. He was not a great eater. He did not converse while eating, nor talk when in bed. Though his food comprised only coarse rice and vegetable broth, he invariably offered a little in sacrifice, and always did so with solemnity.

Excess and deficiency is not restricted to matters of food alone. The famous mystic and theologian al-Ghazali says that egotism and vices appear not only as excess but also as deficiency. The commanding self (nafs al-ammara) may command us to worship ourselves, it may also command us to damage and destroy ourselves. In both cases, it has made sure that we are too involved in thinking and worrying about ourselves, when we should be remembering God. Both excess and deficiency in our character will interfere with our ability to sense God's presence, which is just what the commanding self wants.

al-Ghazali therefore recommends moderation in eating, avoiding both extremes of gluttony and self-starvation. He quotes Abu Sulayman as saying:

If something is put before you in the nature of a desire which you have renounced, then partake of it just a little, but do not give your soul what it hopes for. In this way you will banish a desire without making it pleasurable for your soul.

In the words of the Quran: 'Eat and drink, but do not be extravagant.'

As the Bible says:

> If thou sit at a bountiful table, be not greedy upon it . . . Eat
> as it becometh a man . . . and devour not, lest thou be hated
> . . . Be not insatiable, lest thou offend . . . A very little is
> sufficient for a man well nurtured . . . Sound sleep cometh of
> moderate eating; he resteth early and his wits are with him.

Fasting and Purity

Fasting has been prescribed by many religions as a way of keeping
yourself pure. Fasting cleanses both your body and your mind.
Najmuddin Kubra (d.1220) in his book *al-Siyar al-Hayir* (*The
Bewildered Traveller*) has enumerated twenty-two benefits of
fasting. Among them, he says that by fasting, man resembles
those spiritual beings of God that eat none of the things we
eat, overpower the carnal soul (nafs ammara) that commands
evil, purifies it from sins, washes the psychic dirt from the soul,
banishes the cataracts that afflict the eye of the heart and enables
it to look on the hidden world and help in understanding the
suffering of the hungry with compassion and mercy. Fasting also
helps, says Kubra, in attaining bodily health, in avoiding silly and
foolish speech and in receiving faster aid and help from God.[22]

The Old Testament too had prescribed fasting as a means of
refining one's sattvik nature, subduing rajasik and eradicating
tamasik tendencies:

> Is not this the fast I choose—
> To loose the bonds of wickedness,
> To undo the knots of the yoke,
> To let the oppressed go free,
> And every yoke to snap?

Is it not to share your bread with the hungry,
And the homeless poor to bring home
When you see the naked, to cover him
And to hide not yourself from your own flesh . . .
If you remove from your midst the yoke
The finger of scorn, the mischievous speech,
And share your bread with the hungry,
And satisfy the craving of the afflicted
Then shall your light shine out in darkness
And your gloom shall be as noonday,
And the Lord shall guide you continually
And shall satisfy you with rich nourishment
And your strength shall he renew,
And you shall be like a well-watered garden
Or like a spring of water
Whose waters fail not . . .
And you shall be called 'The rebuilder of broken walls,
The restorer of streets to dwell in.'[23]

While talking of the spiritual significance of fasting, Rumi says it is not merely renouncing of physical food; it is abstaining from all things of this world that pander to the hunger of our baser nature. Fasting helps you in keeping away from tainted food, food that has been obtained through questionable means. Rumi tells the tale of a dervish who had a disciple who used to beg for him. One day, he brought some food for his master. The dervish ate the food, but his sleep was disturbed with carnal dreams. On being questioned, the disciple confessed that the food was given to him by a beautiful woman, perhaps a dancing girl.[24]

One may also recall the confession of Mahatma Gandhi who once ate goat's meat during his student days in England. That night he could not sleep as the goat kept bleating miserably in his stomach! It was tamasik food. And so Prof. Ramaswamy abstained from all rajasik and tamasik food.

I asked him why he had been willing to subject himself to such deprivation in a far off land for so long—was it for money? He smiled at my naive question and said, 'First of all I suffered no deprivation. I liked the food that I ate there—fresh vegetables and fruits cooked with my own hands. It was sattvik food and kept me healthy. Secondly, I did not work for money. I had gone there as I was deputed by the government and it was my duty.' Then he quoted the famous verse of the Gītā:

karmanāy evādhikāras te mā phalesu kadācana
mā karma-phala-hetur bhūr mā te saṅgo 'stv akarmaṇi[25]
You have a right to perform your duty. You have no claim to the fruits thereof. Never consider yourself to be the cause of the results of your activities, and never be attached to not doing your duty.

He did his job because it was a job to be done, even though it was in a far-off land and in days when communication was non-existent and basic amenities in a war-devastated country a luxury—he believed in the lesson of the Gītā: 'You have a right only to the performance of your duty, but not to the fruits thereof. Do not make the fruits of action, your motive, nor incline towards inaction.'

He said, 'This is the philosophy of nishkāma karma, action without attachment to results. All disappointments, all heartburns, all frustrations, all stress and tension arise only because one invests so much emotional capital into the results of action. You go to office punctually every day, you work hard, but you see that someone who has not put in a spot of work gets promotion and recognition. You run a legitimate business observing all the statutory rules and regulations, the mandates of corporate governance and the demands of corporate social responsibility. Yet your business fails.

'You see your rival, who never believed in any ethics of business, who cheated the banks and his suppliers, who exploited his workers and who polluted the environment for years to come, prosper and get the respect of the community. You feel disappointed, frustrated, and angry. You oblige others whenever they approach you, you help your relatives and friends but far from acknowledging it, they repay your favour with hostility, backbiting and downright betrayal.

'All this disappointment, frustration and anger arises out of your attachment to the expected fruits of your action. When you worked hard, when you helped others, when you conferred favours, when you followed all ethical dictates, you expected something in return. You expected profit, promotion and recognition for your work, you expected love and affection from your near and dear ones, and you expected your favours to be returned. When those expectations of the fruits of your actions were not fulfilled, all the negative emotions arose to consume your peace and quiet. That is why Sri Krishna advocates nishkāma karma—action without expectation of rewards.

'Once you achieve that state of mind, you never once feel disappointment, frustration, anger, etc. Since you had no expectations of any rewards for your work, you are not disappointed if your work bears inadequate fruits or no fruits at all.'

I listened to Prof. Ramaswamy's discourse on the philosophy of nishkāma karma. While intellectually I accepted the concept that all disappointments, sorrows, anger and hatred spring from attachment to the fruits of action, how is one to detach oneself from those expectations? Was it not Thomas Hobbes who said,

'No man doeth anything except he gaineth thereby?' Without a personal profit motive, be it in the form of material gain, fame, happiness or emotional satisfaction, all the operations of this world would come to a standstill. Unless this world is full of saints, how does one put the philosophy of nishkāma karma into practice? If I cannot hope for the fruits of my work, I might as well lie back and work no more. Why should I work at all then? All this I asked Prof. Ramaswamy. He was not perturbed at my questions.

'Krishna does not advocate inaction. Nor does he tell you not to gauge the likely result of your action before you undertake it. On the other hand, if you do not consider all the possible consequences of your action before your act, you will become a big cropper in this world. All that Krishna is advocating is that while you do calculate and take into account the results, the fruits of the action, you do not expect those as a matter of right. You do not attach yourself to those expected results. That is why He clearly says that you have no right, adhikar, on the fruits. If the fruits, expected or otherwise, come your way then well and good; you do not spurn them. If they do not accrue, as very often happens in this modern world of non-causality, do not be affected; do not be perturbed or disappointed. Do not jump with joy or ecstasy if the results are far better than what you planned for or expected, as sometimes does happen. The man with sthitaprajna, who does not attach himself to the fruits of his action, will never be disappointed, so will never be disheartened, never be angry, will never hate, never be bewildered, and will preserve his wisdom in all circumstances.'

Much later, I read Marcus Aurelius who said, 'When you have done good and another has benefited, why do you still look, as fools do, for a third thing besides credit for good works, or a return?'[26]

All religions, all philosophies, all mystics have defined one who has achieved sthitaprajna as a pure man—a man who wants nothing from the world, expects nothing from his work, remains in action yet detached from the fruits of action.

Shabistari, in his *Gulshan-e-Raz*, describes such a balanced man in sublime poetry:

Virtue and equity
Courage and temperance
Are the four qualities of the sage
He is not over-cunning or a fool
From cringing and boasting he is free
And from foolhardiness and cowardice.
All virtues lie between
Excess and deficit
A narrow path betwixt
Hell's bottomless abyss
Fine and sharp as a sword blade,
Which permits no lingering
Or turning round.
Equipoise is the summit of perfection
Becoming like a simple essence.[27]

While reading the great Chinese classic Tao Te Ching, I came across the observations of some commentators. The great Chinese mystic Chuang Tzu (or Zhuangzi), a worthy follower of Lao-Tze, who is credited with the spread of Taosim just as St Paul is credited with the spread of Christianity, has defined a pure man thus:

But what is a pure man? The pure men of old acted without calculation, *not* seeking to secure results. They laid no plans. Therefore, failing, they had no cause for regret; succeeding, no cause for congratulation. And thus they could scale heights without fear; enter water without becoming wet, fire without feeling hot. So far had their wisdom advanced towards Tao. The pure men of old slept without dreams and without anxiety. They ate without discrimination, took deep breaths for pure men draw breath from their utmost depths; the vulgar only from their throats. Out of the crooked, words are retched up like vomit. If men's passions are deep, their divinity is shallow.

The pure men of old did not know what it was to love life or to hate death. They did not rejoice in birth, nor strive to put off dissolution. Quickly come and quickly go—no more. They did not forget whence it was they had sprung; neither did they seek to hasten their return thither. Cheerfully, they played their allotted parts, waiting patiently for the end. This is what is called not to lead the heart astray from Tao, nor to let the human seek to supplement the divine. And this is what is meant by a 'pure man'.[28]

In one of the hymns of Adi Granth, the holy Book of Sikhism, we have this definition of a pure man—a man in whom God dwelleth and whose soul mingles with the Lord, that man who in the midst of grief is free from grieving:

And free from fear, and free from the snare of delight
Nor is covetous of gold that he knows to be dust
Who is neither a back-biter nor a flatterer
Nor has greed in his heart, nor
Vanity, nor any worldly attachment
In such a man God dwelleth
The man on whom the grace of the Guru alights
Understands the way of conduct
His soul, O Nanak, is mingled with the Lord
As water mingles with water.[29]

Playing your allotted part cheerfully is what Krishna advocates. He advises Arjuna that this state of nishkāma karma does not apply only to worldly actions. Even devotion to the Lord should not be with expectations of a reward. *Sarva ārambha parityāgi*— renouncing all understandings, he who is devoted to me is dear to me, says Kṛṣṇa.

Even the love of God, for the sake of salvation or paradise, was frowned upon by the true mystics. Rābi'a echoed Kṛṣṇa when she said, 'O God! If I adore you out of fear of Hell, burn me in Hell. If I adore you out of desire for Paradise, lock me out of Paradise. But if I adore you for yourself alone, do not deny me the vision of your eternal beauty.'

This is the philosophy at the very heart of the Gītā which has appealed to generations of Indians, but which only very few follow.

One must however remember that Kṛṣṇa does not advocate abstinence from necessary action, nor does he advocate mere mindless action which could lead to unintended results. Such action could be dangerous both to the doer as well as humanity at large. Action should certainly precede a planned result. But, Kṛṣṇa says, the doer should not be personally involved with the results of the action, he should not act with ulterior, self-serving motives. When you act with expectations of a return, and when that does not come through there is every chance that you will either become vindictive or give up your obliging acts in future. You may even attempt to harm those whom your actions have benefited but who did not even acknowledge those benefits. Man should not act with the intent to hurt or harm anyone. Kṛṣṇa praises that yogi as his most beloved bhakta who harms no one, nor allows anyone to harm him. There is a Hadith of Prophet Muhammad wherein he said, '*La dirar wa la dirar*'—harm not, nor be harmed.

And the Gītā says:

yasmān nodvijate loko lokān nodvijate ca yaḥ
harṣāmarṣa-bhayodvegair mukto yaḥ sa ca me priyaḥ[30]

He who does not inflict harm on others and does not allow the world to harm him, who is free from joy, anger, hatred, fear, anxiety—he is dear to me.

While not harming others is understood, how does one ensure that the world does not harm him? Prophet Muhammad once told his followers, 'Help the oppressed and the oppressor.' The amazed Companions asked him, 'How does one help the oppressor?' He replied, 'by preventing his oppression'. While one does not harm anyone in the world, it is also one's duty to see that oneself is not harmed either.

Ramakrishna Paramahamsa tells the story of a saint who was going on a pilgrimage:

On the outskirts of a village he was warned against using a shorter path as it was inhabited by a large venomous snake which attacked all wayfarers. The saint approached the hole and told the snake that what he was doing was evil and harmful to all and so he should abstain from such evil acts. The snake took the saint's advice to heart.

While returning from the pilgrimage, the saint happened to pass the same way. He found the snake cowering in its hole, wounded and starving. 'What has reduced you to this state?' asked the saint, sympathetically. 'I followed your advice and stopped biting people. Now every passerby throws stones at me. I cannot even stir out to search for food.'

'O foolish creature,' said the saint. 'I told you not to bite. But I did not ask you not to hiss!'[31]

To suffer evil, to suffer oppression and wickedness itself is a sin. A person who allows himself to be harmed without lifting a finger is not dear to God. So Krishna tells Arjuna:

niyataḿ kuru karma tvaḿ karma jyāyo hy akarmaṇaḥ
śarīra-yātrāpi ca te na prasiddhyed akarmaṇaḥ[32]
Do your bounden duty, for action is preferable to inaction.
Even the maintenance of your body will be impossible if
you abandon all activity.

Dil Mohammad explains:

Jo hai farz tera kar us par amal
Ki tark-e amal se hai behtar amal
Amal chode den-e hain tujhko tamaam
To mushkil hai tere badan ka qiyaam

Nor should one, says Krishna, run away from one's ordained duty
out of fear, out of cowardice or just because one faces difficulties,
dangers or inconveniences in its performance.

Woh buzdil jo takleef ke khauf se
Jo karne ka hai kaam us-e tyaag de
Samajh le rajavgun woh tark-e amal
Na haasil ho us tyaag se koi phal.

The Quran also refers to those who when ordered to fight for
their rights and to defend themselves from oppression, cry out,
'*Rabbana lima katabta 'alaynaalqitala lawla akhkhartana ila
ajalinqareeb.*'[33] (Our Lord, why hast Thou ordered us to fight?
Wouldst Thou not grant us respite until our natural term of life?)
But the life of this world is short, says the Lord, one should not
avoid doing one's duty for fear!

Yet again, the Quran exhorts:

Waltakun minkum ommatun yad'aoona ilaalkhayri
waya'muroona bilma'aaroofi wayanhawna 'aanialmunkari
waola—ika humu almuflihoon'[34]
And let there arise from among you a people inviting to all
that is good and enjoining what is right, and forbidding what
is wrong. They are the ones who shall prosper.

And enjoining the right and forbidding the wrong is the duty of
all those who believe in God. And above all, as the Quran says, '*al
fitnatu ak baru min al qatl*'[35] (oppression is worse than warfare).

Anyone who abandons his duty fearing discomfort and
difficulty is not really renouncing action. He is really doing so
out of *rajas*, mere carnal motives. He is not a yogi, says the Gītā:

Kar-e farz ko farz agar jaan kar
Ta-alluq ho uss-e na fikr-e samar
Jo asli hai Arjun yahi tyaag hai
Ki ayn-e sattav gun yahi tyaag hai.
But one who performs his duty knowing it is a duty, without
fear or favour, is really a renouncer! This is sattvik.

Exhorting Arjuna to engage in meaningful action, Krishna goes
on to add in the subsequent shlokas that God himself is constantly
engaged in action. There is nothing in the three worlds that has
not been wrought by God. As the Quran says:

ya'alamu ma feelbarri walbahri wama tasqutu minwaraqatin
illa ya'lamuha wala habbatinfee dhulumati al-ardi wala
ratbinwala yabisin illa fee kitabin mubeen.'[36]
He knoweth whatever there is on earth and in the sea. Not a
leaf falls but with His knowledge; and there is not a grain in the
darkness of the earth which is not there in the Book manifest.

Slumber does not overtake him nor sleep.[37] It is this ceaseless activity that keeps the Universe on course.

Even though God alone has wrought the three worlds, the nether world, the phenomenal world and the next world, or in other words, pāthāl, prthvi and swarga—the animal world, the human world and the spiritual world, yet He is constantly engaged with all the worlds and does not cease from His activity. There is yet another purpose behind this ceaseless activity. As Krishna explains, if He ever ceases from His activity, the world would come to a standstill:

> utsīdeyur ime lokā na kuryāṁ karma ced aham
> saṅkarasya ca kartā syām upahanyām imāḥ prajāḥ[38]
> These worlds would perish if I cease my activity and I would
> be the cause of chaos and destruction of all creation.

Muslim philosophers and theologians basing their opinion on the Quran and Hadith are unanimous in their view that God as a Creator is continuously engaged in the act of creation.

Krishna has yet a third reason for emphasizing God's eternal activity—for he is encouraging Man to cast himself in the image of God.

Prophet Muhammad is reported to have said, 'takhalluqoo bi akhalqillah'—create in yourself the attributes of God. And the Quran says, 'Slumber does not affect him, nor sleep.' If humans believe that God also ceases His activity, they too may be tempted to follow and cease from activity. Inaction of mankind would bring about the collapse of the social order, just as the inaction of a head of a family leads to the perishing of the family.

Allama Iqbal, throughout his poetry, always exhorts man to be active.

He writes:

Junbish se hai zindagi jahaan ki
Yeh rasm qadeem hai yahaan ki
Hai daudta ash-hab-e zamana
Khaa Khaa ke talab ka taaziyana
Iss raah mein maqaam be-mahal hai
Pasheeda qaraar mein ajal hai
Chalne waale nikal gaye hain
Jo thhahre zaraa, kuchal gaye hain
anjaam hai iss khiram ka husn
Aagaaz hai ishq, intihaa husn.
The life of the world depends on activity
This is the primordial custom of the world.
The steed of Time is galloping fast
Driven by the whip of Desire
To stop on the road is inexcusable
For death is lurking in repose
Those who moved managed to succeed
And those who paused awhile are crushed
The end of this journey is Beauty
The start is Love, the Zenith is Beauty.

Iqbal claimed himself to be an acolyte, a follower of Rumi—the relationship that exists between a mystic saint, a pir, and his follower, a murid.

Iqbal's teacher, Rumi again, a committed follower of the Quran and the Prophet, exhorts man to be always striving, acting without concern for the results or the outcome:

koshish-e behooda bih az khuftagi
een dareen rah mitaraash o mikharaash
Taa dam-e aakhir dami farigh mubaash
It is better to strive even vainly, than to sleep; this way

remain, struggling, striving until thy last breath, do not be idle for a moment.

Even if the ordinary man, unaware of the higher purpose of nishkāma karma seeks a profit motive in his actions, Krishna exhorts the wise man, not to interfere with the approach of such simple, ordinary folk. Krishna says:

> *na buddhi-bhedaṁ janayed ajñānāṁ karma-saṅginām*
> *joṣayet sarva-karmāṇi vidvān yuktaḥ samācaran*[39]
> Let not the wise man confuse those who are attached to the fruits of karma. The wise man should persevere in his selfless action so as to provide an example to the ignorant.

Krishna recognizes that it is difficult, if not impossible, for the common man to labour without expecting anything in return. And the majority of humanity consists of the common men. The philosophy of nishkāma karma would be difficult for them to understand, appreciate and follow. The best way to bring them round is not to involve them in scholastic discussion on the philosophy of nishkāma karma but to persuade them by setting them an example. The wise man therefore tries to behave wisely before the common man and sets before them, a goodly example of what the Quran calls *bil hikma* (with wisdom).

Swami Vivekananda summed up the philosophy very succinctly when he wrote:

> If we give up our attachment to this little universe of senses, we shall be free immediately. The only way to come out of bondage is to go beyond the limitations of law, to go beyond causation. But it is most difficult to give up the clinging to the universe—few ever attain to that . . .

The other way is not negative but positive . . . it is to plunge into the world and learn the secret of work . . . Do not fly away from the wheel of the world-machine but stand inside it and learn the secret of work, and that is the way of karma yoga . . . Through proper work done inside, it is also possible to come out.[40]

Krishna had earlier explained to Arjuna that an illuminated man, a wise man has to set a good example in his behaviour, for the ordinary people, the common men, always look up to such a role model. It is therefore incumbent on those who wield authority and power, and have a status in society, to remember that they are role models, and the common folk of the land will follow them in their social, ethical and moral behaviour.

Work Is Worship

Madhavsinh Solanki was one of those persons who had perhaps imbibed many of the lessons of Gītā—control of anger, maintenance of balance in life, equanimity of demeanour, equipoise, sthitaprajna, and retaining a sense of humour in adverse times. He had internalized these lessons, though I have never heard him quote from that book.

I met him when he was a junior minister in the Gujarat government in the early 1960s. I was touring the hilly areas of Banaskantha district in Gujarat, riding out to inspect various villages which were under drought because of the failure of the monsoon. This area of Gujarat bordered on the barren Rann of Kutch on the west and the desert of Sindh (in Pakistan) on the north. It suffered permanently with scanty rainfall and the soil produced but poor crops. Some vegetables were grown in small patches wherever the farmer could garner a few drops of water. His staple diet consisted of bhakri, dry bread, moistened with crushed onions. Whenever I happened to camp among the villagers, as an honoured guest I was usually provided with a glass of warm milk to enable me to swallow the dry bread.

Once when returning to Varahi, the taluka headquarters after an inspection, I was caught in a heavy downpour. I lost my way, as the cart track which I had followed all along was washed away in the flood waters. Dusk had already fallen on the dak bungalow when my bedraggled horse and I reached there utterly exhausted. As I stepped on to the veranda, a gentleman in a clean white kurta and immaculate dhoti stepped out of a room and introduced himself to me. That was my first sight of Madhavsinhbhai.

We remained confined for the next three days to the dak bungalow surviving on a bland and boring diet of chapattis and roast chicken, occasionally relieved by fried chicken and bhakris. No vegetables, not even an onion, could be obtained as the rains were too heavy. Though variety was lacking in the food for the body, Madhavsinhbhai provided a variety of intellectual sustenance. During those three days we discussed a range of topics—Urdu poetry, Gujarati poetry, Sufism, English novels, films, Lata Mangeshkar and Mohammad Rafi, Mirza Ghalib and in between, the problems of district administration in Gujarat. I found Madhavsinhbhai to be an avid reader and it was he who introduced me to Tolkien, Milan Kundera, Gabriel Garcia Marquez and Pablo Neruda. And it was during those three days that we developed a strong bond of friendship that continues to this day.

When his political party returned to power in the next election, Madhavsinhbhai declined a cabinet minister's post, preferring to go back to his law practice. I asked him why he had declined a cabinet post, which so many in politics hankered after. He replied, 'You see Moosa, my five years of ministership were a heavy financial burden. I had to offer hospitality to every visiting constituent of mine, and had to take care of all those from Kheda who required medical assistance and help. That wiped out all my savings. Politics is an uncertain profession and I don't even have a flat of my own. I thought I would take a respite, earn some money in legal practice and once I have a flat and build up some reserves, I might think of returning to politics.'

He did return to politics, first as a cabinet minister and then to take over the reins of the state as chief minister. I worked with him for some time as his principal secretary and had the opportunity of observing him at close quarters. He was the epitome of courtesy, soft-spokenness, self-control and dignity. He would not behave in a vindictive manner even towards his political rivals and was always willing to help his colleagues and subordinates and rarely asked them to do what he could do himself. As his principal secretary, I used to sit late in his sitting room to go over official files. Whenever he needed a glass of water and it was late, he never woke his peon up but would go and fetch it himself. I remember that even during the office hours, when we were working together, he would get up from his chair, walk all the way around the table to my side, bend down and push the call button. To my remonstrance that I could have performed that simple task by lifting a finger, he would smile and say that he did not want to trouble me. I recalled what Confucius had said about a man of honour: 'A man of honour makes demands upon himself; the man without a sense of honour makes demands on others.'

Iqbal, in his *Asrar-e-Khudi* (*Secrets of the Self*), exhorts the reader:

Khud farood aa az shutar misl-e Umar
Al-hazar, az minnat-e ghayr, al-haza
Get down from the camel, as Umar did. Beware of accepting others' obligation! Beware!

This refers to an incident in the life of Umar, the Caliph of Islam. As he was setting out on a journey, he got up on a sitting camel and made it go through all the convoluted motions to stand up. In the process, his whip fell down. He made the camel go through all the motions in reverse, got off, picked up his whip, got on and made the camel go through the motions again. A companion standing by who observed all the trouble Umar went through, remarked, 'O Commander of the faithful, I could have picked up the whip for you.' Umar smiled and said, 'For a simple task like that, why should I ask you to oblige me?'

One day, while I was sitting with Madhavsinhbhai in his chamber, he handed me a slip of paper with a name on it and said, 'That person is an old classmate of mine. We studied together in school in Kheda district. He is today the mamlatdar of Visavadar taluka and has approached me with a request to transfer him to Umreth. I believe the post is vacant or about to fall vacant. Please help him.'

On returning to my chamber, I rang up Mr KNZ, the revenue secretary, who was the transferring authority and conveyed to him the chief minister's request. Mr KNZ, who was my senior, asked me to send him a note. I promptly did so with the details of the request. Mr KNZ sent back a long response, delineating the current transfer policy of the government in relation to mamlatdars and saying how injustice would accrue to other prior claimants for the Umreth post. He desired that a clear directive should be issued to him to deviate from the operative policy. Madhavsinhbhai laughed when he read the note.

'Let him have his way,' he said. 'KNZ is merely doing his duty. I do not want to overrule him.'

KNZ retired during the second stint of Madhavsinhbhai's tenure as the chief minister. He was immediately appointed chairman of the State Public Service Commission that recruited personnel for all state civil services. I asked the chief minister what led to his choice of KNZ for the post. His reply was remarkable.

'A man who refused to transfer a personal friend of the chief minister on a junior post is not going to succumb to any political pressures. The Public Service Commission's integrity is safe in his hands.'

I recalled that the Gītā exhorts that one achieves perfection through action, through right action and not through its avoidance. Doing one's duty and supporting persons in the performance of the right action is also necessary to establish a role model for the guidance of other men, for their protection—lokasamgraham.

To repeat what the Gītā says:

> *yad yad ācarati śreṣṭhas tat tad evetaro janaḥ*
> *sa yat pramāṇaṁ kurute lokas tad anuvartate*[1]
> Whatever a great man does is followed by others. The world follows the example set by him.

Solanki never lost touch with the common man and the poor. In a discussion on good eating places, he once recommended a dhaba on the national highway to Bharuch as a place that served good food. Some years later I was travelling to Bharuch from Baroda. As lunchtime approached, I remembered his recommendation and asked the driver to drive there. And what did I find? The chief minister's car and his personal escort standing outside and Madhavsinhbhai ensconced in the midst of a crowd of truck drivers, Sikhs from Punjab, Muslims from UP and dalits from Tamil Nadu, enjoying a plate of tandoori chicken and nan, and discussing the cost of diesel and oil with them.

In Chapter 12 of the Bhagavad Gītā, Krishna describes the traits of the man who is dear to him:

> *sanniyamyendriya-grāmaṁ sarvatra sama-buddhayaḥ*
> *te prāpnuvanti mām eva sarva-bhūta-hite ratāḥ*[2]
> Restraining all the senses, even minded everywhere, taking pleasure in the welfare of all beings, such a devotee comes to me.

The Gītā emphasizes two qualities here—even-mindedness and service to humanity. The devotee who does not discriminate between the high and the low, between the rich and the poor, between the followers of this religion or that, between members of this caste and that, and is happy to serve all humanity without discrimination is the one who is dear to God.

Some years later, during his second stint as chief minister, I happened to be in Gandhinagar and thought of calling on him. His secretary told me that he was meeting some important shaikhs from the Middle East to persuade them to invest in Gujarat. I took a quick peep into the room and saw him deep in discussion surrounded by the chief secretary, finance secretary, industry secretary and half a dozen Arab gentlemen in their white *kandooras* and *ghutras*. As I was about to withdraw, he noticed me.

'Moosa!' he exclaimed 'What a pleasant surprise. Do come in. We are discussing how to attract investment into Gujarat. Your advice would be welcome.'

So I went in and choosing a vacant corner seat, I sat down and lit a cigarette. Not wanting to participate in a discussion whose head or tail I had no knowledge of, I went off into a reverie. After a few moments, I suddenly noticed an inch of ash trembling on the tip of my cigarette, threatening to fall on to the carpet. I thought of going out in search of an ashtray but even the slightest movement on my part would detach the ash from the cigarette. I was staring at the impending catastrophe, wondering how and where to dispose of the ash without getting up when I noticed a sudden silence in the room. I looked up to see the chief minister himself bringing a small side table with an ashtray on it, for my utterly embarrassed convenience. Madhavsinh Solanki also provided a role model in modesty, humility, total absence of arrogance and any vestige of pride.

This selflessness despite enjoying power and privileges, finds comment in many religions. The Talmudic saying is:

> God loves these three: the person who does not get angry, the one who does not get drunk, and the one who does not insist upon his privileges.

Performance of duty, unaffected by the possible results is called samatvam yoga—equanimity yoga—in the Gītā, because the performer retains his balance (equanimity) in the midst of opposite pulls.

As the Gītā says:

> *yoga-sthah kuru karmāṇi saṅgaṁ tyaktvā dhanañjaya*
> *siddhy-asiddhyoḥ samo bhūtvā samatvaṁ yoga ucyate*[3]
> Do thy work steadfast in devotion, renouncing attachment, be still the same in success and failure with an evenness of mind. This is called samatvam yoga.

Ramakrishna says:

> Be in this world even as a maidservant in a rich man's house. While enjoying the sojourn, she knows in her heart that none of the assets which she uses belong to her. She is not attached to them. So, just as she can relinquish her notional ownership of her master's property, one should also be prepared for separation from such earthly possessions.[4]

al-Ghazali, the most famous mystic of Islam, asks the samatvam yogi to live like a civil servant in a government house, using all the facilities legally placed at his disposal, but never attached to them and ready to leave them all at a moment's notice once the transfer order comes.

Many years later, I met Madhavsinhbhai again, when he and his party had lost power in the state. I happened to be in Ahmedabad and I learnt that he was now living in Navrangpura. Since I was staying with a friend in the vicinity, I thought of calling on him and inquiring after his health. I got hold of his telephone number from his former personal assistant and called him. There was no answer. After several futile tries I decided to walk across to his residence.

He was living in a two-bedroom flat on the second floor of a multi-storey complex. I saw no security man at the door. On my pressing the bell, the door was opened by Madhavsinhbhai himself. The small living room was furnished with a simple sofa and a couple of chairs.

'I am sorry to have barged in like this without notice, sir,' I apologized. 'I rang several times, but perhaps you didn't hear it ring.'

'No, I heard all the rings. But when I picked up the receiver, the connection didn't get made. There is something wrong with the instrument since yesterday. I am able to call others but others are not able to get through. It must be so frustrating to all my friends.'

Then he picked up the receiver and rang the telephone exchange.

'Madam, I have lodged several complaints about my telephone, but without response from you. I have told you my name is Madhavsinh Solanki. I am the ex-chief minister of Gujarat. And I would like to remind you that the post of chief minister is a temporary one. But the post of ex-chief minister is a permanent one!'

I burst out laughing.

'What to do, Moosa,' he said ruefully. 'The lady doesn't seem to have heard of me at all!'

Madhavsinhbhai never showed an iota of regret at the loss of his status, his palatial official bungalow and all the trappings of the most powerful office in the state. That is samvatyoga.

Duty and Non-attachment

Khwaja Ala al Din Attar, a famous Sufi of Central Asia, defined non-attachment thus:

The object of the quest is to rid oneself of all attachments that stand in the way of Truth. Our revered Khwaja Bahauddin Naqshbandi was most careful never to regard any object or state as belonging to him. If he donned a new robe, he would wear it as something borrowed, saying, 'This is so-and-so's robe.'

I had an opportunity to visit the tomb of Khwaja Bahauddin Naqshbandi located near Bukhara, in 1990. Its last *sajjadanashin* lived for decades in exile in Syria, as the Soviets who ruled Bukhara had burnt all the religious books in the library of the monastery and executed most of the disciples of the order who lived there. Yet, the old man received me with great affection and humility and treated me with the meagre hospitality that he could afford. I could see the vestiges of Bahauddin's humility in the visage of his successor—600 years later!

One who can get rid of the consciousness of good and bad results (sukrta and dushkrta) and acts for its own sake, strives for real yoga which is to do the best in all activities.

According to the Gītā:

buddhi-yukto jahātīha ubhe sukṛta-duṣkṛte
tasmād yogāya yujyasva yogaḥ karmasu kauśalam[5]
One who has a balanced mind frees oneself from the pulls

of vice and virtue. Therefore, devote yourself utterly to your duty—for work done to perfection is itself yoga.

This attitude of mind-commitment to action, to do your duty aiming to do it perfectly and yet remain totally detached is also called buddhi yoga by Krishna. Samatvam yoga and buddhi yoga both are attitudes of mind. Swami Vivekananda talks of a yogi seated in a Himalayan cave who allows his mind to wander by thinking of unwanted things. On the other hand, a cobbler sitting at a corner of a busy crossing is absorbed in mending a shoe, with total concentration, intent on doing a good job as an act of service. Of these two, says Vivekananda, the latter is a better yogi than the former.

So Krishna does not advocate mere performance of duty without attachment to its fruits, but goes one step further and advocates that such duty should be performed to the best of one's ability.

'Yoga karmasu koushalam' is the motto adopted by the Indian Administrative Service which unfortunately is honoured more in breach than in observance nowadays.[6]

Junayd Baghdadi is known as the greatest exponent of the 'sober' school of Sufism[7] as opposed to the 'ecstatic' typified by Hallaj and Bayazid in Baghdad and Sarmad in India. Farid al-Din, his biographer, tells of an anecdote in the life of Junayd. A thief had been hanged in Baghdad. Junayd went and kissed his feet.

'Why did you do that?' he was asked.

'A thousand compassions be upon him!' he replied. 'He proved himself to be a true man at his trade. He did his work so perfectly that he gave his life for it.'

From childhood I had been brought up on such and similar other stories. So when I learnt from the Gītā that yoga consists in doing whatever duty is cast on you to its utmost perfection, the shloka appealed to me. And I have attempted to follow it not only in my own personal life, but in persuading others, my family and colleagues, to follow it too.

During the early 1980s, I was posted as the chairman and managing director of the Gujarat State Fertilizer Company, one of the largest fertilizer and chemical companies of India. Within weeks of my joining, I found during a review meeting that one of the company's twenty plants producing caprolactam, the raw material of which nylon is made, was functioning far below its nameplate capacity—at a mere 40 per cent. But much worse, it was producing caprolactam of an inferior quality—with an unacceptable PN number of 2000 against the international norm of 20,000!

The technical director argued defensively that the original technology was defective and that even after the ongoing quality improvement program (QIP), the plant would not function beyond 60 per cent capacity because of the insurmountable problems of wrong technology, low-capacity reactors and poor catalysts. It was thus claimed that all the reasons for failure were external and beyond remedy. Since the losses were mounting month by month, I thought I had to do something to either improve the situation or close down the plant permanently. I invited a British expert from the UK, Mr Shaw, a retired caprolactam technologist, at a nominal cost under the ODA (Overseas Development Assistance) to come and study our plant and give us his expert advice.

He stayed for a month and observed the functioning of the plant and its intricacies and then asked for a one-to-one meeting with me—without any of my officers present. He told me that making caprolactam was not a science. It was an art. It required total commitment and dedication of the staff at all duty points—any carelessness, casual approach or negligence would make a lot of difference both to the quality and quantity produced. Unless each and every staff member put in his work with total dedication and sincerity, neither the operations nor the quality would improve. The reasons were not merely technological or related to machinery. They had more to do with the morale of the staff. He said all the fifty or so staff members working in the plant were rejects from other plants—recalcitrant staff—disobedient, obstructive and argumentative and hence transferred as punishment to the caprolactam plant, which was already condemned as a write-off by the management. My officers, he said, had no rapport with the operating staff and rarely visited the plant. They did not want to enter into any discussions with the staff, since they believed that the plant was a hopeless case and the staff, write-offs.

I went to the plant, talked to all of them at length, listened to their reasons for the deficiencies and found out that they had some minor grievances mostly related to working conditions, absence of basic amenities and delayed promotions. Since they felt condemned and neglected, they reacted like condemned convicts—sullen, truculent, defiant and contentious. So in turn they neglected the plant. I redressed some of their grievances on the spot and promised to look into the others in time. I also talked to them in detail of the Gītā and *karmanievadhikaraste,* samatvam yoga, buddhi yoga and *yoga karamasu kaushalam.* While they were argumentative and bellicose, they were basically devout and religious by commitment. They were the more intelligent of the staff, and hence the most discontented. The concept of yoga karamasu kaushalam appealed to their inner consciousness. 'Yoga consists in performing all your actions with competence and commitment,' I told them. Nobody had condemned them or convicted them. We just had to let them work with the consciousness of good work being its own reward and rewards would automatically follow without their asking for it. I asked the senior officers to visit the plant regularly and redress their grievances expeditiously and occasionally I dropped in at the plant in the middle of the night to sit and chat with the control room staff.

Even before the QIP was complete, production went up, quality improved and within three months the plant was working at 80 per cent capacity. By the time the QIP was commissioned, it had crossed 100 per cent capacity and today it is functioning at 120 to 130 per cent capacity and producing caprolactam of a 22,000 PN number, which is on a par with international standards.

Many years later after demitting office, when I visited the plant at the invitation of my successor, I found a wooden board at the entrance to the control room with 'Yoga karamasu kaushalam' painted on it in prominent colours! My successor said that the staff there was the best!

Krishna says buddhi yoga is superior to mere action—it is non-attachment, a combination of a mental attitude (sānkhya) and a way of action. Buddhi yoga involves acting with a mental attitude of non-attachment to the action as also its results. Buddhi yoga therefore would comprise of both jnāna yoga and karma yoga.

Prof. Ramaswamy was a buddhi yogi. One fine morning, I came to the college and saw a strange man, an almost unrecognizable Ramaswamy with a shaven head, a tuft at the crown, a prominent caste mark on his forehead, a plain kurta from which the janeve, the sacred Brahminical thread, was visible, a dhoti tied in the traditional style and wooden pattens on the feet! Gone were his three-piece tweed suit, his tie, his centre-parted hair and his shoes with woollen socks!

All the students were amazed and consumed with curiosity. What had wrought this transformation? Even his colleague, Prof. Jagadeesan called it a 'translation', in Shakespearean terms.

Dorairaj called it a 'metamorphosis' in Kafkaesque terms. I was chosen by my fellow students to go into the lion's den or rather the 'yogic cave' and discover the secret of the metamorphosis.

With great trepidation, I knocked on the door and was asked to come in. 'Yes?' he said, inviting me in with a quizzical look on his face. I sat silent, tongue-tied, not knowing how to frame the question. He was amused. With a twinkle in his eye and a gentle smile, he said, 'You and your friends are curious and want to know why I have shed my suit and shorn my hair?'

I said 'Yes sir, we didn't recognize you.'

'In fact, the departmental peon too didn't recognize me. I had to convince him of my identity before he would let me in,' he said. Then he told me the story.

The paramacharya of Kanchi, the late senior, was camping at Ennore near Chennai and Prof. Ramaswamy had gone to listen to the discourse on Gītā as was his wont, straight from the college. He was a favourite disciple of the paramacharya and had once even taken me to visit him.

During the discourse, the paramacharya was explaining the sixteenth adhyaya. He spoke at length of people who were too involved in the world, who were caught in the net of ambition and lust, who earned money by unlawful means and squandered it in enjoyment and luxuries, who went from fulfilling one desire to the next, who prided themselves on amassing wealth and believed that it would keep them company permanently, who took pleasure in putting down one rival after another, who boasted of their bloodline and pedigree and above all, who performed even sacrifices for the sake of earning name and fame, out of mere hypocrisy.

As Krishna says that bound by a hundred ties of hope, caught in the snares of lust and anger, people adopt all unlawful means to gather wealth for their sensual enjoyment:[8]

idam adya mayā labdham imaṁ prāpsye manoratham
idam astīdam api me bhavisyati punar dhanam
asau mayā hataḥ śatrur hanisye cāparān api
īśvaro'ham ahaṁ bhogī siddho'haṁ balavān sukhī
āḍhyo'bhijanavān asmi ko 'nyo 'sti sadṛśo mayā
yakṣye dāsyāmi modiṣya ity ajñāna-vimohitāḥ[9]

This, say they, 'I have gained today; that desire of my heart I shall obtain. This possession is now mine, and that shall be mine tomorrow. He is my enemy, and I have killed him; and my other enemy will also be killed. I am the lord of everything. I am the enjoyer. I am perfect, powerful and happy.

aneka-citta-vibhrāntā moha-jāla-samāvrtāḥ
prasaktāḥ kāma-bhogesu patanti narake'śucau[10]

Tossed to and fro by many thoughts, enveloped in the meshes of delusion, devoted to the enjoyment of their lust, even sacrifices they offer with hypocrisy, without the sincerity of purpose.

The paramacharya quoted Krishna's condemnation of *dambhena* (with pride), ostentation, deceit and hypocrisy—especially the hypocrisy of performing yajna (holy sacrifice) for the sake of name, fame and recognition.

The paramacharya would have quoted Jesus Christ, had he recalled what Jesus said about fasting:

When you fast, do not put on a gloomy look, like the hypocrites, for they neglect their personal appearance to let people see that they are fasting. I tell you, that is all the reward they will get. But when you fast, perfume your hair and wash your face, so that no one may see you are fasting, except your father who is unseen, and your father who sees what is secret, will reward you.

dambho darpo'bhimānaś ca krodhaḥ pārusyam eva ca
ajñānaṁ cābhijātasya pārtha sampadam āsurīm[11]
Ostentation, arrogance and self-conceit, anger and also harshness and ignorance belong to one who is born, O Partha, of a demoniac state.

When the discourse reached this last line, Prof. Ramaswamy felt that the paramacharya was looking at him directly, at his appearance and attire. Ramaswamy felt that it was a message to him to give up all ostentation and hypocrisy and become a humble yogi—to bring his outward in consonance with his inward, for as the Gītā says, what a great man does is followed by the common folk. Therefore the Gītā casts a greater responsibility on the men of knowledge—gyanis and men of discernment rather than on the common man. Straight from the discourse, Ramaswamy went to the barber, had his head shaved and adopted the traditional Brahmin attire. That was a transformation.

I would often visit Prof. Ramaswamy in the early mornings. He would be performing his pooja and his wife would direct me to the pooja room, a plain unadorned room with bare walls. He would be squatting on a wooden plank, bare-chested, and performing aarti. He would cast a casual glance at me and signal me to sit against the wall. I would squat on the floor until he had completed his devotions and then he would turn and greet me.

Even though Prof. Ramaswamy was a strict Brahmin, observing all the religious rituals and following all the Brahminic laws, he never entertained an iota of prejudice against other religions, or made any denigrative or contemptuous gesture. He exemplified the even-mindedness that the Gītā advocated. Even though he knew I was a Muslim, he invited me into his pooja room and allowed me to sit with him during his devotions. He was a living lesson in tolerance, respect for all dharmas, yet a strong believer in his own dharma. Ramaswamy was quite fond of quoting from the writings of Christian saints. Often we discussed Islam and its contributions to the building of the concept of India.

Contrary to all the false propaganda and misconceptions about Islam, it is a religion which has taught tolerance, respect for other religions, inclusivity and pluralism. Without these qualities, Islam would not have spread so rapidly in the world and continue to claim new adherents every day.

Right from the days of the Prophet, the lessons of tolerance and respect for other faiths was emphasized both in words and actions. There is a well-known story of the visit of the Christians of Najran to Medina during the time of the Prophet. A delegation of Christian priests, more than a score in number, led by Bishop Haris came over to negotiate a peace treaty with Prophet Muhammad. He put them up in the mosque, today the second-most holy mosque of Islam. During the parleys (perhaps it was a Sunday) the time for the Christian prayers came. Bishop Haris asked the Prophet to show him a place where he and his companions could perform their prayers.

'You can do so right here,' said the Prophet. 'For this is a house of God.'

'But we pray with bells, incense and chanting,' said the Bishop.

'To each community, their way of prayer,' said the Prophet.

And the Christians performed their mass in one of the holiest mosques of Islam, in their own way, in accordance with their own dharma.

As a corollary to the Prophet allowing the mass to be performed in what later came to be known as Masjid Nabwi—the Prophet's mosque—we have the story of the Prophet's close Companion

Umar who became the second Caliph of Islam. When Jerusalem, the holiest city of Christianity, surrendered to Umar, he was being taken around all the important sites of the city. Bishop Nestorius, the Patriarch of Jerusalem, took Caliph Umar into the church of the Holy Sepulchre, which enclosed the place where Jesus Christ was crucified and buried. Just then, the hour of Muslim prayer struck and Caliph Umar asked Bishop Nestorius where he could perform his noon prayers. Bishop Nestorius courteously told him to perform his prayers in the church. Caliph Umar however refused.

'If I perform my prayers here, Muslims of subsequent generations may decide to convert the church into a mosque,' he said. Muslims ruled over Jerusalem for over thirteen centuries. The Holy Sepulchre has continued to remain a church to this day under the control of six denominations of Christians. Though the Christians of the various denominations have fought, and continue to fight, for every foot of space inside the church, the Muslims never claimed even an inch of it.

Farid al-Din Attar[12] tells an anecdote in the life of Abu Bakr al-Shibli.[13] Once Shibli announced to his followers that he required a thousand dirhams to buy shoes for the poor and equip them for the Haj pilgrimage. Before anyone could respond a Christian jumped up and volunteered 'I will give them, but on one condition, that you take me with you.' Shibli hesitated, since the young man was a Christian and so was not allowed into Mecca.

'There is no mule in your caravan,' the youth replied. 'Take me along as your mule.'

The dervishes set out, the Christian along with them, loins girded to the trail.

'How are you faring, young man?' asked Shibli.

'I am so happy at the thought of accompanying you that I cannot sleep,' he replied.

On the road, the Christian took a broom and at every halting place he swept the floor for the pilgrims and plucked out the thorns. When the time came for putting on the ihram, the white pilgrim robes, he saw what the rest were doing and followed their example. At last the party arrived at the Kaaba.

'With your girdle, I cannot let you enter the Holy Precincts,' Shibli told the Christian.

'O, God,' the Christian cried, laying his head on the threshold. 'Shibli says he will not allow me into thy House.'

'Shibli,' came a voice out of heaven. 'We have brought him here from Baghdad, kindling the fire of love in his heart. We have dragged him to our House with the chain of loving kindness. Shibli, get out of the way! You friend, come in!'

The Christian entered the Holy House and performed the rituals. The rest of the party then entered and in due course emerged, but the youth still did not come out.

'Young man, come out!' Shibli called.

'He will not let me out,' the youth wailed. 'Every time I make for the door of the House I find it shut. What will become of me?'[14]

This was an example of Shibli's tolerant faith in taking a Christian into the Kaaba itself and God appreciating the sincerity of the Christian's devotion. Such tolerance and such sincerity of devotion have become rare.

Hypocrisy

In contrast to Prof. Ramaswamy, I have encountered some men whom Krishna condemns in no uncertain terms. These are the rajasik and tamasik men who take pleasure in harming others when they are enjoying their brief moments of power, who take umbrage at the slightest imagined defiance of their authority, who use their position to be vindictive, who believe that only *their* caste deserves to be favoured and people of other castes, religions and regions are to be sidelined.

There was once a senior colleague of mine under whom I had had the misfortune to serve for some years. Every officer under him was mortally afraid of him, except the chosen few who belonged to his caste. Unfortunately, he rose to the highest position in the state administration. Once I was called to meet him at his house for some official work in the early morning. He was in his pooja room. I sat on the veranda and waited a couple of hours for him to complete his long-drawn pooja, though he had given me a specific time to come to his house. He boasted to me when he came out that he got up daily at 5 a.m. to perform his devotions. But he did not apologize to me for keeping me waiting for two hours.

He talked of the Makrana marble he got transported from Rajasthan and the value of the gold and pearls he used in adorning the raiments of the deity. He showed me round the large and magnificent mansion he had built for himself. He took me to the threshold of the pooja room without allowing me to get in (since I was a Muslim) to catch a glimpse of the magnificence of the marble sanctum, with gold and silver ornaments. I saw that he performed his devotion as though he was conferring a great favour on the deity and he expected the deity to confer material benefits on him manifold times. The moment he emerged from the pooja, he got engaged in thinking up original ways of showing his perceived rivals their place and wreaking vengeance on all those who he believed had defied him. He was a living contradiction of the Gītā's definition of a devotee dear to God.[15]

This man was always trying to cultivate a reputation of piety and godliness, but he could not hide his true nature. All his colleagues, his superiors and his subordinates knew his true nature. It is about such hypocrites that the famous Tamil saint Thiruvalluvar wrote:

If a man hides himself in the garb of piety and under that garb commits sins, he descends to the level of the bird catcher

who hides behind a bush to trap innocent birds. Is not the
cruel arrow smooth and straight, while the curved lyre it is
that makes sweet music? So judge not on appearance, but
on conduct.[16]

I have known this man consorting with the rich and the powerful
on the one hand, and remaining closeted with men of God, sages
who claimed to have renounced the world, in seaside resorts on
weekends. But all the good company he kept had not changed
this man for the better in any way. His insincere attempts to free
himself from the rajasik and tamasik coils by spending time in
the company of sattvik people only backfired.

As the Gītā says:

karmendriyāṇi saṁyamya ya āste manasā smaran
indriyārthān vimūḍhātmā mithyācāraḥ sa ucyate[17]
That man is called a hypocrite (mithyachari) who sits
restraining the organs of his actions but dwelling in his mind
on (attaining) the objects of his senses.

The so-called knowledge these mithyacharis acquire is also vain
knowledge which does not help them to discriminate between
right and wrong. The Gītā castigates such a person as partaking
of the nature of rakshas or asura of a tamasik constitution.[18]
Such persons of a demonic nature cannot distinguish between
right and wrong, truth and falsehood; they do not believe that
this Universe is real, created in Truth and that there is a God
who governs it.[19] They are continuously involved in gratifying
their lust, anger and ambition while using all means, fair or foul,
to amass wealth.[20] They boast of their wealth, high birth and of
their power to destroy their enemies.[21] The Bhagavad Gītā
castigates the hypocrites of a demonic nature who, on the strength

of their power and wealth, defy God and the teachings of the scriptures.

But there is another breed of self-deluded hypocrites, who convince themselves that they are acting for the sake of God and the hereafter; but in reality, their motives are different. In a Hadith Qudsi, quoted by Imam Nawawi,[22] God speaking through the Prophet says:

> There will come a time and a people who will seek the world in the name of religion, who will put on lambskin for the sake of appearance, with tongues sweeter than sugar and hearts like those of wolves.
>
> On the Day of Judgement, Allah will call a martyr who will claim that he died for the sake of Allah. Allah will tell him, 'No, you fought and died for the glory of being termed a brave warrior.'
>
> Next will be a scholar who will claim that he acquired knowledge, taught it and recited the Quran for the sake of God. God will say, 'No, you acquired, taught and recited the Quran so that people would say "here is a scholar and reciter of Quran."'
>
> Next will come a rich man who will claim that he gave his wealth to the poor for the sake of God. 'Nay,' God will say, 'you did so to claim a reputation of generosity.'

The Quran also calls such mithyacharis the munafiqoon—when called to believe in God, they turn away their faces,[23] hold it in ridicule,[24] and claim that religion has misled the believers.[25] They enjoin evil, forbid what is just and keep a closed fist. They have forgotten God and God has forgotten them,[26] they stir up rebellion and sedition,[27] they have pleasing exteriors and beguiling words, but they are as worthless as a hollow piece of timber, propped up, always believing they are a persecuted lot[28] and their abundance of provision deludes them even until they reach their graves.[29]

These hypocrites, mithyacharis or munafiqoon, illustrate the prime examples of those who are controlled by their nafs ammara or carnal selves.

So what is the remedy? How does one subdue the nafs ammara?

The Prophet of Islam won a historic battle—the Battle of Badr—which was a turning point in the history of Islam. As the victorious army was returning to Medina, some warriors complimented the Prophet on a great victory won. The Prophet replied, 'We are going from a minor skirmish to a greater battle.' His companions, jolted out of their complacent joy, asked him 'And what is that greater battle—jihad akbar—O Prophet of God?' He replied, 'The battle with our carnal selves.'

Krishna advised Arjuna on how to fight the carnal self. He says:

> He who, casting aside the ordinances of the scriptures, acts on impulse of desire, attains not perfection, nor happiness, nor the supreme goal (*sukham* and *param gathi*). Therefore, let the scriptures be your authority in deciding what ought to be done and what ought not to be done. Having known what is said in the ordinance of scriptures, you should act, here.[30]

Throughout the Gītā, Krishna has delineated what is sattvik and what is tamasik—what is to be done and what is not to be done. Those are the ordinances.

Islam talks of halal and haram—what is permissible and what is prohibited.

The Gītā recommends moderation in eating, sleeping, recreation and in all other actions:

nāty-aśnatas'tu yogo'sti na caikāntam anaśnataḥ
na cāti-svapna-śīlasya jāgrato naiva cārjuna[31]

Yoga is not possible for him who eats too much or for him who abstains too much from eating; it is not for him, O Arjuna, who sleeps too much or too little.

And a Hadith Qudsi says:

God says, '*qillat al ta'am*'—there is nothing more effective in my sight than eating frugally.

The Quran goes further and says:

Waqsid fee mashyika waghdudmin sawtika inna ankara al-aswaati lasawtualhameer[32]
And be moderate in thy pace and lower thy voice: for the harshest of sounds without doubt is the braying of the ass.

The New Testament tells us, above all, to do all this only for the glory of God:

Whether therefore you eat or drink or whatsoever ye do, do all to the glory of God.[33]

Arjuna continues to ponder how to control the mind—restless mind that hankers after the pleasures of the senses, gives in to anger and refuses to concentrate on the pursuit of goodness. Krishna acknowledges that the mind indeed is restless and hard to control. But by practice and non-attachment, it can be controlled.[34]

And the starting point for this, says Islam, is to follow the Islamic way of life—the shariat. The shariat tells you how to lead your life according to the ordinance of God, what Krishna said about letting the scriptures be your authority.

In one Hadith Qudsi, quoted in Ibn Saniy, God speaks to his servants through the Prophet. 'My servant does not come close to me except when he performs his prescribed duties (faraid). And he draws even closer when he performs supererogatory acts.' In yet another similar Hadith, God says, 'No man worships me except by performing what I have made obligatory.'

Shaikh Muzaffar Ozak al-Jarrahi, is the head of the Sufi Order of Khalwatiya in Istanbul. Over forty years, he wrote nine books containing the essence of his spiritual teaching. In *The University of Love*, he writes about how to control the carnal self or as he calls it the Domineering Self, the nafs ammara, by observing the laws of God:

The Domineering Self always leads man to the things forbidden by God, Exalted is He, and keeps him from those He has commanded. This is the self that finds the Sacred Law bitter and hard to bear. Those controlled by this self dislike the law and try to evade it. This is the Self—possessed by unbelievers, rebellious sinners and immoral people (about whom Gītā said, 'They say, the Universe is unreal without a moral basis, without a God.').[35] By bringing this Self to submission with the sword of the Sacred Law—shariat—man gains the upper hand over this great enemy of his; since he is outwardly human, it means that outwardly also he has stepped upon the first rung of the ladder of humanity and begun to climb upwards. If, on the contrary, man lapses into the Domineering Self, he gets lost in an animalistic way of life and may even sink lower than the animal level . . . It is only the Sacred Law that makes man truly human . . . the first gate of the Sacred Law . . . Then they become engaged in the struggle with the Domineering Self, the Greater Jihad.

The people who followed the sacred law were always the simple folk—people like my father and mother who did not delve into logic and philosophy, the whys and wherefores of things, who were content with what they had been given, who did not hanker after wealth and luxury, who were neither jealous of the rich and powerful, nor contemptuous of the poor or those below them, and those who were happy in their own station in life.

I learnt more of the Quran and Gītā from such ordinary people, simple folk who actually lived the life of the holy books, who had actually given up all desire for results, and who did not hanker for wealth, name, fame, power or authority. They lived a life of simplicity, rendering selfless service to the oppressed and the weak, to the destitute and the helpless. I met one such person, who had controlled his nafs ammara many years ago in a small village in the interiors of India.

Panditji was a Sanskrit scholar and social worker. He lived in an ashram near a small village with a few of his students, but served the surrounding community. My duties as district magistrate took me to various places and this village fell on the way, so I used to drop in on him occasionally to pay my respects. There were no chairs or tables in his small cottage. My unannounced visits often embarrassed him, as he could not offer me a chair or a glass of warm milk. As I sat on the reed mat on the ground and listened to him, his discourses on Sanskrit literature were hospitality enough. He remembered Kalidasa's *Abhijnyāna Shākuntalam* and *Meghdoot* by heart, he could recite the entire Gītā, and most parts of the Ramayana and the Mahabharata in the original Sanskrit. He often quoted the vivid similes and metaphors of Kalidasa and I learnt that long before T.S. Eliot coined the metaphor of the patient etherized on the table, or the fog curling up in a corner of the room and going to sleep, Kalidasa had set the trend.

It was from him that I learnt the fundamentals of a balanced life as taught by the Gītā—that man lifts himself up by his own self, by his own inner strength, and debases himself, lowers himself, through his own self. Man is his own best friend and worst enemy. He who conquers his baser self through his divine attributes, his ego becomes his best friend. But for him who allows his baser self to conquer his divine essence, his self becomes his enemy. And what are the attributes of this divine self in man? This divine self remains unaffected by cold or heat, pleasure and pain, honour and dishonour. It maintains *samahita* in all these states. This *paramātmā*, this *tṛptātmā* (self-realized) which has conquered the weaknesses of the senses remains unshaken by the allurements of this world. To this soul a clod, a stone or a piece of gold are all equal. Such a person finds happiness within his own self and does not seek it in the external phenomenal world. So the Gītā says that the one whose happiness is within, who is active within, who rejoices within and is illumined within is actually the perfect mystic. He is liberated in the Supreme, and ultimately he attains the Supreme.[36]

Once Confucius, the great Chinese sage, was travelling with his disciples over Mount T'ai when he caught sight of an aged man roaming in the wilds. He was clothed in a deerskin, girded with a rope, and was singing as he played on a lute.

'My friend,' said Confucius, 'what is it that makes you so happy?'

The old man replied, 'I have a great deal to make me happy. God created all things, and of all his creations man is the noblest. It has fallen to my lot to be a man; that is my first ground for happiness. Then there is a distinction between male and female, the former being rated more highly than the latter. Therefore it is better to be a male; and since I am one, I have a second ground for happiness. Furthermore, some are born who never behold the sun or the moon, and who never emerge from their swaddling clothes. But I have already walked the earth for the space of ninety years. That is my third ground for happiness. Poverty is the normal lot of the scholar, death the appointed end for all human beings. Abiding in the normal state and reaching at last the appointed end, what is there that should make me unhappy?'

'What an excellent thing it is,' cried Confucius, 'to be able to find a source of consolation in oneself!'

The Quran, centuries later, confirmed this: *Wa'amma biniamati rabbika fahaddith.*[37] So count the blessings of your Lord, constantly!

Find the source of your happiness within yourself. Such a contented soul looks at friend and foe with equal regard. He looks at his companions, his acquaintances, his mediators, those who hate him, his relatives, and all saints and sinners with samabuddhi, an equanimous mind.

The great Roman emperor Marcus Aurelius, talking of the sources of happiness in his *Meditations*, says:

> Men seek retreats for themselves—in the country, by the sea, in the hills [sounds so contemporary, after eighteen centuries] . . . No retreat offers someone more quiet and relaxation than that into his own mind, especially if he can dip into thoughts there which put him at immediate and complete ease. Remember this retreat into your own little territory within yourself, above all no agonies, no tensions. Be your own master, and look at things as a man, as a human being, as a citizen, as a mortal creature . . . anxieties can only come from your internal judgment.

The Gītā says:

> *uddhared ātmanātmānam nātmānam avasādayet*
> *ātmaiva hy ātmano bandhur ātmaiva ripur ātmanaḥ*[38]
> Man should raise himself by his own self. He should not debase himself, for man is his own best friend and (worst) foe.

'Man should raise himself by his own self,' says the Gītā. And Iqbal, the greatest exponent of the khudi, the self, in Persian and Urdu poetry has expounded this Philosophy in *Javid Nama*:

> Art thou a mere particle of dust?
> Tighten the knot of thy Self
> And hold fast thy tiny being!
> How glorious to burnish one's Self
> And to test its luster in the presence of the Sun!
> Rechisel, then, thine ancient frame
> And build up a new being.
> Such being is real being;
> Or else thy Self is a mere ring of smoke!

And what was man after all in origin? And what stages did he pass through in his evolutionary journey? And if he continues to rise, what ultimate goal will he reach?

Rumi has an answer:

> I died as mineral and became a plant
> I died as a plant and rose to an animal
> I died as animal and I was Man.
> Why should I fear? When was I less by dying?
> Yet once more I shall die as Man, to soar
> With angels blest, but even from angelhood
> I must pass on;
> All except God doth perish
> When I have sacrificed my angel-soul
> I shall become what no mind e'er conceived.
> O, Let me not exist! For non-existence
> Proclaims in organ tones 'To Him we shall return.'[39]

We return to the Gītā:

bandhur ātmātmanas tasya yenātmaivātmanā jitaḥ
anātmanas tu śatrutve vartetātmaiva śatru-vat[40]
To him who has conquered his own self, the self is his friend.
But to him who has no control over his self, the self is an
enemy.

Dil Mohammad proceeds to explain that the sovereign spirit of the
man who has conquered his self remains unaffected by cold and
heat, by pain or pleasure, by honour or dishonour. The one who
is content with knowledge and wisdom, steadfast and unshaken,
who has conquered the senses, treats alike a clod, a stone or a
piece of gold. He is deemed supreme who regards equally friends
and companions, enemies and strangers, neutrals and arbiters,
kindred and saints and sinners.[41]

This aspect of the ātman, which the Sufis call nafs, is like a
high-spirited thoroughbred. If the rider is a novice and negligent the
horse bucks and cavorts, throwing its rider down. But if the rider is
in control, the horse behaves well and can take him long distances.

Rumi said, 'When the nafs says "meow" like the cat, I put it
in the bag like the cat.'[42]

The Arabic word nafs is variously translated as 'soul', 'self',
'ego', etc. Sufis hold that it has seven stages of development. By
purifying the self at every stage, the soul (ātma) reaches perfection.
These stages are:

1. *nafs al-ammara*—this is the basic 'self'—atman—that
every man possesses and is born with—the commanding or
compulsive—obsessive self, also known as the carnal or animal
self, *anima bruta*, and it is entirely governed by its desires, passions
and instincts. This is what the Gītā describes as the atman of the
person who is governed by the quality of tamas.

The Gītā says:

aprakāś 'pravrttiś ca pramādo moha eva ca
tamasy etāni jāyante vivrddhe kuru-nandana[43]
Darkness, inertness, and also stupidity and bewilderment—
these are produced, O son of Kuru, when darkness intensifies.

When the nafs al-ammara is in control, the results are aprakash (darkness), apravittih (inertia), pramadah (heedlessness), moha (illusory desires), ajnānam (ignorance) and finally a descent into perdition.

Elsewhere, the Gītā describes this state:

cañcalam hi manah krsna pramāthi balavad drdham
tasyāham nigraham manye vāyor iva su-duskaram[44]
For the mind is restless, turbulent, obstinate and very strong,
O Krishna, and to subdue it, it seems to me, is more difficult
than controlling the wind.

The Gītā, among other attributes of this nafs ammara, pinpoints three major constituents—gates of hell, viz., lust, anger and greed, and the man who overcomes kāma, krodha and lobha, achieves the Supreme Good, *paramgathi*.[45]

The Quran also calls this baser self nafs al-ammara bi su—the self that inclines one to evil. When Prophet Joseph was tempted by the Egyptian princess and he resisted her seductions, he exclaimed, 'Allah does not allow the designs of the treacherous to succeed. I do not seek to acquit myself; for surely one self-prompts one to evil, except him to whom my Lord may show mercy. Verily my Lord is Ever-forgiving, Most-merciful.'[46]

It is this very self that inclines man to hawa—evil desires[47] and which requires to be kept under control and content.[48] Joseph did not allow his carnal self to conquer him, though he must have been sorely tempted by the wiles of a beautiful and powerful woman, a princess to boot. Joseph refused to enter the first gate of darkness—lust, kāma.

Rumi talks about this carnal self, the nafs ammara, as the mother of all idols—idols of pride, selfishness, hatred, egotism, anger, lust, etc. While this nafs that yearns after material things, he says, is a snake, there is a nafs which is more evil than the material nafs. This is the pride of having achieved a high spiritual status. This nafs, Rumi says, is a dragon.

The Pharaoh prided himself on his power and his glory. He believed he was God—he could give and take life. It was this pride that compelled him to pursue Moses across the Red Sea. It was this nafs that deceived him.

Rumi tells us how this carnal self deceives us at every step and how it creates a hundred Pharaohs of pride and arrogance, of self-aggrandizement and ego. But it is the carnal self that also drowns its followers when they blindly follow it into the illusory parting seas.

While this carnal self cannot be utterly destroyed, nor is it possible or even necessary to do so, it can be subdued in the initial stage and with effort and help of God, it can be sublimated.

Ibn Sina (known as Avicenna in the West) and al-Ghazali, interpret anger and lust, manifestations of nafs ammara, as aggressive and sexual instincts of man. They are natural constituents of the human psyche and are as such ineradicable. Nor do they need to be eradicated, for if they are totally eradicated the human being would lose a part of what makes him human. But each should be controlled and used to temper the other.

These instincts are not in themselves evil and al-Ghazali (in his *Kimiya-e-Saadat* or *Alchemy of Happiness*) compares them respectively to a wild animal and a pack animal. The mystic Junayd Baghdadi while discussing the human psyche probably had these two faculties in mind, anger and lust, which 'principally contributed to loss of self-control, a condition, as C.G. Jung points out, when one is no longer "oneself", when one "forgets oneself" or is "beside oneself". The remedy is to recognize it for what it is and once recognized be subjected to reason or in Jung's words "the conscious mind".'

A famous Sufi, Ahmad Samani, who was a contemporary of al-Ghazali and San'ai, took a positive view of the nafs ammara. In his *Rauh al-Arwah* (*Happiness of Souls*), he observes:

The self that commands to evil which every human being must confront, makes possible the ascent beyond the heavens to God. If a palace does not have a garbage pit next to it, it is incomplete. There must be a garbage pit next to a lofty palace so that all the refuse and filth that gather in the palace can be thrown there. In the same way, whenever God formed a heart by means of the light of purity, he placed this impure self next to it as a dustbin. The black spot of 'ignorance' flies on the same wings as the jewel of purity. There needs to be a bit of corruption so that purity can be built upon it. A straight arrow needs a crooked bow . . . When they place the dress of purity on the heart, they show the heart that black spot of wrongdoing and ignorance so that it will remember itself and know who it is. When a peacock spreads out all its feathers, it gains a different joy from each feather. But as soon as it looks down at its own feet, it becomes embarrassed. That black spot of ignorance is the peacock's foot that always stays with you.

2. *nafs al-lawwama*—The second stage is the accusing or blaming self. It corresponds to the awakening of the conscience

and a realization of the extent to which one's actions are controlled by the nafs al-ammara. Once the nafs al-lawwama is awakened in man, he is on the way to realization.

3. *nafs al-mulhama*—The third stage is the inspired or balanced self. It marks the beginning of genuine spiritual integration and a release of the self from the tyranny of physical instincts and the desires of the ego. In this stage, though anger, greed, jealousy and other baser emotions are still present, they are under control.

In this state, even though the self is subject to the bodily needs, it has however conquered the urgings of the nafs ammara. The Gītā says:

He who, even before he quits his body, controls his lust and anger, he is a yogi, a happy man.[49]

4. *nafs al-mutmainna*—The fourth stage is the tranquil self or self at peace, as its name implies. It has attained a degree of detachment from worldly concerns and an increasing awareness of the Presence of God in all things. 'Mutmain' in Arabic means 'content', where the atman has come to terms with itself and is at rest. This is when the soul gets the direct attention of God and intimations of His Love. And it is love, divine love, which transforms the nafs al-ammara, the anima bruta, into the nafs al-mutmainna, the self at peace.

Rumi addresses love and says:

You enter the ugly jinn and make him a Yusuf
You enter the wolf's character and make him a shepherd.

This is also the stage where the soul is content remembering God, day and night, and passes beyond the desire of the pomp and glitter of this life.

As the Quran says:

wasbir nafsaka ma'alladhizina yad'oonarabbahum bilghadati
wala'ashiyyiyuridoona wajhahu wala ta'du aynaka 'anhum
turidu zeenata alhayati addunya wala tuti'aman aghfalna
qalbahu, 'an dhikrinawattaba 'ahawahu wakana amruhu
furuta[50]

And keep yourself patient [by being] with those who call upon their Lord in the morning and the evening, seeking His countenance. And let not your eyes pass beyond them, desiring adornments of the worldly life, and do not obey one whose heart we have made heedless of Our remembrance and who follows his desire and whose affair is ever [in] neglect.

This is the state where the Gītā says, the self is dominated by sattvik characteristics—*urdhavam gacchanti sattvastha.*

From sattva arises divine knowledge[51] and he who is fixed in sattva rises upward. Sattva creates light of knowledge, for the atman in this stage partakes of the nature of light.

> *Sattogun se irfaan ka paida ho noor*
> *Sattogun ki fitrat he pakeeza noor*

This is the nafs al-mutmainna—the tranquil soul.
In the words of the Gītā:

> *yadā viniyatam cittam ātmany evāvatiṣṭhate*
> *nispṛhaḥ sarva-kāmebhyo yukta ity ucyate tadā*[52]

When the disciplined mind controls the self and dwells inwardly, free from all desires, then alone is it established in yoga.

St Francis of Assisi writes in *Laudes*:

The soul that is untroubled by passions—which means not that it is absolutely impassive, but that it is always fixed on God, whence the exclusion of 'worldly', egoistic and pretentious movements of the soul which nevertheless remains open to holy joy, holy sadness and holy anger—the soul then which is not carried away by passions, is 'pure' without however being exempt from the natural condition of the human microcosm, since a plane of existence cannot cease to be what it is by definition. The soul in a state of 'pure simplicity' is the receptacle of the Divine Presence, being neither determined nor soiled by anything which is beneath its nature.[53]

al-Ghazali recalls in his *Ihya-ul-uloom* (*Revival of Learning*), the vision of God 'makes those brought nigh (mugarrubun) forget the *houris* and ends in supreme union. It is only the distance that makes you see the gardens flowing with milk and honey and inhabited by *houris*. Once you have achieved the "proximity" to God, you live in God where there is only the supreme union and nothing else.'[54]

This is also the state of abiding in Brahma, extinction in Brahma (brahmanirvana). This 'extinction' has to be understood only in the context of what Gītā has said:

pārtha naiveha nāmutra vināśas tasya vidyate
na hi kalyāṇa-kṛt kaścid durgatiṁ tāta gacchati[55]
O Partha, neither here nor hereafter is there destruction for him, for none that does righteousness, my son, comes to evil state.

5. *nafs al-radiyaa*—In the fifth stage, the soul is fulfilled or satisfied with the initial merging or union of the individual with God.

The Gītā says:

śaknotīhaiva yaḥ soḍhuṁ prāk śarīra-vimokṣaṇāt
kāma-krodhodbhavaṁ vegaṁ sa yuktaḥ sa sukhī naraḥ[56]
That yogi who has an illumined heart, happy within his
own self, he is closest to divine grace and has achieved the
merger with brahma—nirvana.

Many Sufis reached this stage and some have expressed it in
beautiful poetry. Shabistari, in his poem 'The Beloved Guest'
from *Gulshan-e-Raz* (*The Secret Garden*) writes:

Cast away your existence entirely
for it is nothing but weeds and refuse
Go, clear out your heart's chamber;
arrange it as the abiding place of the Beloved
When you go forth, He will come in
And to you with self discarded
He will unveil his beauty.[57]

By 'self', Shabistari here means the domineering self, the nafs
ammara.

6. *nafs al-mardiyya*—the fulfilling or satisfying self also
described as the self of total submission, is the merging of God
with the individual soul.

7. *nafs al-kamila*—the perfected and complete self is the
state of total union with God and the attainment of universal
consciousness. This state is the final one, where the yogi has
attained union with God, Fana fillah.

The Gītā describes this well:

yo mam pasyati sarvatra sarvam ca mayi pasyati
tasyaham na pranasyami sa ca me na pranasyati[58]

He who sees Me everywhere and sees all in Me, he never becomes lost to me, nor am I ever lost to him. He, who is fully established in my Unity, worships me as abiding in all beings, that yogi abides in me howsoever he lives.

Another Sufi saint, Abu Said ibn al Khayr, put it romantically:

> *Hama jamal-i tu binam, chu dida bāz kunam*
> *Hama tanam dil gardad, ki bā rāz kunam*
> *Harām dāram ba digaran sukhan guftan*
> *Kuja hadith-i tu aamad sukhan daraaz kunam*
> I see all your beauty, when I open my eyes. All my body becomes heart, in communion with you. I regard it as forbidden to speak with other. When talk turns to you, I discourse at length.

This stage which the Gītā describes as 'yog' (which literally means 'union') is also described by the famous Sufi al-Ahraar of Bukhara:

> As soon as the faithful disciple has cleansed and polished all worldly allure from the mirror of his heart and has purified its innermost apartment of all but God, he immediately begins to experience a selfless rapture which obliterates his own being and that of the unreal world. This purification is the prelude to selflessness. *Such loss is true finding*.

The Sufis call this self-forgetting non-being (adam) or absence (ghaiba). This state is the prelude to the dawn of bliss and union (what the Gītā calls yog). After losing himself in this fashion and discovering a genuine form of being, a dervish is incapable of reverting to ordinary human existence. He has truly found satchitananada—the supreme union of truth and bliss in the consciousness.

Once one has acquired a divinely endowed mode of being, one is liberated from the troubles of personal and worldly existence. This state is called 'permanence after annihilation' (*baqaa ba'da al fanaa*).

My meetings with panditji gave me the impression that he had achieved the state of satchidananda and detachment which the sages of yore are said to have achieved.

I was so grateful to him for the inner knowledge of Sanskrit literature which he imparted to me that I thought I should do something for him. He was not interested in accepting any favours from anyone, much less from the government. He merely wanted to be left alone in his ashram doing his work. But my gratitude compelled me to collect all information about him and recommend his name for a government award—for his services to the Sanskrit language. I spoke to the legislators of the area and the powers that be and the government was pleased to confer an award on him. It fell to my lot to obtain his consent. I should have known his response. He was just not interested. For him, awards were meaningless. But I knew that a flat refusal by him would have been most embarrassing for me and those who had recommended his name at my instance. It was with great difficulty that he was persuaded to accept the award.

I learnt later that he refused to leave his ashram to receive the award and it had to be delivered to him by my successor in office.

Jugatram Dave, a Gandhian and another follower of the Gītā, used to live in the forest near Surat in Gujarat, where I was collector in the 1960s. He too ran an ashram at Vedchi for the benefit of the landless tribals of the area known as the Dublas, training them to become self-sufficient in agriculture, horticulture and other village industries. In 1935, Gandhiji had written to him, advising him to tell the raniparaj, the forest dwellers, that they were not dependent on the cities but that the city dwellers were dependent on them. He wrote, 'If at all they want to preserve their self-respect, they

should themselves meet all their requirements and be self-reliant.'
At the ashram, Dave was trying to carry out this mission even after
three decades. When Governor Shriman Narayan wanted to visit
the ashram with his wife and camp there for three days, Jugatramji
was most embarrassed. It took me all my persuasive eloquence to
convince Jugatramji to accept a visit from the Governor. A true
Sufi feels that his equanimity and his atman is compromised by
association with rulers and holders of worldly authority.

When Emperor Tughlaq expressed his wish to call on the saint,
Nizamuddin Aulia, the latter sent word that if the king entered
his monastery by the main door, he would exit by the back door!

Another gyani was Rangildas Kapadia who lived in a small
town of Gujarat. His house was located in the old part of Gandevi
town and whenever I visited him, my driver found it difficult to
manoeuvre the jeep and park it opposite his house. Rangildas was
an active freedom fighter, had participated in the movement for
the independence of India and had gone to jail for his patriotic
activities. He had also been secretary to Sardar Vallabhbhai
Patel who became the first home minister of free India. Had he
wanted, he could have stayed on in Delhi and enjoyed the plums
of office and would have perhaps been appointed as Governor
of some state. But he chose to resign his post and come back
to his hometown and ancestral house. I have described in my
previous book *Of Nawabs and Nightingales* how he helped me in
controlling a communal riot in 1969 when the whole of Gujarat
was burning. Many of the political leaders of the state used to call
on him while passing through Gandevi, but I had never heard of
his visiting any of the ministers or Governors in the state capital.
In fact he once told me that he did not much appreciate these
visits as the caravan of cars and possés of policemen disturbed
his neighbours whose ingress and egress from their houses was
blocked during such visits.

In my search for a true Sufi, I had visited many holy men, some who had renounced this world and some who still lived in this world and served humanity.

One such liberated soul whom I had the good fortune to meet and spend some time with was Syed Abul Hasan Ali of Nadwa in Lucknow, popularly known as Ali Miyan. He was renowned as a great Islamic scholar, fluent in Islamic law, the science of Tafsir and Hadith, the Arabic language and other Islamic sciences. Because of his erudition and scholarship, he was held in very high esteem all over the world of Islam and was received by kings and presidents when he went abroad.

When I desired to call on him, one of his companions accompanied me to Lucknow and put me up in the guest house of the Darul-ul-Uloom, the Islamic University of Nadwa. Ali Miyan was its rector and had the administrative responsibility for the welfare, physical and religious, of some eight or nine thousand resident students, teachers and supporting staff.

After freshening up in the sparsely furnished room, I repaired to where Ali Miyan lived. It was a single room, even more sparsely furnished than the guest house. A cotton dhurrie, somewhat frayed at the edges, covered the floor. A string cot was propped up against the bare wall. Ali Miyan slept on it with a cotton pillow and during the day it was stood up against the wall to make room for visitors. The single room served as his bedroom, living room, dining room and reception room and prayer hall. My first impression of Ali Miyan created feelings similar to what Dr Carret experienced when he first met Shaikh Alawi in Algeria. Ali Miyan exuded spirituality, contentment, detachment and a kind of selflessness. There were close to a dozen people who had come to see him.

Squatting on the dhurrie with his back to the wall, the frail old man listened to each one of them intently and gave his advice quietly in a few words. Though I was sitting a couple of feet away, I could not hear a word of what he said. After his brief discourse, I asked him some questions. He gave very brief replies in the same low voice and referred me to his books—he had written extensively though he spoke little.

The next morning I joined him for the dawn prayers. I thought he would lead the prayers. But his health perhaps did not permit him to do so. One of his companions led the small congregation, all that the room could accommodate. I had hoped to have a one-to-one meeting with him and was wondering how to word the request. Perhaps he sensed my desire intuitively, for at an unseen signal the room emptied, leaving the two of us alone. I again asked him questions about faith and doubt, about prayers and God's answer to them and all the issues that were agitating my mind.

He took both my hands in his while he answered my questions briefly. Then he taught me a few *awraad*, a few prayers from the Quran, to recite immediately after my morning prayers. By the time he finished speaking, perhaps in response to another unseen signal, the visitors, the professors, the deans of the vast university he was managing all trooped in to take guidance from him. I felt he was the last of the Sufis of India that I had the great fortune to meet and get guidance from.

Prayer, Faith and Surrender

Way back in the early 1970s, I put a rather embarrassing question to Panditji. In one of my visits to him in the ashram I found him sitting on a reed mat, half naked, totally absorbed in contemplation. Two of the inmates who were looking after him asked me to wait in the veranda of the ashram until he came out of his contemplation. It was very hot outside and since the ashram did not have electricity or fans, not even chairs, I sat on a backless wooden bench for more than an hour before I could meet panditji. It was amazing to see that even though I was perspiring from every pore of my body, Panditji looked as though he had just had a bath, fresh and blooming.

'Tell me, Panditji. What were you absorbed in for the last hour or so while I waited outside?' I asked him after the preliminaries. He smiled gently and replied, 'I was contemplating myself.'

'What does that mean? How does one contemplate oneself?'

'One contemplates oneself by emptying one's mind of all thoughts.'

'Is that ever possible? How is it possible for anyone to sit for an hour or more without a single thought crossing his mind?'

'Yes. It is possible,' he said. 'But it cannot be done by a novice. It takes years of practice to empty yourself of your own self and reach a stage where you become zero, you become nothing, you don't exist. That is the stage when you contemplate yourself because the self, which actually is the universal self, takes over your individual self. You cease to exist and only the universal self remains.'

To be honest I did not understand much of what Panditji conveyed. I could not think of a stage in which I was conscious yet I had no thought in my mind. Every moment of my life, except when I was asleep, I was always full of thoughts—sometimes thinking rationally, consistently, systematically, and sometimes my thoughts were just a jumble of various strains criss-crossing each other, often leaving me confused.

'When the universal self takes over, Panditji, do you feel that you have become God?' I asked him. He smiled and remained silent. 'There are these so many god-men—Mehrbaba, Satya Sai Baba, Maharshi Mahesh Yogi and the earlier ones like Ramakrishna Paramahamsa, Ramanuja, Madhava and even Sankara—did they all become divine when they shed their carnal selves and attained to the level of the divine universal self? They have many devotees today who all believe that these were divine incarnations. Does this happen in reality?' Panditji then told me that none of the persons that I had named, ever overtly claimed that they were gods or divine incarnations. It was their followers and devotees who deified them, either during their lifetimes or in later years. For, a person who really sheds his own self and reaches a stage where his self gets merged in the divine self never stands up and beats any drums about it. The very happiness that he achieves through reaching that stage is more than enough for him than any acclaim from the followers or the devotees. In any case the secret that one has achieved that status of submergence in the universal self is better not revealed to the world at large. There is always the danger that the world may not recognize this and go to the extent of punishing one for having made such a claim.

I had put the very same question to Prof. Noorulla who was one of my Arabic teachers, a Sufi in his own right. He had studied Ibn al Arabi in great depth and absorbed his philosophy of *Wahdat al Wujud*, unity of being, and used to expound it to a group of followers who used to gather around him in the mosque after the ritual prayers. Often, I used to drop in on these discourses and Prof. Noorulla would sit there after the evening prayers for an hour or so, and talk about how to destroy your carnal self through dhikr to reach a stage where nothing remained except God. Over a period of time I noticed that his visits to the mosque became more and more infrequent. Somebody from his group told me that he had resigned from his job in the college, and was seen wandering about in scanty clothes in the streets of Chennai. I was shocked on hearing this and wondered what had happened to him. One day I came across the professor on the street wearing a tattered shirt, with unkempt hair and barefooted. I greeted him but he did not recognize me. I asked him why he was not coming to the mosque any more. He gave a strange laugh, more a cackle. 'Why should I come to the mosque? What is there in the mosque?'

'You used to come for prayers there,' I said.

'I don't need to pray any more. People should pray to me,' he said.

This appeared to me to be a rather crazy statement. I thought that Prof. Noorulla had gone mad and I walked away.

People who made such claims came to bad ends. It was therefore better to keep such secrets to yourself, if you ever reach a stage of divine submergence.

Mansur al Hallaj, the Persian Sufi, was accused of heresy and executed by the Abbasid Caliph Al-Muqtadir. One of the accusations against Hallaj was blasphemy. In a letter, he was accused of writing, 'If a man would go on pilgrimage (haj) and cannot, let him set apart in his house some square construction to be touched by no unclean thing, and let no one have access to it. When the day of the pilgrimage rites comes, let him make his circuits around it (as he would have done around the Kaaba) and perform all the same ceremonies as he would perform at Mecca. Then let him gather together thirty orphans for whom he has prepared the most exquisite feast he can get; let him bring them to his house and serve them that feast after waiting on them himself, and washing their hands as a servant himself. Let him present each of them with a new dress, and give them each seven dirhams. This will be a substitute for pilgrimage.'

The judge, Abu Umar, asked Hallaj, 'Where did you get this doctrine from?'

'From Hasan of Basra's *Book of Devotions*,' Hallaj replied.

'That is a lie,' the judge said, and declared Hallaj an apostate and an atheist, without giving any opportunity to Hallaj to explain. Hallaj was then taken to the gallows.

From the gallows, as his hands and feet were being cut off, he declared, 'O our God! Who dost glow in all places and art not in any place, I beseech Thee by the Truth of Thy word which declares that I am, by the truth of this my word which declares that Thou art, I beseech Thee my Master, give me grace to be grateful for this happiness of Thy giving, that Thou didst hide from others what was unveiled to me, the raging fires of thy face, and forbid them to look, as I was permitted to look, into things hidden in the Mystery of Thee. And these Thy servants, who are gathered to slay me, in zeal for Thy religion, longing to win Thy favour, forgive them, Lord. Have mercy on them. Surely, if thou hadst shown them what thou hast shown me, they would never have done what they have done; hadst thou kept from me what thou hast kept from them, I should not have suffered this tribulation.'

Just when he was about to be decapitated, Hallaj exclaimed, 'All who have known ecstasy long for this . . . the loneliness of the Only one . . . alone with the Alone.'

The Gītā says:

sarva-bhūta-sthitaṁ yo māṁ bhajaty ekatvam āsthitaḥ
sarvathā vartamāno'pisa yogī mayi vartate[1]

The yogi who knows that I and the Super-soul within all
creatures are one worships Me and remains always in Me in
all circumstances.

The greatest lesson that both the Gītā and the Quran taught
me was to see the underlying unity in the multiplicity of God's
creation.

The Quran says, '*innaa khalaqnaakum min nafsun wahida*'[2]
(verily we have created you from a single soul). The Quran also
says that mankind is but a single community, *ummatan wahida*
(*vasudaiva kutumbakam*). It says that God has created tribes, clans
and nations so that you may be distinguished from each other.
But the most honoured in God's sight amongst you is he who
holds Him in the greatest awe:

ya ayyuhannasu innaa khalaqnakum min dhakrin wa untha
wa ja'alnakum shu'uban wa qabaila lita'arafu inna akramakum
inda Allahi atqakum inna Allaha aleemun khabeer[3]
O mankind, indeed We have created you from male and
female and made you peoples and tribes that you may know
one another. Indeed, the most noble of you in the sight of
Allah is the most righteous of you. Indeed, Allah is Knowing
and Acquainted.

'Ponder the creation,' says the Quran.

araayat al ibl, kaifa khuliqat, wal ard kaifa sutihat, wal jibaal
kaifa nusibat, was samaa kaifa rufiat[4]
Observe the clouds, how they are created, the earth how it is
spread out, the mountains how they are affixed, the heavens
how they are raised.

The Gītā says:

> He who sees Me everywhere and everything in Me, him I
> forsake not, and he forsakes not Me.[5]

The presence of divinity in all beings is affirmed unequivocally by
the Gītā—*sarvabhutasthitam* (abiding in all beings). Similarly, in
the same breath, the Gītā affirms—*bhajatayekatvam asthitah*—
established in oneness. The Gītā says that anyone denying this
unity of humanity, this unity of existence, this unity of God is
steeped in ignorance—ajnānam.

The Sufi also sees God, in every atom, every speck and every
drop of water. Shabistari in his beautiful poem 'The Mirror' in
his *Gulshan-e-Raz* says:

> Your eye has not strength enough
> to gaze at the burning sun
> but you can see its burning light
> by watching its reflection
> mirrored in the water.
> So the reflection of Absolute Being
> can be viewed in the mirror of Not-Being
> for non-existence, being opposite Reality
> instantly catches its reflection
> Know the world from end to end is mirror
> in each atom a hundred suns are concealed
> If you pierce the heart of a single drop of water
> from it will flow a hundred clear oceans
> if you look at each speck of dust intently
> in it you will see a thousand beings
> A gnat in its limbs is like an elephant

In name a drop of water resembles the Nile
In the heart of a barley-corn is stored a hundred
Harvests
Within a millet seed a world exists.
In an insect's wing is an ocean of life
A heaven is concealed in the pupil of an eye
The core at the centre of the heart is small
Yet the Lord of both the worlds will enter there.[6]

Sankara the monist bemoaned:

O Lord! Pardon my three sins.
I have in contemplation clothed in form Thee who art
formless.
I have in praise described Thee who art ineffable.
And in visiting temples ignored Thy omnipresence.

The Gītā affirms unequivocally the unity of God, Being and
Humanity. This is what the Quran and the Sufis taught me as well.
He who believes that God is One, and that human beings because
of the limitations imposed by geography, climate, language and
time call Him by different names, *will never discriminate against
people on the basis of religion, caste, creed and ethnicity*. All humanity
is created from a single soul and belongs to one family. That is
what the Quran repeatedly informs us and that is what Prophet
Muhammad announced in his last sermon from the Mount of
Mercy in his last pilgrimage to Mecca. He said:

All mankind is from Adam and Eve. An Arab is not superior
to a non-Arab, nor does a non-Arab have any superiority
over an Arab. A white has no superiority over a black, nor
a black has superiority over a white, except through piety

and good deeds. All mankind is therefore bound together as one family—*vasudaiva kutumbakam*—and one cannot gain profit, happiness and nirvana by causing loss, sorrow and spiritual damage to another.

As John Donne, the mystic poet of England, put it, 'No man is an island unto himself . . . each man is a part of a continent.'

The Gītā also taught me to maintain equanimity and mental balance at all times, to keep my soul unaffected by desire, anger, instability and all influences that would affect my rationality, especially in the face of calamities and adversities. That is also what the Quran taught me, that those who maintain their fortitude in times of calamity and disasters are the real followers of truth, they are the men of real piety.

The Gītā taught me to fix my mind on Him alone and obtain His Grace by abandoning my ego and to seek refuge in Him alone with all my heart. A well-known sacred saying, Hadith Qudsi, told me in divine words, 'My love belongs by right to those who love one another in Me, to those who sit together (in fellowship in Me), to those who visit one another in Me and to those who give generously to one another in Me.'

But having given these lessons to Arjuna, the Gītā comes to the most important lesson of all. In a mysterious and highly debated shloka, interpreted variously by karmayogis and bhaktimargis, by philosophers and linguists, by pandits and scholars for centuries—the Gītā exhorts all believers to renounce all other paths and repose faith and devotion in God alone:

sarva-dharmān parityajya mām ekaṁ śaraṇaṁ vraja
ahaṁ tvāṁ sarva-pāpebhyo mokṣayiṣyāmi mā śucaḥ[7]
Abandon all varieties of religion and just surrender unto Me. I shall deliver you from all sinful reaction. Do not fear.

Sankara sees this verse in the sense of transcendence and notes that what is intended is total renunciation of all actions, as is enjoined in the Vedas and Smritis—like 'Give up religion and irreligion.' This shloka teaches freedom from 'all duties', *sarva dharma*, lawful and unlawful, religious and irreligious.

Abandon all dharmas, 'Surrender unto me alone.'

Earlier, Krishna had said, *'tam eva sharanam gachcha'* (in Him only seek refuge)—this evokes the prayer recited by the Muslims five times a day, *'iyyaaka na'abudu'*, (You alone do we worship) and *'iyyaaka nastayeen'* (from You alone we ask for help). By seeking refuge in Him alone, and asking for succour from Him only, you gain supreme peace and *shasvat sthānam*, eternal abode.

Ramanuja's followers consider this, the sixty-sixth shloka, as the final verse, the charama shloka—a summary of the whole Gītā doctrine. In contrast to Sankara, Ramanuja believes that this shloka reinforces Krishna's advice that total surrender to God, and absolute love and faith in Him releases man from all chains, all trammels and travails, all fears and all sins.

One may recall that the Gītā had earlier said:

ye bhajanti tu mām bhaktyā mayi te teṣu cāpy aham[8]
But those who worship Me with devotion they are in Me and I also in them.

And also:

api cet su-durācāro bhajate mām ananya—bhāk
sādhur eva sa mantavyaḥsamyag vyavasito hi saḥ[9]
Even if a man of the most sinful conduct worships Me with undeviating devotion, he must be reckoned as righteous, for he has judged rightly.

In a Hadith Qudsi, quoted by both Tirmidhi and Ibn Hanbal, God speaking through the Prophet says:

> O son of Adam, so long as you call upon Me and ask me, I shall forgive you for what you have done and I shall not mind. O son of Adam, were your sins to reach the clouds of the sky and were you then to ask forgiveness of Me, I would forgive you. O son of Adam, were you to me with sins nearly as great as the earth and were you then to face me, ascribing no partner to me (that is, acknowledging Me and Me alone), I would grant you forgiveness nearly as great as it.

Krishna himself realizes that the doctrine he is teaching is a revolutionary doctrine—a doctrine which was not suitable for the ears of those who are not committed to austerity (atapasya) nor to one who has not already followed the other paths and has not devoted himself to God (abhakta), nor to one who is not willing to serve humanity and is heedless to teaching (asusrusu) nor one who criticizes divine providence (abhyasuyuta):

> *idam te nātapaskāya nābhaktāya kadācana*
> *na cāśuśrūṣave vācyam na ca mām yo 'bhyasūyati*[10]
> This secret is never to be revealed to anyone who is not austere and devoted and who is heedless and reviles God.

Earlier also, Krishna had warned against interfering with the faith and practice of the simple folk—those without the deep knowledge of the mysteries of the Divine.

> *na buddhi-bhedam janayed ajñānām karma-saṅginām*
> *joṣayet sarva-karmāṇi vidvān yuktaḥ samācaran*[11]

Let not the wise disrupt the minds of the ignorant who are attached to fruitive action, they should not be encouraged to refrain from work, but to engage in work in the spirit of devotion.

So, Krishna warns Arjuna here not to reveal this secret of total surrender to God to the ignorant, the self-willed, the obdurate, the selfish and scoffers.

Many Sufis had lost their lives by revealing this secret to the common man. Hallaj abandoned all rituals and went about crying '*anal haq*' (I am the Truth) and for that he was crucified, quartered, burnt and his ashes were thrown into the Tigris. Had Hallaj read the Bhagavad Gītā and heeded to the advice of Krishna that such secrets are not to be revealed to the general public, for the common man's faith too is dear to the Creator and should not be shaken, he would perhaps not have gone about the streets of Baghdad crying '*anal haq*'. His teacher Junayd held him culpable for revealing a secret which was best kept hidden from the common man. On another occasion, when Hallaj's ecstatic saying—*shattiyat*—was reported to him, Junayd replied, 'What else could he have said? He could not have very well proclaimed "I am the Falsehood! I am the Falsehood," could he?'

The rulers in Baghdad banned the buying and selling of all books of Hallaj.

There were other Sufis too who had learnt the same secret that Hallaj had proclaimed. But they were discreet enough to not reveal it openly.

Bayazid and Junayd cried, '*Subhaani, maa aazama shani.*' (Glory be to me, how great is my majesty.) But they both communicated this to only a select few and escaped being lynched at the hands of the mob. Ibn al Arabi in his *al-Futūḥāt al-Makkiah* restrained himself in expressing some of his deeper experiences or couched them in obscure language, to avoid serious charges of heresy, and sharing the fate of Hallaj. In fact, in his journal *Al-Fanaa Fil Mushaahadah*, he warns, 'This kind of spiritual insight and knowledge must be hidden from the majority of men by reason of its sublimity. For its depths are far-reaching and the dangers involved great.' Inspite of this, he could not refrain from revealing this secret, albeit partially, in his *Bezels of Wisdom* and *Meccan Illuminations*. And for that, even though he is called the *Shaikh al Akbar*—the Great Shaikh—his books are ritually burnt annually in Egypt!

But all these persecutors, these interpreters of only one aspect of Divine Unity, forgot that even the Prophet of Islam, in a moment of ecstasy, said '*Man qala la ilah illa Allah, fa dakhl al jannah*' (he who declares 'there is no god but God enters Paradise'). But Umar, his later successor and a practical thinker cautioned against such ecstatic utterances as the common man would give up all good deeds if the acknowledgement of God's unity alone guaranteed salvation. This was not a call to pay mere lip service to the Unity of God, but to surrender to Him totally, to the exclusion of all other idols of heart and mind.

Maulana Azad in his impeccable and poetic Urdu tells the story of Sarmad Shaheed, the martyr of Delhi.[12] Sarmad was one of those who had learnt no lesson from Hallaj, Suhrawardy, and al-Ghazali. It was during the reign of Shah Jahan, the Mughal emperor that Sarmad came to India via Sindh. He was probably an Armenian Jew and was bringing some merchandise from Iran for sale in India. At Thatta, in Sindh, he underwent a profoundly spiritual experience which transformed him from a merchant into a Sufi. When he reached Shahjahanabad (now Old Delhi), he encountered the spiritually inclined heir apparent, Dara Shukoh. Dara was as much devoted to Muslim dervishes as he was to Hindu sages and sadhus. Dara regularly visited Sarmad in his retreat to derive spiritual sustenance.

Unfortunately for both of them, Shah Jahan fell ill and Aurangzeb took over the reigns of the kingdom. When Dara Shukoh retreated to Gujarat in exile, some of his companions and friends left with him. But Sarmad remained behind. Sarmad, in his mystic ecstasy, had gone beyond the constraints of organized religions. In one of his Persian quatrains, he wrote:

> *Har kas ki sirre haqiqatash padar shud*
> *Il pahan tar az siphar pahnawar shud*
> *Mulla goyad ki bar falak shud Ahmad*
> *Sarmad goyad falak be Ahmad dar shud.*
> In the second couplet the mullah says Ahmad went to the heavens. Sarmad says, the Heavens came to Ahmad.

The last two lines refer to Prophet Muhammad's (who is also known as Ahmad) Ascension to Heaven (mi'raj).

This was held by the orthodox Muslim clergy to be a denial of the bodily ascension of the Prophet to Heaven, and they clamoured for his head. Aurangzeb was also bent upon eliminating Sarmad, less for religious and more for political considerations. Sarmad had become very popular in Delhi and this popularity was helping the cause of Dara Shukoh in exile. Aurangzeb sent his representative to Sarmad to ask him why he went about naked in Delhi whenever he stirred out, which was not often. When Aurangzeb's chief Qazi, Qawi Khan (which meant 'strong' Khan), met Sarmad and asked him why he exposed his private parts which was against the Islamic shariat, Sarmad answered with a pun on the jurist's name Qawi and said, 'What could I do, the Devil is strong.'

Qawi Khan angrily reported to Aurangzeb that there was enough evidence to prove that Sarmad and his apostasy could be put to death.

But Aurangzeb, a shrewd politician, knew that stronger grounds were needed to execute such a popular Sufi as Sarmad who was loved by the people. So he convened an assembly of jurists and summoned Sarmad to appear before it. Sarmad was asked to recite the Kalima, the Muslim profession of faith: 'There is no god but God, and Muhammad is his Prophet.'

As was his wont, Sarmad simply recited '*la ilaha*' (there is no deity) and stopped. The assembly cried that that was affirmation of denial.

Sarmad said, 'I am still at the stage of negation and have not reached the stage of affirmation. So how can my lips express something which my heart does not believe?' The assembly clamoured that this was a clear case of *kufr*—infidelity—and so Sarmad should be put to death.

In the poetic prose of Maulana Azad: these worshippers of mere appearances little knew that Sarmad was far above the debate between faith and denial, and was not frightened at the prospect of death. These fabricators of infidelity stood in their mosques and madrasas and wondered at the status of Sarmad. But Sarmad was perched at the top of that minaret from where he saw that the temple and mosque faced each other and the flag of faith and denial fly together. There are some who affirm a faith that they have actually experienced and have seen God face-to-face. So how could Sarmad affirm what he had not actually seen? People who travel this path come to such crossroads at some point in their lives. The crime of Sarmad was that he confessed openly a dilemma that others discuss in secrecy. So when Sarmad refused to recant and recite the Kalima in the way the clergy desired, he was sentenced to death. When he was taken to the place of execution, just opposite the gate of the Jama Masjid in Delhi, the whole city came out on the streets and it was difficult to walk through the throng. But Sarmad had hardly any concern to spare a glance.

When the executioner came forward, flourishing his naked sword, Sarmad exclaimed:

> *biya biya ki tu behar surate ki mi aayi*
> *man tura khub mishanasam*
> Come, come, in whatever guise you come, I recognize you very well.

And then he calmly put his head on the block. He is buried close to the spot where he was executed.

Many tales are told of his martyrdom. It is reported that his head, as it rolled down from the block, exclaimed '*illa Allah*' (except God), thus completing the Kalima, for at the very moment of death he saw his Creator!

Hallaj and Sarmad lost their lives for openly declaring the secret of Unity, of total surrender to that Unity. This was too much knowledge for the common man. Such knowledge, misunderstood and misinterpreted, had led some mystics to abandon this world, to abandon the path of karma yoga altogether, eschewing all rules of society, smoking opium and hemp, and ending up as parasites in society. Since Judaism, Christianity and Islam all had an orthodox creed, any deviation from that creed invited the charge of heresy. Depending on the age and the political clime they lived in, some mystics got away despite revealing the secret. Among them were Ibn al Arabi and Rumi. Despite their utterances and in the case of Rumi his ecstatic dances in the streets of Konya, the large following he had among all religions and creeds and the tolerant political climate saved them. Hinduism had no orthodox creed and therefore no heresy. Mira, Ramakrishna, Madhava and a myriad others faced no persecution. On the contrary they were acknowledged, some of them, as saints in their own lifetime.

Orthodoxy demanded, and continues to demand, adherence

to the exoteric interpretations of religious scriptures. It demands adherence to the confession of faith, ritual prayer, fasting, prescribed charity, pilgrimage and so on. But mystics, highly individualistic in their nature, developed esoteric interpretations. Many of the famous mystics of Islam, while subscribing to the exoteric format of religion practised their esoteric rituals in their hospices, khangahs, to the disapproval, and often consternation, of the orthodox ulema.

The Secret of Unity

The story of Farid al-Din Attar, a Sufi saint of the twelfth and thirteenth centuries, and his initiation into Sufism is told by his biographer:

> Farid al-Din Attar was sitting one day at his door with a friend when a dervish, or religious mendicant, approached the shop. Looking closely into the well-furnished shop and inhaling the sweet scent of the drugs and perfumes with which it was loaded, the dervish heaved a deep sigh and began to shed tears. Attar assumed he was doing this to arouse pity in order to get alms and therefore asked the dervish to leave.
>
> 'I have no difficulty in leaving as I only have this,' said the dervish, pointing to his ragged cloak, 'but oh merchant! How will you leave this world with all this?' pointing to Attar's well-stocked and fragrant shop.
>
> Surprised, Attar replied, 'My soul will leave my body just as your soul will leave yours.'
>
> The dervish said, 'My soul will leave like this,' and he put his bowl on the ground and laying his head on it he recited the Kalima and gave up his soul to his Creator.
>
> Attar was deeply moved by this incident, gave up his business, renounced all worldly concerns, became a disciple of Shaikh Rukn ad-Din and became a Sufi.

Whether accurate or not, this story reflects the deep belief the dervish had in God and his total surrender to his Lord. But how does an ordinary mortal surrender to God, abandoning, renouncing all dharmas? Only the rishis and Sufis understood this secret fully. That path is the path of silence, the path of love, the path of utter unquestioning faith arrived at through the heart, not through reason, by surrender and not by argument or logic, nor by mere ritual observance without the total commitment of one's self to God.

Shabistari exhorts his disciples:

> Let reason go. For His light
> Burns reason up from head to foot.
> If you wish to see that face
> seek another eye. The philosopher
> with his two eyes sees double
> so is unable to see the unity of Truth
> As His light burns up the angels
> even so does it consume reason.
> As the light of our eyes is to the sun
> So is the light of reason to the Light of Lights.

Rumi asserts in his *Fihi ma fihi*:

> Faith is better than ritual prayer, for prayer is obligatory five times a day, whereas faith is continuous. Ritual prayer can be neglected if there is a valid excuse, and it may also be postponed under certain circumstances . . . But faith cannot be neglected for any excuse, nor are there any circumstances under which it may be postponed. Faith without prayer is (still) beneficial whereas there is no benefit in prayer without faith, as is the case of prayer of hypocrites. Furthermore,

ritual prayer differs from one religion to the next, whereas faith does not change at all; its inner states, its orientation and so forth are immutable.

This is what Ghalib had to say:

Wafaadaari bashart-e ustwaari asl-e imaan hai
Marey butkhaaney mein to Kaaba mein gaadho
Brahmin ko.
Steadfast loyalty is the essence of faith. If the Brahmin lays down his life in the temple, he deserves to be buried inside the Kaaba.

Earlier, the Bhagavad Gītā had emphasized the importance of single-minded devotion to God:

mahātmānas tu māṁ pārtha daivīṁ prakṛtim āśritāḥ
bhajanty ananya-manaso jñātvā bhūtādim avyayam
satataṁ kīrtayanto māṁ yatantaś ca dṛḍha-vratāḥ
namasyantaś ca māṁ bhaktyā nitya-yuktā upāsate[1]
O Partha, those who are not deluded, the great souls, partaking of the divine nature, worship Me with a single mind, knowing Me as the immutable and the source of all beings, glorifying Me always, striving firm in vows, prostrating before me they worship Me with steadfast devotion.

ahaṁ sarvasya prabhavo mattaḥ sarvaṁ pravartate
iti matvā bhajante māṁ budhā bhāva-samanvitāḥ
mac-cittā mad-gata-prāṇā bodhayantaḥ parasparam
kathayantaś ca māṁ nityaṁ tuṣyanti ca ramanti ca[2]
I am the origin of all; from Me all things evolve. The

wise know this and adore Me with all their heart. With
their minds fixed on Me, with their life absorbed in Me,
enlightening each other and ever speaking of Me, they are
contented and delighted.

mayy eva mana ādhatsva mayi buddhiṁ niveśaya
nivasiṣyasi mayy eva ata ūrdhvaṁ na samśayaḥ[3]
Fix your mind on Me alone, let your thoughts dwell in Me.
You will hereafter live in Me alone. Of this there is no doubt.

In these verses, Krishna has emphasized the integration of faith
and worship, devotion and prayer.

While Rumi placed faith above ritual prayer, this was a purely
Sufi response to the tendency of those who believe in prayer,
mere ritual prayer, devoid of the element of ehsaan in it, which
the Hadith al Ehsaan emphasized. So what is essential is imbuing
the act of ritual prayer with the consciousness of the presence of
God when one is performing it.

One of the many questions faced by a believer in his quest is:
Can one find salvation through faith alone without observing the
law, the ordinances prescribed by the scriptures? At the beginning
of Chapter 17 of the Gītā, Arjuna asks:

ye śāstra—vidhim utsṛjya yajante śraddhayānvitāḥ
teṣām niṣṭhā tu kā kṛṣṇa sattvam āho rajas tamaḥ[4]
What is the state of those who leave aside the ordinances of
the scriptures (sastras) but worship with faith (shraddha)?

In other words, is it essential to observe all the requirements
prescribed by the Law, if one has an unwavering faith in God?—
the question of Islam, Iman and Ehsaan.

Krishna answers this question:

tasmāc chāstram pramāṇam te kāryākārya-vyavasthitau
jñātvā śāstra-vidhānoktam karma kartum ihārhasī[5]
Therefore let the scriptures be your authority in deciding
what ought to be done and what ought not to be done.
Having known what is said in the ordinances of the
scriptures, you should act here.

But mere observance of the ordinances is not sufficient, however
meticulously you perform them. Something more is required.
And that something is faith. Krishna says:

aśraddhayā hutam dattam tapas taptam kṛtam ca yat
asad ity ucyate pārtha na ca tat pretya no ihā[6]
Whatever offering or gift is made, whatever austerity is
practised, whatever ritual is performed, if it is done without
Faith, it is called asat, a falsehood, O Partha. It is of no
account here or hereafter.

Therefore what is emphasized here is to observe the law and the
ordinances which help to keep you on the right path and to do
so with sincere faith which take you to God.

As the Quran says, '*fiddunya hasanathan wafil aakhirati hasana*'
(the well-being in this world and happiness in the hereafter).

Nurcholish Madjid, an Indonesian scholar of Islam, in his *Worship
as an Institution of Faith* writes eloquently on this integration:

People often raise the question, 'Isn't it enough for someone
to have faith and do good works, without also having to
worship?' We might note that a question of this type suggests
an attitude both logical and reasonable. Moreover, the Holy
Book (Quran) itself always speaks about faith and good
works as two associated values that people must possess.

Nurcholish then analyses that no system of beliefs has ever appeared in the world that has not introduced some kind of rituals to a greater or lesser extent. Even communism which has no pretence to religiosity and which in fact strives to eliminate religion altogether has developed its own ritual system, showing respect to party symbols, etc.

One of the spiritual dimensions of faith is the expression of devotion through a system of worship. Such devotional acts, he says, strengthen the feeling of belief and produce a higher consciousness. They also help in developing a feeling of closeness to God.

Nurcholish concludes:

> For abstract faith to move someone in the direction of performing good works, it must posses a warmth and intimacy in the soul of the believer, and this can be achieved by way of activity of worship . . . Otherwise, faith would become a kind of abstract formulation without the ability to motivate the individual inwardly to do something at the level of genuine sincerity.[7]

The act of worship is to bring the worshipper close to God.

As the Quran says, '*wasjud wa aqtarib*' (So worship Him and draw near).[8]

But this worship should also be solely for the love of God, not with any other motive. And this worship, this prayer should be with passion and sincerity.

Frithjof Schuon writes in *Understanding Islam*:

> Let us now consider prayer in its most general sense; call to God, if it is to be perfect and 'sincere' must be fervent, just as concentration if it is to be perfect must be pure; now at

the level of emotive piety, the key to concentration is fervour
. . . the very fact of our existence is a prayer and compels us
to prayer so that it could indeed be said, 'I am, therefore I
pray; sum ergo oro.'[9]

Rābi'a al-Adawiyya or Rābi'a Basri, the famous saint of Islam, lived
in Basra in the eighth century. The only way to God, she used to say,
is in total surrender and total love. For her, love (hubb or mahabba)
meant concentration on God to the exclusion of all else. When
Sufyan Thawri asked Rābi'a what was the reality of her faith, she
replied, 'I have not worshipped Him from fear of His fire, nor for
love of His Paradise, so that I should be like a mere paid servant;
rather I have worshipped Him for love of Him and longing for Him.
 She sang:

I love You with two loves;
A selfish love and a love of which You are worthy
That love which is a selfish love
Is only remembrance of You and nothing else.
But as for that love of which You are worthy
Ah, then You have torn the veils for me so I see You.
There is no praise for me in either love
But praise is Yours in this love and that.

Once you have done the act of total surrender, God frees you of
your sins—for one who has totally surrendered cannot sin. For
him, his inward and outward become one.

The famous Persian poet Saib put it succinctly in a
quatrain:

Neest shu ta hastiyat az vay rasad
Ta tu hasti hast dar tu kay rasad

Ta nagardi mahv-i khwaari u fanaa
Kay rasad isbaaat az uzz-u baqa
Become nothing so that your being may come from Him; as
long as *you* exist, how can (real) existence come to you? As
long as you are not absorbed, obliterated and annihilated,
how can affirmation ever be granted you by the Almighty
and Eternal?

In the Bhagavad Gītā, Krishna presents a third and the most effective
alternative to the path of Action (karma mārga) and the path of
Knowledge (jnāna mārga). Man can seek and find his salvation in
God, *Fana fillah* as the Sufis would call it, by total, wholehearted
devotion to the Lord. While the Gītā does not exhort man to give
up the other two paths—action and knowledge—Krishna counsels
man to offer all his actions too to God as a sacrifice:

yat karoṣi yad aśnāsi yaj juhoṣi dadāsi yat
yat tapasyasi kaunteyatat kuruṣva mad-arpaṇam [10]
Whatever thou dost, whatever thou eatest, whatever thou
offerest in oblation or givest, whatever austerities thou
performest, son of Kunti, that do as an offering to me.

śubhāśubha-phalair evaṁ mokṣyase karma-bandhanaiḥ
sannyāsa-yoga-yuktātmā vimukto mām upaiṣyasi [11]
In this way you will be freed from all reactions to good and
evil deeds, and by this principle of renunciation you will be
liberated and come to Me.

The Gītā teaches that a spiritual man is he who has transcended
cause and effect, who acts without desire, who has no attachment
to the consequences of performing his duty, who has devoted
himself and all his acts to the Lord, but who nevertheless has

not abandoned the world, who remains in society, performs his duty faithfully and conscientiously and is conscious of his social responsibilities.

The Gītā too has advocated action, karma yoga, as one way of achieving Reality. Krishna has advocated ceaseless activity—God's own nature as an example to man!

Once again I cannot help but quote the *Yogavāsishta*:

Liberation cannot be attained by merely living in a forest, far away from human society, by undergoing penances[12] by performance or renunciation of any particular action, by undergoing any prescribed rules of discipline of any sect, by pilgrimage to the sacred places, by making religious gifts by bathing in sacred rivers, by learning, by the concentration of the mind, by some kind of yogic feats, by penances, by sacrifices,[13] by reading scriptures, by obeying the orders of a perceptor, by good luck, by religious acts, by means of wealth, or by the help and kindness of friends and relatives.[14]

Yogavāsishta, of course, advocates one extreme view—for Vasishta here asks the seeker after truth to abandon all paths which smack of rituals and regulations, penances and sacrifices, even recitation of scriptures and other religious rites and rules. So how does the seeker after Truth achieve his goal?

Says Vasishta:

Knowledge of Reality, acquired through one's own efforts at right thinking, together with living by the enlightenment one gets from that knowledge, is the only method of crossing over the ocean of misery and reaching the land of happiness.[15]

This finds an echo in the words of Prophet Muhammad, *La*

ruhbaniyat fil Islam (There is no monkhood in Islam). Islam prohibits total abandonment of action, retiring to a monastery or a cave and devoting oneself utterly to God, washing one's hands of humanity.

One of the most famous Sufis, Abu Sai'd Abul Khayr was approached by a critic who wanted to belittle his spiritual attainments.

'So-and-so flies in the air,' he said implying that Abu Sai'd could not.

'Yes, crows, pigeons and birds do fly in the air,' commented Abu Sai'd.

'So-and-so walks on water,' persisted the critic to drive in the point.

'Yes, water insects and frogs do walk on water,' commented Abu Sai'd.

'So-and-so travels from Damascus to Baghdad in a few moments,' said the critic yet again.

'Satan is reputed to travel from the east to the west in the blink of an eye. Flying in the air, walking on water or going from east to west in a moment is not spirituality. True spirituality lies in living in this world, marrying and having children, buying and selling—yet doing all these actions in the utter consciousness that you are performing them in the presence of God.'

Farid al-Din Attar in his *Tadhkirat al-Auliya'* (Memorial of the Saints) tells of an episode in the life of the famous saint Sari Saqati.

Sari was the first man to preach in Baghdad on the mystic truths and the Sufi 'unity'. Most of the Sufi Shaikhs of Iraq were his disciples. He was the uncle of Junayd Baghdadi. He lived in Baghdad and ran a shop. Hanging a curtain over the door of his shop, he would go in and pray.

One day a man came from Mount Lokam to visit him. Lifting aside the curtain he greeted Sari.

'Shaikh so-and-so from Mount Lokam greets you,' he said. 'He dwells in the mountains,' commented Sari, 'so his efforts amount to nothing. A man ought to be able to live in the midst of the market, and be so preoccupied with God, that not for a single instant is he absent from God.[16]

The Madness of Love

It is said about Mirabai (1498–1546), the sixteenth-century Rajput princess-turned-Krishna devotee and bhakti poet, that she fell in love with Girdhar (another name for Krishna) as a child. Even when she was betrothed to a Rajput prince, a Rana, from another state and took the seven pheras with her around the fire, the mantras she said in her heart were all directed to her spiritual husband, Girdhar. The only dowry she took with her from her maternal home was the image of Krishna, which was her most beloved possession. And when she arrived at her matrimonial home, she refused to pray to the family's deity. She associated herself with the wandering sadhus. Her sister-in-law tried to dissuade her from this but to no avail. The Rana, hearing of this, sent her a cup of poison in the guise of nectar as an offering for Krishna. But after she touched it to her Lord's feet and drank it, the poison turned into nectar.

She wrote:

Drink the nectar of the Divine Name, O human! Drink the nectar of the Divine Name!
Leave the bad company, always sit among righteous company.
Hearken to the mention of God (for your own sake).
Concupiscence, anger, pride, greed, attachment: wash these out of your consciousness.
Mira's Lord is the Mountain-Holder, the suave lover.
Soak yourself in the dye of His colour.[1]

Many saints and Sufis, rishis and sants have held that the path of total surrender to God in love, bhakti yoga, is superior to mere intellectual knowledge and a rational commitment to His transcendence, jnāna yoga, and single-minded pursuit of God through action and devotion to duty, karma yoga. This bhakti yoga is what all mystics achieved—Hallaj and Junayd, Rumi and Ramakrishna, Rābi'a and Mira, Bayazid and Chaitanya, Attar and Kabir, Tukaram and Chishti. As Swami Vivekananda has summed up, 'In the end it is not the philosophy that takes you to salvation. Even the Gītā, the great philosophy itself, does not compare with that madness (what the Sufis called jazb or junoon). For in the Gītā, the disciple is taught slowly how to walk towards God, but here is the madness of enjoyment, the drunkenness of love, where disciples and teachers and teachings and books and all these things become one, even the ideas of fear and God and Heaven.'

One may recall Rābi'a's ecstatic outburst: 'to burn the garden of Paradise and douse the fires of Hell so that people should not pray for the sake of Paradise or out of fear of punishment. It should be only for love of God.'

'Everything has been thrown away,' continues Vivekananda, 'what remains is madness of love. It is forgetfulness of everything, and the lover sees nothing in the world except that Krishna and Krishna alone, when the face of everything becomes Krishna, his own face looks like Krishna's when his soul has become tinged with Krishna's colour.'

The Bhagavad Gītā advocated the bhakti mārga, total devotion to the Supreme Lord as the path to nirvana. Many centuries later this bhakti mārga inspired many saints in India to devote themselves to the Supreme Lord totally and unconditionally.

Manikka Vachaka, a saint from south India wrote:

Into my vile body of flesh
You came, as though it were a temple of gold,
And soothed me wholly and saved me,
O Lord of Grace, O Gem most pure,
Sorrow and birth and death and illusion
You took from me, and set me free.
O Bliss! O Light! I have taken refuge in you,
And never can I be parted from you.[2]

And one finds the echo of Krishna's exhortation, *sarvadharmān parityajya mām ekam saranam vraja* (abandon all dharma and devote yourself to me alone), in Allama Prabhu's cry:

Feed the poor
Tell the truth
Make water-places
For the thirsty
And build tanks for the torn
You may then go to heaven
After death, but you will get nowhere
Near the truth of our Lord
And the man who knows our Lord,
He gets no results.[3]

Many of the Tamil and Kannada saints sang of God, of Krishna, not in his aspect of world-destroying Time but in the intimate manifestation of the Krishna of Vrindavan, of the gopis and Radha. Sometimes, in their poetry they even claimed that the true devotee cannot serve God and society at the same time. Gopis became models of devotional excellence and Radha became the ideal devotee, to be emulated and followed. Some of the saints in effect became Radha in their devotions, sometimes even the erotic Radha of Jayadeva's *Geeta Govinda*.[4]

This devotion was manifested in several ways. Some saints, like Vishnu Puri[5] wrote in the *Bhakti-ratnavali*, based on the *Bhagwat Purāna*:

> The thief, the wine drinker, the betrayer of his friend, the killer of a Brahmin, the polluter of the bed of his guru, the killer of women and of cows, a regicide, a patricide and other sinners, the expiation of the sin of all these sinners is made by the uttering of the name of Vishnu . . . the name of Hari has been spoken of as destructive of sins.

Recall the ecstatic words of the Prophet Muhammad when he exclaimed '*man qala la ilaha ill Allah, fa dakhl al jannah*' (he, who says there is no God but Allah, enters Paradise).

Bhakti was seen by the saints not as a means to an end but as an end in itself. It was an expression of man's highest and essential nature. Even moksha was an unworthy goal.

Rābi'a Basri exclaimed:

> O my Lord,
> the stars glitter
> and the eyes of men are closed.
> Kings have locked their doors
> And each lover is alone with his love.
> Here, I am alone with you.[6]

With total surrender to God comes bhakti, which is to revel in bliss, to dance uncontrollably under the intoxicating influence of God. When God takes over your soul, when you are alone with God, your beloved, the devotee goes into a frenzy, weeping, laughing and dancing almost on the verge of madness.

As T.S. Eliot wrote in *Burnt Norton*, 'At the still point of the turning world . . . there is only the dance.'

Krishna Chaitanya (1486–1533) was a mystic who lived in eastern India in the sixteenth century and in his early life was known as a scholar and debater. However, meeting his guru, Ishwara Puri, proved to be a turning point in his life as he was initiated into the Krishna mantra. He believed in total absorption in Krishna's consciousness through chanting His name. Though he left no written body of work behind, his method of non-ritualistic mysticism through music and dance has been legendary among the Vaishnavites of Orissa. By the very force of his personality, he became a role model devotee of Krishna. In his devotion to Krishna, he identified himself with Radha, the ideal bhakta who devoted herself—body and soul, to the worship of Krishna. Chaitanya often appeared as Radha to his companions. He wore anklets, a necklace, a sari, a garland and earrings. He saw Krishna everywhere and was reminded of Krishna when he saw the blue neck of a peacock or when he heard the flute of a cowherd boy he 'forgot himself entire in the holy frenzy of love'.

Sometimes, 'overcome by ecstasy and madness, the Lord (Chaitanya) would not be still. Everything he said and did was symptomatic of madness,' so says the *Madhya-lila* about Chaitanya. In the twentieth century, Swami Bhaktivedanta popularized Chaitanya's bhakti movement through the cult of Krishna Consciousness. In this ecstatic state, Chaitanya's devotees themselves saw Krishna in him: 'All the signs of Godhead exist fully in our Lord Chaitanya.'

Another great devotee of Krishna who absorbed the lessons of Gītā in himself was Ramakrishna Paramahamsa. Though three and a half centuries separate Ramakrishna from Chaitanya, in their utter devotion they show essentially the same commitment. Ramakrishna saw Krishna, like Chaitanya, in every manifestation. When he worshipped the child Ramlala for example, he immersed himself in the mood of a mother. His heart became so filled with motherly tenderness that he began to regard himself as a woman. Even his speech and gestures changed. When he worshipped the child Krishna, in the form of one of his own disciples Rakhal, he in essence became Yashoda, the foster-mother of Krishna. Rakhal also felt towards Ramakrishna as a child feels towards its mother.

But when Ramakrishna engaged in the practice of madhur bhava, he dressed himself as a woman, using women's clothes and ornaments, a skirt, a gauze scarf and a bodice. The consciousness that he was a male disappeared from his behaviour and his thoughts. His every word, movement and thought became feminine. He would then become Radha incarnate and would see her in his visions. Sometimes, when Ramakrishna became ecstatic in his devotions, his behaviour bordered on madness and his moods would become unpredictable.

Centuries before Ramakrishna, another devotee of God, Jalaluddin Rumi too had similar ecstatic visions. Just as Chaitanya and Ramakrishna could see the beauty of Krishna in an ordinary human being, an urchin, Rumi saw the divine light in the countenance of his friend, Shams Tabriz. For Rumi, love appeared personified in his guru, his mystical master Shams whom he raised to supernatural and cosmic heights.

He sang:

You are the river that moves the green wheel of the sky!
You are the face that amazes the moon and venus!
You are the princely polo stick that alone on the

Playground
of the mind sets all balls into motion
O thou before whom angels and kings
are one poorer than the other,
O you, the adored one of my soul—Shams al-Din.

Rumi introduced dance into the Sufi seance, and his followers later established the Order of the Whirling Dervishes. Poetry, music and dance are all combined in the cosmic dance of the Whirling Dervishes of the Mevlevi order of Sufism.

An ecstatic Rumi had written:

My love for you intoxicated me and made me dance
I am intoxicated and in ecstasy (*bekhudi*) what can I do?
I will render the thanks of earth and Heaven
for I was earth, He made me Heaven.

As Burgel describes it:

The whirling of the Mevlevis is certainly the most persuasive, most beautiful incarnation of the two polar principles of ecstasy and control. The rite is certainly performed with the aim of reaching ecstasy, mystical unity or in other words the repletion with the divine mightiness.[7]

Most scholars agree that the whirling dance was taught to Rumi by his spiritual teacher and friend Shams. It is symbolic of the celestial spheres whirling around in the universe creating the music of the spheres, and at the same time the dance symbolizes the circular motion of the soul when the Sufi's entire existence gets focused on a single point of consciousness, that is, God.

Rumi in one of his poems describes it thus:

Sound drum and mellow flute,
resounding Allah Hu
Dance, ruddy dawn,
in gladness bounding Allah Hu
Sound exalted in the center, o thou streaming light
Soul of all wheeling planets rounding Allah Hu

This sama of the Mevlevi Dervishes has been described by Annemarie Schimmel as 'an expression of the sweetest and deepest secrets of mystical love. The dervishes after slowly walking around the room thrice, each time kissing the Master's (Pir's) hand suddenly throw off their black gowns (thin earthly bodies as it were) and emerge in their white gowns of eternal light, spinning around their axels as well as whirling around the centre, as though the atoms were dancing around the sun which attracts them to set them in motion—heavenly dance, dance of immortality, as the Mawlana (Rumi) had described it in so many of his verses.'[8]

While the Mevlevi Order of Whirling Dervishes has been keeping this tradition of the spiritual dance alive in their monasteries and hospices for over six hundred years, in his own lifetime the Mawlana himself was reviled as a 'madman' when he went round ecstatically dancing in the streets of Konya after the disappearance of Shams from his life.

His own son describes the scene vividly:

Day and night he danced in ecstasy
On the earth he revolved like the Heavens.
His (ecstatic) cries reached the zenith of the skies
And were heard by all and sundry.
He showered gold and silver on the musicians;
He gave away whatever he had
Never for a moment was he without music and

ecstasy.
Never for a moment was he at rest
There was an uproar (of protest) in the city.
Nay the whole world resounded with that uproar
(They were surprised that) such a great Qutb and
Mufti of Islam
who was the accepted leader of the two Universes
Should be raving like a madman –
In public and in private[9]

But Rumi was least concerned with what the world thought of
his ecstatic whirling.
He wrote:

Come, come! Let us whirl about in the rose garden.
Let us whirl like a compass around that point of
divine grace!
We have sowed many seeds in the ground
and turned about the barren place.
Let us now whirl about the grain which no granary
Comprehends

In one of the greatest lyrics of Rumi, he uses the word 'sama', the
round dance, itself as the refrain.

Come, come, o thou, who are the soul
of the soul of the round dance!
Come thou who are the walking cypress
in the garden of the round dance.
Come thou, under whose feet is the fountain of light,
who hast a thousand venuses in the heaven of the
round dance!

You leave the two worlds when you enter the round
dance!
Beyond the two worlds in this world of the round
dance
The roof of the seventh heaven is certainly high,
Yet this roof does not reach where lies
the ladder of the round dance!

Matching Rumi's ardour that impelled him to dance in his ecstasy
of love, two centuries later Mirabai, the princess of Rajputana,
also danced in her intoxication of love for Krishna. She sang:

Mira danced with ankle-bells on her feet
People said Mira was mad; my mother-in-law said
ruined the family's repute
Rana sent me a cup of poison and Mira drank it
laughing.
I dedicated my body and soul at the feet of Hari
I am thirsty for the nectar of the sight of him
Mira's lord is Giridhar Nagar; I will come for refuge
to him.[10]

Mira in her 'sober' moments, if she ever had any, knew that she
was permanently intoxicated with Krishna's love. Like Rumi, she
was aware of her intoxication:

Friend, I am completely dyed in Krishna's colour
I drank the cup of immortal bliss, and became drunk.
My inebriation never goes away, however
many millions of ways I try.[11]

On a different occasion, Mira uses the image of a butterfly and every flower on which she hovers dancing is Krishna for her:

> As a butterfly in sunshine filled with light in blue air hovers,
> thus I dance . . . Love inflamed I dance into the Light of
> Blessed Krishna.[12]

Ramdas, Tukaram, Bilvamangal were all such absorbed devotees
that their contemporaries looked on them as mad. So did the
people of Baghdad, Shiraz and Isfahan who looked at the ones
who were God-intoxicated and called them majzub and majnun.

Mahmud Shabistari wrote in *Gulshan-e-Raz*:

> Allah brought forth this creation in a twinkling of an eye.
> As His creation, the world is said to be a 'dizzy whirl' having
> only a simulated existence/its state is but an insubstantial
> pageant and a farce.

This view is close to what Krishna claims for maya and the wheel
of maya which God is constantly turning. For Shabistari, the
divine dispensation is beyond the confines of cause and effect, and
the whole world is a wine house of Allah and the entire creation
is intoxicated by His influence.

Here is Shabistari at his most ecstatic:

> The whole universe is as His wine house,
> The heart of every atom as His wine cup
> Reason is drunk, earth drunk, heaven drunk
> The heavens giddy with his wine are reeling
> to and fro
> Desiring in their heart to smell its perfume
> The angels drinking it pure from pure vessels
> Pour the dregs of their draught upon this

world.
The elements becoming light-headed from
that draught
Fall now into the fire, now into the water.
From the scent of its dregs which fell on the
Earth
Man ascends up till he reaches heaven
From its reflection the withered body
becomes a living soul.
From its heat the frozen soul is warmed to life
and motion.
The creature world is ever dizzy therewith.

There are two great proponents of atheism today in the world—
Richard Dawkins and Stephen Hawking. While Dawkins is an
active missionary of atheism, Hawking attempts to demolish belief
in God through more scientific arguments. Yet, it is poetic irony
that the writings of both have led many an agnostic into faith in
God. One of them happens to be my daughter, Shahla, who was
tending towards rationalism. She borrowed Dawkins's book *The
God Delusion* from me and one of the passages she mentioned,
affected her. That surprised me.

'Which particular part of Dawkins's argument affected you?'
I asked.

'Dawkins believes that this universe is friendly to human life.
So is the planet earth. The fact that there is life on earth means
that the laws of physics are friendly enough to allow it to happen,'
she replied.

'Could that not have happened as a logical consequence of
creation, as Dawkins argued?' I interrupted her.

'No,' she said, 'in addition, Dawkins further argues that the very
creation of the stars led to the existence of most of the chemical

elements. In fact, life would be impossible without the availability of those chemicals.'

I quote further from that particular passage:

Physicists have calculated that if the laws and constants had been even slightly different, the Universe would have developed in such a way that Life would have been impossible. Martin Rees, in *Just Six Numbers*, lists six fundamental constants, which are believed to hold all around the universe. Each of these six numbers is finely tuned in the sense that, if it were slightly different, the universe would be comprehensively different and presumably unfriendly to life.[13]

Dawkins goes on to give examples of how the six critical numbers range in such a narrow range that if one number had been 0.006 or 0.008 instead of being exactly 0.007, there would have been no hydrogen, no oxygen, no water and no life. He says, 'It is as though God had six knobs that he could twiddle, and he carefully tuned each knob to its Goldilocks valve.' Yet he denies that there is a power that creates those six relationships between the various forces that govern the creation of the universe and life in it. His only lame comment is, 'When we finally reach the long hoped-for theory of everything, we shall see that the six key numbers depend upon each other, or on *something else yet unknown*.' But Dawkins still refuses to acknowledge that that as 'yet unknown' could be God, Divine Providence!

Stephen Hawking, in his *Grand Design*, goes into great detail to explain the design behind the creation of the universe and life in it. At the end, Hawking quotes another Nobel-winning physicist, Fred Hoyle, 'I do not believe any scientist who examined the evidence would fail to draw the inference that the *laws of nuclear physics have been deliberately designed* with regard to the consequences they produce inside the stars' (emphasis added). And Hawking further writes, 'Such calculations show that a change of as little as 0.5 per cent in the strength of the strong nuclear force, or 4 per cent in the electric force, would destroy either nearly all carbon or all oxygen in every star, and hence the possibility of life as we know it. Change those rules of our Universe just a bit and the conditions for our existence disappear.'[14] And yet, all these, this extremely delicately balanced universe leads Hawking to argue that God does not exist!

I am reminded of the eighteenth-century Urdu poet, Mir Taqi Mir:

Le saans bhi aahista ke nazuk hai bahut kaam
Aaafaaq ki is kaargahe sheeshagari ka.
Draw even your breath very gently in this glasswork house,
for everything here is delicately poised and finely carved.

To anyone other than a Dawkins or a Hawking, the very existence of the universe, the myriad galaxies, stars, planetary system and the teaming life on earth, dancing to the divine tune and singing paeans to His glory every moment is proof enough of the existence of God and the six knobs he twiddles to create the music of eternity.

Perhaps, taking his cue from the Old Testament,[15] St Bernard, the Christian mystic, envisioned Jesus Christ as a dance master. He writes:

Jesus the dancer's master is,
A great skill at the dance is his
He turns to right, he turns to left
All must follow his teaching deft

Another song in which Jesus sees his crucifixion as a dance of love for God is:

> Tomorrow shall be my dancing day;
> I would my true love did so chance
> To see the legend of my play
> To call my true love to my dance
> Sing, O my love, O my love, my love;
> This have I done for my true love.

Rumi in his ecstatic moment cried, '*Allah, Allah, kun ki Allah mishavad*' (Recite Allah, Allah, until you yourself become Allah) and Bulleh Shah, the eighteenth-century mystic cried, *Ranjha, Ranjha kar di ninh men ape Ranjha hui* (Repeating Ranjha, Ranjha in my mind, I myself have become Ranjha).

The Prophet of Islam is also reported to have said as much earlier. Abdullah ibn Busr reported that a man said, 'O Messenger of Allah, the laws of Islam are too many for me, so tell me something that I may cling to.' He replied, 'Let your tongue never cease to be moist from invoking Allah.'

Sanjaya called the discourse between Krishna and Arjuna hair-raising—*roma harsanam*. All scriptures, once felt by the heart, are hair-raising and the Gītā is first amongst them all.

When a Sufi is wholly absorbed in God, and nothing but love for God remains in his heart, he sings with Rumi:

> *Ishq ast dar aasman paridan*
> *Sad parda b'har nafas dareedan*
> *Awwal nafas az nafas gusastan*
> *Aakhir qadam as qadam baridan*
> *Na dida giraftan een jahan ra*
> *Mur dida-e kheesh ra n'didan*

Zaan su-e nazar nazara kardan
Dar koocha-e seena'ha dawidan
What is Love? To soar into the very Heavens; with every
breath to rend a hundred veils; with the first breath to pass
beyond one's self; with the last step to go beyond all bounds.
To behold this world without seeing it; to close your eyes to
what they see; to look beyond the bounds of vision; to delve
deep into the labyrinth of the heart.

And when the Sufi reaches into the bounds beyond all boundaries,
after rending a hundred veils what does he find?
Rumi replies:

Az kufr ze islam beroon saharaeest
Mara bemiyane aan fiza saudaeest
Arif chun bedaan raseed sar ra benahad
Na kufr na islam na aanja jaaeest
Beyond belief and unbelief lies a vast expanse; I wander
carefree in that clime, when the Seer, reaching there, rests
his head, he finds neither belief nor unbelief there.

Once a seer realizes the Unity of God—the real spirit of tawhid—
and comprehends the concept of the Unity of Mankind—
ummatan wahida, as the Quran puts it—he can harbour no
discrimination in his heart, for he goes beyond the narrow
definitions which separate mankind into warring groups, based
on caste, creed, colour, race and clime.[16]
    One of the most telling lessons that the Gītā teaches is that
Man is a microcosm in which the whole of creation is contained.
It is only through spiritual knowledge that one can see the whole
of creation in one's own self, one's ātman, and in God, of course.

yaj jñātvā na punar moham evaṁ yāsyasi pāṇḍava
yena bhūtāny aśeṣāṇi drakṣyasy ātmany atho mayi[17]

Knowing this, O Pandava, you will not again fall into this
confusion; by this you will see the whole of the creation in
your own self and in Me.

In *Yogavāsishta*, Vasishta tells Rama:

> The idea that this man is my brother and that one is not,
> is entertained by only petty-minded people. How can one
> be said to be a brother and another not, when the same
> Self pervades all? All classes of creatures, O Rama, are your
> brothers. There is none here who is absolutely unrelated
> to you.

While the sage taught Rama about the brotherhood of man and
the concept of humankind as belonging to one family, vasudaiva
kutumbakam, the Quran taught the same lesson. Mankind was a
single community—ummatan wahida—affirmed the Quran and
as a corollary said that the killing of one innocent man was like
killing humanity as a whole, and the saving of one innocent life
is like saving humanity as a whole.

Sufis and saints have sought for God in the hearts of man—that
is where he resides.

Centuries later, another Sufi saint of India, Kabir, sang:

> O servant, where does thou seek me
> Lo! I am beside thee.
> I am neither in temple nor in mosque;
> I am neither in Kaaba nor in Kailash
> Neither am I in rites and ceremonies
> Nor in yoga or renunciation

> If thou art a true seeker, thou
> shalt at once see me, thou
> shalt meet me in a moment of time[18]

Kabir also says: 'O Sadhu! God is the breath of all breath.'[19]

Earlier, Krishna had exhorted Arjuna that such knowledge as enables man to see the whole of creation in one's own self can be taught only by the wise, the visionary, the seer into the Truth. And for that, what is needed is constant prayer, (*prani patena*), by discourse (*prani prasnena*) and by selfless service (sevā).

And what is this self in which one can see the whole of creation? It is the individual ātman, which in reality is also the Brahman, the Supreme Lord. For the self is that one, immutable, all-pervading, all-containing self-existing reality or Brahman hidden behind our mental being into which our consciousness widens when it is liberated from the ego. He is God, the Divine, the Purshottama. To Him we offer everything as a sacrifice; into His hands we give up our actions; in His existence we live and move; unified with him in our nature and with all existence in Him, we become one soul and one Power of being with Him and with all beings.

This finds reflection in Prophet Muhammad's remark, '*man arafa nafsahu, arafa rabbuhu*' (he who knows himself, knows God); The ancient Greeks said, '*gnothi seauton*' (know thyself) and the Upanishads exhorted, '*ātmānam viddhi*' (know yourself).

Ibn al Arabi, the great seer, remarks, 'The knowledge of things necessarily precedes the knowledge of God. The goal is to know God in his capacity as Lord of the world and this knowledge only becomes accessible once prior knowledge of the world has already been obtained.'

'Do not approach the gates of the sultan,' so admonished Ibn al Arabi. And he was totally inflexible where this principle was concerned. Everything that in one way or the other is linked with power is to be held in contempt. Once Sultan Abdul Ala, the ruler of Ceuta where Ibn al Arabi was residing at that time, sent two loads of food when the Shaikh was not in. Some visitors who had come to see the Great Shaikh helped themselves to it, though his own disciples refrained. The next evening, the Sultan again sent two more loads of food, which the Shaikh neither accepted nor refused. Some visitors, who had heard that the Sultan was sending loads of food, came visiting. Without touching the food, the Shaikh gave the call for congregational prayers. Whereupon, one of the visitors quoted, 'One does not perform the prayer when the meal is served.'

When the Shaikh remained silent, the silence angered the mass. The Shaikh told the man that he had not accepted the food and had no intention of eating it because as far as he was concerned it was illicit (haram) and he could not possibly tell his visitors to eat it because he wanted for them what he wanted for himself. He also said that those who considered the food licit (halal) could eat it. This act of the Shaikh was reported to the Sultan. But the Sultan held the Shaikh in such high regard that he disregarded this. One of the Shaikh's colleagues advised him, 'diplomacy, first of all'. The Shaikh replied, 'Agreed—provided the essential is preserved.'

The Gītā further tells us:

ye yathā māṁ prapadyante tāṁs tathaiva bhajāmy aham
mama vartmānuvartante manuṣyāḥ pārtha sarvaśaḥ[20]
In whatever way men approach Me, even so do I render to them. In every way, O Partha, the path men follow is mine.

The Gītā affirms that in whatsoever way you worship, you are worshipping God, for all roads of devotion lead only to God.

And many centuries later, Ghalib wrote:

Maayeen wa zauq-e-sajda cheh masjid cheh buthkada
Dar ishq neest kufr z'imaan shanaqtan.
When passion moves you to prostrate yourself
What matters a mosque or a temple?
Love does not distinguish
Between faith and infidelity.

What I Learnt

There is a legend that when Adam left Paradise he carried the Black Stone with him and this stone travelled all the way from Sri Lanka, via south India, to Mecca where it is fixed in a corner of the most sacred Muslim mosque, the Kaaba. Every Muslim who goes to Mecca on pilgrimage considers it a great blessing if he manages to kiss the Black Stone. There is also a tradition, not counted as very authentic, that the Prophet once said, 'I feel a divine breeze from India.' Allama Iqbal refers to this in his patriotic poem on India:

Wahdat ki lay suni thhi duniya ne jis makan se
Mir-e Arab ko aayi thhandi hawa jahan se
Mera watan wahi hai, mera watan wahi hai
The world had heard the song of Unity from this place; The Leader of Arabia had felt a cool breeze from this place. That is my native land! That is my native land.

The first encounter of Muslims with the religions of India on the soil of north India was in 711 CE when Muhammad bin Qasim was sent by the Omayyad governor of Iraq to teach a lesson to Raja Dahir of Sindh, who was reported to be harbouring some Medh pirates. These pirates were given to attacking pilgrim ships going to Arabia and making slaves of Muslim women and children. Muhammad bin Qasim ended up by capturing Sindh. That was the first time an invading Muslim army encountered Hindus on

Indian soil. Muhammad bin Qasim consulted the ulema about the treatment to be given to Hindus. He was clearly aware that the Christians and Jews were to be taxed with jizya, the poll tax levied from the People of the Book in lieu of military service and zakat levied from Muslims. But he did not know where to place the Hindus in the political spectrum. After some internal discussions, the ulema recommended that Hindus be treated as the People of the Book for '*ma al budd illa kakanais al nasara, wal yahud wa buyut niran al majus* (the temple is similar to the Church of the Christian, the Synagogue of the Jews and the Agiari of the Zoroastrians).' As all three traditionally accepted People of the Book were treated alike, the Hindus were also classified as People of the Book. Muhammad bin Qasim exempted the local Brahmins and temple priests from this poll tax and confirmed the existing Hindu nobility in their positions.

After the conquest of Sindh by Muhammad bin Qasim in 711 CE, the province came under the rule of the Abbassid Caliph Mansur (753–774 CE). It is reported that he received embassies from the Hindu chieftains, and among them were some Hindu scholars who brought with them two books, the *Siddhanta* of Brahmagupta and his *Khandakyaka*. These books of astronomy were translated into Arabic and proved to be influential in the development of Arab astronomy. In addition, numerous books on Indian medicine too were imported during the reign of al-Mansur.

The next Caliph to take an interest in India and Hindu philosophy and science was Harun al Rashid (786–808 CE). His prime minister, Yahya Barmaki (the name Barmak is said to be of Indian origin ['pramukh'], as Yahya's ancestors were said to be high priests of Naubehar—Nava Vihara in Afghanistan) is said to have sent Arab scholars to Sindh and also invited Indian scholars to Baghdad. During the Abbassid period and especially during the reign of Harun's son, al-Mamun (813–833 CE) many Sanskrit books on the subjects of medicine, pharmacology, mathematics, philosophy and astrology were translated into Arabic and enriched Arab thought. Many of these books were in the libraries of Khwarizm (modern Khiva in Uzbekistan), Ghazna and perhaps were read by the great scholar Al Beruni before he entered India.

The Persian geographer Ibn Khurdadbih (d. 894) included learned accounts of the Indian topography with occasional references to Indian religions. The early Arab accounts of India never employ any term equivalent to 'Hinduism' to describe the religions of India. The term 'Hindu' as the ancient Persian word 'river' (Sanskrit 'sindhu') applied above all to the greatest of the rivers then known to the ancients, namely, the Indus. The word India took its origin from 'the region where the Indus flowed'. In Arabic, the general term for the subcontinent is 'hind', another variation of the term 'sindhu', and Hindustan in Persian refers to the northern plains of India. It is only after the advent of Mahmud Ghaznavi and the Turkish invasion that the term Hindu emerged in Persian, first as an ethnic and later as a religious term.

***

Al Beruni was born in 973 CE in Khwarizm. Even in his early years Al Beruni distinguished himself in science, philosophy and religion. In 1017 CE, when Mahmud Ghaznavi conquered Khwarizm, Al Beruni was taken to Ghazna to become the Sultan's adviser. He entered India with Mahmud, but instead of participating in his raids, he preferred to study India, especially Indian philosophy, science and religion. Al Beruni refers in his writings to one al-Iranshahri who lived in the ninth century as the only writer to have aimed at objectivity in his account of the religious beliefs of the Indians. Unfortunately, the works of al-Iranshahri are lost. But another famous Ismaili scholar, Nasir-i-

Khusro, states that al-Razi, the polymath, took from al-Iranshahri, some of his views on matter, space and time. Al-Razi was an extremely bold scholar for his times and believed in striking an original path.

As Majid Fakhri writes in his *A History of Islamic Philosophy*, 'the most distinctive aspect of his view of man and the world is his belief in five eternal principles encompassing every aspect of the world, his conception of the atomic composition of bodies, and perhaps, for a Muslim his boldest view, belief in the transmigration of the Soul.' Fakhri believes that Razi was perhaps influenced by Indian philosophy in his views of matter and Soul.

Later Al Beruni wrote the now famous *Kitab al-Hind* which is perhaps the first critical study of India by a Muslim scholar. Al Beruni spent years studying Sanskrit with Indian pandits and mastered the religions, philosophical scientific and geographical literature of India. From his copious commentary, with long quotations from Indian classics, it is obvious that Al Beruni had made an in-depth study of the Hindu religion with the help of Sanskrit pandits, Kapila's Sāmkhya, Patanjali, the Bhagavad Gītā, Vishnu dharma, *Vishnu Purāna, Matsya Purāna, Āditya Purāna*, etc.

His knowledge of the Gītā appears to have been rather extensive.

Talking of the Hindus' belief about God, Al Beruni quotes from the conversation of Vasudeva (Krishna) and Arjuna:

I am the unwise, without a beginning by being born, or without an end by dying. I do not aim by whatever I do at any recompense . . . I have given to each one in my creation what is sufficient for him in all his functions. Therefore, whoever knows me in this capacity, and tries to become similar to me by keeping desire apart from his action, his fetters will be loosened and he will easily be saved and freed.

Describing the belief in reincarnation and the immortality of the soul, Al Beruni quotes Vasudeva's peroration at the very beginning of the Gītā:

> How can a man think of death and being killed who knows that the soul is eternal, not having been born and not perishing; that the soul is something stable and constant, that no sword can cut it, no fire burn it, no water extinguish it and no wind wither? The soul migrates from its body after it has become old, into another, a different one as the body when its dress has become old, is clad in another. What then is your sorrow about a soul which does not perish? Both life and death are not your concern. They are in the hands of God, from whom all things come and to whom they return.

The way Al Beruni quotes Krishna echoes the words of the Quran, 'inna lillahi wa inna ilaihi rajioon.'

Then again, perhaps expatiating on jnāna yoga, Al Beruni quotes the Gītā:

> Man is created for the purpose of knowing; and because knowing is always the same, man has been gifted with the same organs. If man were created for the purpose of *acting* his organs would be different in consequence of the difference of the *three primary forces*. However, bodily nature is bent upon *acting* on account of its essential opposition to *knowing*. Besides, it wishes to invest action with *pleasures* which in reality are pains . . . How is man to obtain liberation who disperses his heart and does not concentrate it alone upon God, and does not exclusively direct his action toward Him? . . . Pain and pleasure have no effect on the real world, just as the continuous flow of streams to the ocean does not

affect its water. How could anyone ascend this mountain pass save him who has conquered *cupidity* and *wrath* and rendered them inert?

Though Al Beruni claims to be quoting from the Gītā, it often appears that he is actually paraphrasing the various shlokas of the Gītā, and sometimes adding his own commentary thereon.

He quotes Vasudeva who spoke to Arjuna:

If you want the absolute good, take care of the nine doors of thy body, and know what is going in and out through them . . . Do not take perception of the senses for anything but the nature immanent in their organs, and therefore beware of following it.

The Gītā distributes the duties of worship among the body, the voice and the heart.

What the body has to do is fast, pray, fulfil the law, perform service towards the angels and the sages among the Brahmans, keep the body clean, stay aloof from killing under all circumstances and never look at another man's wife and other property.

What the voice has to do is recite the holy texts, praise God, always seek the truth, address people mildly, guide them, and order them to do good.

What the heart has to do is to have straight, honest intentions, avoid haughtiness, always be patient, keep the senses under control and have a cheerful mind.

Al Beruni's paraphrase of the Gītā may almost sound like a commentary on the Quran in the paragraphs quoted above. What he is attempting to do here, whether subconsciously or deliberately, is to bring the essence of the Gītā close to the essence of Islam.

Al Beruni distinguishes the Hinduism of the Brahmins of his day from popular Hinduism. While upholding the superiority of Islam, he concedes that the Brahmin belief was monotheistic, while popular belief tended towards idolatry. He maintains that the emergence of idolatry was based on the fact that the uneducated common people (*al-awaam*) tend to be impressed only by the concrete (*mahsoos*) and fail to appreciate the abstract (*maqool*). Many religious communities, such as the Jews, the Christians and the Manicheans, says Al Beruni, have therefore introduced pictorial representations (*tasweer*) into their places of worship. Similarly, the Hindu idols have been erected only for the benefit of the uneducated. He says:

> For those who march on the path of liberation, or those who study philosophy and theology, and who desire abstract truth which they call *sara*, are entirely free from worshipping anything but God alone, and would never dream of worshipping an image manufactured to represent Him.

At another place in *al-Hind*, Al Beruni further observes: The first cause of idolatry was the desire of commemorating the dead and consoling the living but on this basis it has developed and has finally become a tool and pernicious abuse.

Writings on Hindu Beliefs after Al Beruni

After Al Beruni, there is a long interregnum occupied by the reigns of the Slave Dynasty, the Khiljis and the Lodhis. The next scholar of note who wrote of the Hindu beliefs on monotheism is Amir Khusrau Dihlavi (1253–1325 CE). His famous *mathnawi* entitled *Nuh Sipihr* pays glowing tribute to India and to the intellectual achievements of its inhabitants. Amir Khusrau was the first to give literary expression to the belief that Adam first descended into India and in his seven poetical arguments demonstrated that India is indeed paradise on earth. Though the Hindu does not belong to the same religion as the Muslim, observes Amir Khusrau, he holds the same beliefs as Muslims on many points. He believes in the oneness, existence and eternity (of God), and in His power to create out of nothing (*qudrat-e ijad-e hama bade adam*). The Hindu believes in all this in contradiction to the followers of many other creeds who persist in false beliefs, like for example, those who believe in the eternity of the world (*dahriyya*), the dualists (*thanawiyya*), those who attribute to God, spirit and progeny and those who worship the stars.

Amir Khusrau's master, Nizamuddin Aulia, the famous saint of Delhi, got up one morning to offer his dawn prayers. He turned to the west, towards the Kaaba, and made his prostrations and then turned to see men standing on the banks of the Yamuna facing east and offering their prayers, the Surya namaskar with fervour equal to his own. Involuntarily, a couplet sprang to his lips and he exclaimed:

Har qaum raast raahe
Deene wa qibla gaahe
Every people is on the right path, in their faith and in the direction of their prayer.

Nizamuddin Aulia must have had in mind that he was only echoing the Quran: 'Everyone has a direction to which he turns; so excel one another in good works.'

Not until Akbar ascended the throne do we find any real Muslim interest in the Hindu religious books, especially the Ramayana, the Mahabharata, the Upanishads and the Gītā. Faizi (d. 1595), Akbar's court poet and a great scholar of Persian and Arabic, translated the Gītā into Persian verse. Instead of trying to find independent, non-connotational terminology, he has translated the Sanskrit Vedic vocabulary into Sufi mystic terminology. Faizi's brother, Abul Fazal (d. 1602) is credited with yet another Persian translation of the Gītā. Some modern scholars, especially among the orientalists, believe that this translation was actually done by Dara Shukoh (1615–1659), the great-grandson of Akbar, and not by Abul Fazal. This translation, unlike that of Faizi, is closer to the original and renders the Sanskrit terminology into simple non-technical Persian. The introduction claims that the translation was intended to educate the Muslim community concerning the wisdom and tradition on which Hinduism was based.

Dara Shukoh was not only a great Persian scholar, but had imbibed the tenets of Sufism and attempted to bring Islam and Hindu Upanishadic thought closer to each other. This is no wonder for his grandfather Emperor Jehangir was also keenly interested in the philosophy of Vedanta. A contemporary of Jehangir, the sanyasi Jadroop, had abandoned the world and lived in a cave in the mountains. Jehangir once went to meet him. His horse could not negotiate the steep climb. So Jahangir climbed three miles on foot to the cave. He writes about Jadroop in his *Tuzk Jehangiri*:

> He was well versed in Vedant, which is Sufism, and I spent six hours in his company, discussing the good subject and his discourse impressed my heart deeply.

Dara Shukoh translated the Upanishads in his *Sirr-I Akbar* (The Great Secret). In his *Majma al Bahrain* (Confluence of the Two Oceans), Dara attempted to bring Islamic Sufism and Hindu Vedanta together into a confluence of two oceans. In the introduction to *Sirr-I Akbar*, Dara refers to the Upanishads as 'without doubt the very first Celestial Book, the fountain of reality and the ocean of monotheism, being in complete accord with the Glorious Quran on which moreover it is a commentary.' For this belief, he paid with his life.

Three hundred years before Dara Shukoh, the famous mystic Mahmud Shabistari (1240–1350), could get away by declaiming in his *Gulshan-e-Raz*:

What are 'I' and 'You'
Just lattices
In the niches of a lamp
Through the one light radiates
'I' and 'You' are the veil
Between heaven and earth
Lift this veil and you will see
How all sects and religions are one.
Lift this veil and you will ask
When 'I' and 'You' do not exist
What is Mosque?
What is Synagogue?
What is Fire Temple?

The Upanishads have said:

Ekam sat, viprā bahudā vadanti
(Truth is only One, the Wise call it by many names).

'There is only one religion,' remarked Bernard Shaw in the preface to *Plays Pleasant*, 'though there are a hundred versions of it.'

Rumi tells the story that attending merely to names and outward forms rather than to the spirit and essence of religion, leads men into errors and delusions. Four persons, a Persian, an

Arab, a Turk and a Greek were travelling together, and received a present of a dirham. The Persian said he would buy 'angoor' with it, the Arab differed and wanted to buy 'inab', while the Turk proposed to buy 'uzum', and the Greek to buy 'staphyle'. Ignorant of each other's language, they did not realize that all the four words meant one and the same thing— grape. Subsequently, a violent quarrel arose between them. At last, a wise man, perhaps a Sufi who knew all their languages came up and explained that they were all wishing for the same thing.

Abdur Rahman Chishti, a contemporary of Dara Shukoh, set out to translate the Bhagavad Gītā (actually a commentary on the Gītā) under the title *Mirat al Haqaiq*. He claimed that his main aim for producing the *Haqaiq* was to do for the Gītā what Shaikh Sufi Qubjahani had done for *Yogavāsishta* in his *Kashf-al-Kunuz*. Earlier, Nizamuddin Panipati is reported to have translated the *Yogavāsishta* (*Jug Bashisht*, under the orders of Akbar, Jahangir and Dara Shukoh). In the introduction Abdur Rahman states that the Bhagavad Gītā is the book in which 'Krishna explained to Arjuna by analogy the secrets of tawhid.' Tawhid means the oneness of God, and in Sufi terminology it means the Unity of Being—*Wahdat al Wujud*.

Mazhar Jan-e Janaan was a famous Naqshbandi Sufi saint of the eighteenth century. He was also initiated into the Qadiri, Chishti and Suhrawardi orders, but he is considered to be a central figure in the late Naqshbandi Sufism in India. M. Mujeeb and Mushirul Haq both believe that Mazhar Jan-e Janaan attempts to bring the Indian Muslims and Hindus closer together ideologically. Mazhar regarded the Vedas as divinely inspired and the Hindus as monotheists. Like Dara Shukoh, Jan-e Janaan admits the antiquity and divine origin of the Vedas which, he says were revealed at the beginning of the creation of mankind. He believes that the sages (mujtahidan) of the Hindus derived from the Vedas the six systems (shish madhhab) of their philosophy. All their sects agree that God is one, hold that the world was created and will vanish and believe in resurrection and retribution. Their idolatry does not involve association (of partners with God). It is in a way similar to some dhikr ceremonies of the Sufis who meditate on the person of their pir (*Burat-e pir ra taswwar mi-kunand*) in order to obtain in this way spiritual benefit, but refrain from making idols of the pirs.

The Hindus make representations of certain angels, says Jan-e Janaan, of the spirits of perfect individuals and of persons who are, in their opinion, endowed with the gift of eternal life. They concentrate their thought on these representations and thereby create a link with the entities represented by them, and attain their material and spiritual needs. Jan-e Janaan further adds, they even prostrate themselves before them but this is a prostration of greeting (*sajda-e tahiyyat*) and not a prostration of worship (*sajda-e ubudiyyat*). By this prostration called *dand'vat*, they also greet their parents and spiritual leaders. All this bears no resemblance to the beliefs of the Arab infidels of *jahiliyya* who thought that the idols were independent agents, effective by themselves. According to their beliefs the idols are the gods of the earth, while Allah is the God of heaven. This is association of partners to God (*shirk*). The Quran has clearly affirmed that no community on earth was left without prophetic guidance. It is therefore certain, says Jan-e Janaan, that prophets were also sent to India. It accepts that prophethood was vested in certain persons who figure in ancient Indian traditions. In this trail of thought, he mentions Krishna and Rama 'whom the Hindus call avatar; in the language of Islamic tradition, this word may be translated as "messenger", "prophet" or "saint" (*bi zabaan-e shar' rasool, ya nabi ya wali tawan guft*)'.

While Jan-e Janaan as a true Muslim, and a revered Muslim Sufi saint, affirms and asserts the truth of Islam and the finality of prophethood in Prophet Muhammad, he frowns upon Muslims passing judgement on anyone, much less the Indian prophets.

This inclusivity of the interpretation of Mazhar Jan-e Janaan led to the spread of the Naqshbandi Sufi mysticism among Hindus and one of those influenced by his teachings, Rama Chandra, founded the order of Naqshbandiyya Ramchandriyya which today under the name of Naqshbandia Mujaddidia Mazharia Ramchandria continues to flourish all over India. The order has more than 1500 centres in India and hundreds of others in Europe, the USA and Canada.

Annemarie Schimmel, one of the foremost scholars of Islam, in her book *Islam in the Indian Subcontinent* refers to several stories that attempt to show that even during the lifetime of the Prophet, a south Indian king, influenced by the Prophet's miracle of the splitting of the moon, converted to Islam. Ibn Battuta's travels refer to this prevalent story and Tim McKintosh-Smith who followed in the footsteps of Ibn Battuta has even located the alleged tomb of the king on the coast of southern Arabia. There is also the popular legend of the Indian merchant Ratan Sen who is said to have served Prophet Muhammad at Medina, and being blessed with miraculous longevity continued to relate Hadith which he had personally heard from the Prophet, for the next six hundred years!

It is believed that India, more precisely Sri Lanka, known as Serendip in early Islamic literature, was the site of Adam's descent to earth after his expulsion from Paradise. Adam's Peak, the place where Adam is supposed to have done penance for 200 years after his expulsion from Paradise, became a place of pilgrimage for Muslims in Serendip (Sri Lanka) and remains so to this day. Pilgrims from other religions too pay homage to the massive footprints on the rock. They are variously ascribed to Adam, Shiva, Buddha, etc.

Azad Bilgrami, the famous Muslim scholar who studied the

Quran, its exegesis and the Prophet's Hadith extensively, both in India and in the holy cities of Mecca and Medina, wrote a book in Arabic, *Subhat al-marjan* (*The Coral Rosary*), which he completed in 1764. This book consists of four parts, dealing with references to India in the sayings of Prophet Muhammad, biographical notes on eminent Muslim scholars, Arabic and Sanskrit rhetoric and poetry in Hindu and Islamic literature. From the evidence collected by him from many sources, including al-Ghazali and Suyuti, Azad Bilgrami has concluded that India was the site of the first revelation, the first mosque on earth and the place from where the first Haj was performed. Azad also described India as the place where, in Sufi terms, the eternal light of Muhammad—*noor-e-Muhammadi*—first manifested in Adam. Arabia is the land where this light found its final physical expression in Muhammad, the Prophet. The Black Stone, which adorns the corner of Kaaba and is venerated by all pilgrims to this day, descended with Adam in India, the miraculous staff of Moses with which are performed many miracles including the cleaving of the Red Sea, grew from a myrtle that Adam planted on the peak in Serendip. While modern historical criticism dismisses these stories as legends, based on weak traditions, they are still remarkable in showing how India was placed as a sacred Islamic land in the geography of Islam. Here Azad, a scholar of Hadith, was only attempting to describe Hind—India—as a realm of vice-regency (*dar al khilafa*), since it was in India that Adam first exercised the authority that God gave mankind over the earth.

Unity of Mankind

Right from the beginning of revelation, the Quran has clearly, not once but in several chapters reiterated the oneness of creation, unity of mankind and non-discrimination.

The Quran says:

> O mankind, we created you all from a male and a female
> and made you into nations and tribes so that you may know
> each other. Verily, the noblest in the sight of God is the most
> God-fearing among you.[1]

With this single verse, the Quran affirms the creation of man
from a single parenthood, whether brown, black, yellow or white,
whether living in India, Africa, China, Europe or America. Of
course, geography and climate played a role in the racial and
physical distinction of one nation from the other, one tribe
and clan from another tribe and clan, and one individual from
another. The Quran also explains that this physical distinction
is meant only to enable mutual recognition, understanding and
appreciation—*la taarafu*.

The verb *taarafu* used in the verse has been inadequately
translated as 'know', due to the limitation of the English language.
The verb *arafa* in its various derivatives has occurred more than
seventy times in the Quran in senses ranging from 'knowing',
'comprehending', 'appreciating', 'recognizing', 'establishing
rapport', etc. So the separation of mankind into various nations
and tribes is to enable them to appreciate each other, to establish
mutual rapport and camaraderie. However, having said that,
the Quran, in the very next clause, clarifies that the noblest of
mankind is not one who is born white or black, Arab or non-Arab,
but one who is most God-fearing—one who is obedient to God
and His commandment and who observes the purpose for which
God has created distinct nations and tribes.

But how does mankind 'know' God himself and His
commandments? And what are those commandments that God
wants mankind to obey?

The Quran says that once all human beings were but a single community and then they differed among themselves.[2] So God sent his messengers among them announcing the glad tidings of His mercy and love and also warning them. He also sent down this law to them, His book of Truth, so that it might decide the disputes among men.[3] God raised a messenger in every community asking it to 'serve God and shun Evil' (*taghoot*). Some accepted the guidance and others fell into error.[4] Before the advent of Prophet Muhammad, God had sent many messengers. Some of them He has described (in the Quran) and some He has not.[5] And every such messenger that God has sent to the various people He sent him with a message comprehensible to them. As the Quran says, 'We sent not a messenger except in the language of his own people so as to make things clear to them.'[6] God's message to mankind was therefore revealed not in any one language, but in almost all languages of the recipient nations.

The message that was sent to all the various people of the world—to every country and to every clime and at all times and in all languages—bore the same purport: 'No apostle have we sent before you to whom we did not reveal. "Verily there is no God beside Me; therefore serve Me."'[7]

A Hadith of the Prophet says that altogether God sent one hundred and twenty-four thousand prophets to the world. Out of these, only about thirty are mentioned in the Quran by name. God Himself tells in the Quran that he has revealed the names of some of the messengers and not of others. The Hadith clearly corroborates the affirmation of the Quran that God has sent His messengers, from the beginning of humanity, to every people of the world. And since China, India, Africa and Asia have always been the most populous of the countries of the world from time immemorial, far more populous than Palestine and Arabia ever, obviously many thousand of prophets must have been sent to the people of these countries at different times in their history. Unfortunately, the passage of time, the neglect and recalcitrance of humanity and the short memory of man has not preserved for us the names and histories of these prophets. We can but reconstruct some of their teachings from the scanty and mutilated records that have come down to us preserved, in the form of hieroglyphic writings, ideographs, cuneiform stone inscriptions, broken frescoes, ceramic shards, clay tablets and palm leaves, and as also whatever authentic revelations are preserved in the various scriptures of the world.

The Quran exhorts all believers:

Say, we believe in Allah and in what has been revealed to us and what was revealed to Abraham, and Ishmael, Isaac, Jacob and the Tribes, and what is given to Moses and Jesus, and the Prophets from their Lord. We make no distinction between one and the other among them, and to Him we submit ourselves.[8]

In this remarkable passage God affirms the truth of all revelations, including those given to the tribes and prophets, both those named in the Quran and those sent in other times to other climes and countries, and exhorts the people of the Quran to believe in all of them. God also affirms that there is no distinction between one and the other. The Quran further recognizes that there are, among the People of the Book, and by extension among all those to whom prophets have been sent, people who believe in God, bow down to Him in humility, do not sell God's signs for a pittance; and God assures all of them with a due reward, for He settles accounts expeditiously.[9]

One recalls the *Yogavāsishta* in this regard. The sage wrote:

All the various views arising at different times and in different countries, however, lead to the same Supreme Truth and misunderstanding of the different views that cause their followers to quarrel with one another with bitter animosity. They consider their own particular dogmas to be the best, as every traveler may think, though wrongly, his own path to be the only or the best path.[10]

The Quran also denies the claim of exclusivity that the adherents of some religions have arrogated for themselves.

Says the Quran:

They say, 'None shall enter the Garden unless he be a Jew or a Christian.' These are their vain beliefs. They say, 'Bring your proof if you are speaking the truth.' *Whoever submits himself to God and does good, will find his reward with his Lord. No fear shall come upon him, nor shall he grieve.*[11]

So the basic requirement laid down for all people is belief in God and performance of good deeds to assure salvation.

The Quran reiterates:

And those who believe, and whether they are Jews or Christians or Sabaeans—all those who believe in God and in the Day of Judgment and do good deeds their reward is secure with their Lord—they need have no fear, nor grieve.'[12]

The Sabaeans were a sect of semi-Christians who included the stars in their worship. Some historians call them star worshippers!

***

'To you, your religion and to me, mine.'

So how does a Muslim deal with the presence of so much diversity of religious beliefs prevailing in the world? A true Muslim will fall back on the words of the Quran:

> To each among you we have prescribed a law and an open way. If Allah had so willed He would have made you a single people, but He tested you in what He has given you. So strive in all virtues. It is He that will show you the truth in what you differ.[13]

And addressing even the Prophet himself, the Quran says:

> And if the Lord had pleased, verily all who are in the land would have collectively believed. What! Will you compel men to become believers?[14]

The Quran advises us to avoid strident disputes:

> Argue not with the people of the book except in the fairest manner and say to them 'we believe in what was revealed to us and what was revealed to you. And your God and our God is one and we submit to Him.'[15]

But the duty is cast upon all of us to invite people to the way of our Lord—but with wisdom, goodly discourse and fair argument.[16] This again is echoed by Vasishta in his discourse:

> All that is expressed in sweet and graceful words, and with easily comprehensible argument, similes and illustrations goes direct to the heart (what the Quran has called *mow'izatul*

hasana, goodly discourse) of the listener, and expands there, just as a little drop of oil expands on the surface of the water . . . it is only through appropriate similes and illustrations that subtle themes which are worthy of being known, can be made popular as it has been done in all great works.[17]

The Quran is full of similes, metaphors, parables and stories of prophets, sages and wise people and attempts at every stage to— *wa jadalahum billati hiya ahsan*—discourse with them with fair arguments. And if all these fail, then one has to content oneself and say, *'To you, your religion and to me, mine.'*[18] There shall be freedom of conscience and there shall be no compulsion in religion—*la ikraaha fiddeen.*[19]

One is reminded of what a great scholar of Islam, Maulana Abul Kalam Azad, had to say on the diversity of religious beliefs:

If revelation directs all mankind to but one and the same truth, or the founders of different religions have preached but one and the same principle of life, how come differences which exist between religion and religion? And why is it that one and the same code of law, conduct and ceremonials and ritual is not prescribed by one and all? And why again is the form of worship observed in one religion different from that in another, and why the laws in one differ in style from those in another?[20]

Having asked this question, Azad proceeds to answer it himself:

The Quran points out that the teaching of a religion is two-fold. One constitutes its spirit; the other its outward manifestation. The former is primary in importance, the latter secondary. The first is called Din; the second Shar'a or Minhaj or nusk. Shar'a and Minhaj mean the outward form of observance; and nusk the manner or ceremonial of devotion. In practice, however shar'a has come to mean the law prescribed by religion and nusk merely the form of devotion or worship. The Quran states that the differences which exist between one religion and another are not differences in Din, the basic provision, but in the manner of giving effect to it, or in the shar'a or minhaj, not in the spirit of religion, but in its outward form.

That is why the Quran observes:

For every people we have prescribed a mode of worship (*mansak*) which they follow. Let them not dispute with you concerning this.[21]

This mansak or way or mode naturally differs from people to people, religion to religion.

So the Quran further observes:

Everyone has a direction to which he turns. So bring you all together wherever you might be; for He has power over everything.[22]

So, as God has warned, we need not dispute about the modes of worship and the direction of prayer. So says Maulana Azad.

We may recall the story of Moses and the shepherd. Moses had rebuked the shepherd for praying to God to come down so that he could wash his feet and comb his lice. 'Blasphemy!' Moses had cried, and the shepherd had been abashed. God rebuked Moses for interfering with the simple faith of the shepherd, and then, as Rumi continues:

Har kasi ra seerati binihadah am
Har kasi ra istilahi dadeh am
Hinduwan ra istilahe Hind madh
Sindhiyan ra istilahe Sindh madh
To each person have I allotted peculiar forms
To each have I given particular usages
What is praiseworthy in thee is blameable in him.
What is poison for thee is honey for him.
What is good in him is bad in thee
What is fair in him is repulsive in thee.
I am exempt from all purity and impurity,
I heed not the laziness and alacrity of my people
I created not men to gain a profit from them,
But to shower my beneficence upon them
In the men of Hind, the usages of Hind are
praiseworthy.
In the men of Sind, those of Sind.
I am not purified by their praises
It is they who become pure and shining thereby
I regard not the outside and the words
I regard the inside and the state of heart
I look at the heart if it be humble
Though the words may be reverse of humble
Because the heart is substance, and words accidents
Accidents are only a means, substance is the final
cause.
How long wilt thou dwell on words and
superficialities?
A burning heart is what I want, consort with
burning!

And to drive home the essence of religion, the Quran says:

Righteousness is not that you turn your faces towards the
East or the West; but righteousness is this, that one believes
in God, in the day of judgement, in the angels, in the books
and the Prophets, and for the love of God gives of his wealth
to his kindred and to orphans and to the needy and to the
way-farer, and to those who ask, and to effect the freedom
of the slave, and observes the prayer and pays the poor-tax,
and keeps faith where he makes a promise and endures with
fortitude poverty, distress and moments of peril – these are
they who are true in their faith and these are they who are
truly righteous.[23]

As Maulana Abul Kalam Azad observes:

The Quran therefore set before itself three distinct objectives
(1) It made faith and deed the sole means of salvation, (and
not affiliation to any particular group), (2) It emphasized
the fact that the religion revealed by God was but one for
all mankind, (and this religion was Islam – total surrender,
submission to God) and that therefore every deviation
from this was a clear aberration, and (3) It emphasized that
real religion was direct worship of but one God, without
any mediating agency, and that this was the teaching of all
Prophets, and that every belief and practice which conflicted
with it was therefore a deviation from it and a denial of
it . . . *Din* or the real religion was thus devotion to God
and righteous living, (that is Islam). It was not a name for
any group formation. Whatever the race or community or
country one belonged to, if only he believed in God and did
righteous deeds, he was a follower of the Din of God and
salvation was his reward.[24]

And where does the Bhagavad Gītā, the Song Celestial, fit into the teaching of the Quran which, as we have seen, repeatedly and consistently advocates inclusivity, pluralism, and universalism and which exhorts the believers to repose faith in the message given to mankind from time to time from Adam onwards?

Has the Bhagavad Gītā reached us in the pristine form and language in which Krishna delivered it to Arjuna on the battlefield of Kurukshetra? One wonders, as there were only the two of them in the chariot when the discourse took place. Were the passages which appear to support the caste system and Brahminism later interpolations by vested interests?

We must remember that the whole of the Bhagavad Gītā is, in its entirety, a report given to Dhritrashtra by Sanjaya who is watching the field of Kurukshetra from a distance with his spiritual eye, and listening to the dialogue between Krishna and Arjuna with his spiritual ear. What he is seeing and hearing with his all too human eyes and ears, even though endowed with special powers, he is conveying orally to Dhritrashtra, the blind listener. Sanjaya is neither a prophet nor a seer. He is merely the charioteer of Dhritrashtra also functioning as his minister. And this reportage of Sanjaya to Dhritrashtra was later reduced to writing at some indeterminate time. The authorship of the Gītā is attributed to Vyasa. But very little is known about Vyasa himself. The origin of the book is placed around 5 BCE to 300 BCE, although some scholars place it in 300 CE.

Be that as it may, scholarship around the world has been unanimous in praising this Song Celestial as one of the finest of religious texts, both in its language and in its content.

The description of God:

aham kratur aham yajñaḥ svadh ham aham auṣadham
mantro 'ham aham evājyam aham agnir aham hutam

pitāham asya jagato mātā dhātā pitāmahaḥ
vedyaṁ pavitram omākāra ṛk sāma yajur eva ca
gatir bhartā prabhuḥ sākṣī nivāsaḥ śaraṇaṁ suhṛt
prabhavaḥ pralayaḥ sthānaṁ nidhānaṁ bījam avyayam
tapāmy aham ahaṁ varṣaṁ nigṛhṇāmy utsṛjāmi ca
amṛtaṁ caiva mṛtyuś ca sad asac cāham arjuna[25]

I am the ritual and the worship, the medicine and the mantra, the butter burnt in the fire, and I am the flame that consumes it. I am the father of the universe, and its mother, essence and goal of all knowledge, the refiner, the sacred Om, and the threefold Vedas. I am the beginning and the end, origin and dissolution, refuge, home, true lover, womb and imperishable seed. I am the heat of the sun; I hold back the rain and release it. I am death and the deathless, and all that is or is not.

Such language evokes the passages in the Quran that describe God and the poetry of Rumi, Shabistari and the prose of Ibn al Arabi and Hallaj.

And describing God's mercy towards those who love Him, here is one of the most magnificent passages of the Gītā:

api cet su-durācāro bhajate māṁ ananya-bhāk
sādhur eva sa mantavyaḥ samyag vyavasito hi saḥ
kṣipraṁ bhavati dharmātmā śaśvac-chāntiṁ nigacchati
kaunteya pratijānīhi na me bhaktaḥ praṇaśyati
māṁ hi pārtha vyapāśritya ye 'pi syuḥ pāpa-yonayaḥ
striyo vaiśyās tathā śūdrās te 'pi yānti parāṁ gatim[26]

Even the heartless criminal if he loves me with all his heart, will certainly grow into sainthood as he moves towards me on his path. Quickly that man becomes pure, his heart finds eternal peace. Partha, no one who truly loves me will ever be lost. All those who love and trust me, even the lowest of the low—prostitutes, beggars, slaves—will attain the ultimate goal.

The enlightened Muslim scholars and saints from Al Beruni to Maulana Azad have given a broad perspective of religion. And the narrative of Azad Bilgrami, *The Coral Rosary*, gives us some idea of the place of India in the geography of Islam.

It is therefore in this overall backdrop of the Quran's inclusivity and the Gītā's spirituality that Muslims will find a place for Krishna and his celestial song in their consciousness.

My search through various religions showed me that there were a million ways to reach God, but the end of the journey was the same whichever road you took.

Notes

Introduction

[1] The relationship between India and Arabia pre-dates the Arab conquerors' arrival at Sindh. Even as early as the first century CE, six hundred years before the advent of Islam, the Indian Ocean trade had brought the Arabs and the Indians together. This has persisted through trade, religion and marriage especially in coastal India and especially in the western and the southern coasts. The communities and practices that rose from these contacts can still be found in these areas. Similarly, during the eighth century CE, the religious practices of Indians have been in circulation among the Arabs through an anonymous treatise that Ibn Nadim records in his bibliographical dictionary – one of the source books of early Islamic literature.

[2] Hans Kung, *Islam: Past, Present and Future*, translated by John Bowden, One World, 2004, 2007.

[3] Quran 2:115.

[4] Quran 17:110.

[5] Rig Veda 1:164:46.

Learning to Believe

[1] Gītā 3:21.

[2] Jalaluddin Rumi, *Mathnavi e Ma'navi*, Book VI, translated by R.A. Nicholson.

[3] Quran 42:13.

[4] Quran 60:18.

[5] *Yogavāsishta* is a text that explores questions on truth, purpose and reality. The dramatic situation contextualizing the discourse is that of Rāma in despair after protecting Viswāmitra's yajna against the asura attacks. He

raises questions of teleological angst. Sage Vasishta, his guru, answers to dissolve his despair. The answers compose the core of this text and hence an expository side text to Rāmayana.

The authorship or the scribing of *Yogavāsishta* is often attributed to Vālmiki.

[6] *Yogavāsishta* II 18: 2/3.

[7] *Yogavāsishta* VI b. 130.2.

Speaking to God

[1] *Mathnavi e Ma'navi* Book II, Story VII.

[2] *Mathnavi e Ma'navi* Book III.

[3] Adi Shankara or Śaṅkara Bhagavatpādācārya was a philosopher and saint professing advaita Vedānta. As the founder of Dashanāmi order of non-dualistic order, and Shanmata tradition of theology, his works have had profound impact in the Hindu schools of orthodoxy.

[4] Gītā 18:66.

[5] Rāmānujācārya was the founder of the Srivaishnava school of theology and a proponent of viśiṣṭādvaita—qualified non-dualism. He is known to have attempted democratizing the schools of orthodoxy that existed in south India during his period.

[6] Vallabhacarya (1479–1531) was the founder of the Pushti cult. He belonged to the Vishnuswami tradition of teachers and has been a major influence on the prevailing schools of non-dualist theology.

[7] Madhvācārya (1238–1317) was a saint proponent of Tattvavāda—the philosophy of reality. An important influence on the bhakti movement, he was the founder of the Dvaita or the dualist school of philosophy.

[8] Abdur Rahman ibn Abdur Rasul Abbassi Alawi Chishti, a Muslim mystic who lived in the seventeenth century and was a contemporary of Dara Shukoh, was a shaikh of the Sabiri branch of the Chishti Order. He became the head of the Order on the death of his brother Hamid in 1628 and is believed to have been a hundred years old when he died in 1683. He lies buried in Dhanithi, near Lucknow. He traced his spiritual lineage from Ghazi Miyan (1033), Abdul Qadir Gilani (1078–1166) and Bahauddin Naqshband (1318–89). He wrote a commentary on the Gītā in Persian—*Mirat al Haqaiq*—in which he interpreted the Gītā in terms of the monistic philosophy of Ibn al Arabi. Abdur Rahman was

well versed in all the classical texts of Sufism such as the *Bezels of Wisdom* of Ibn al Arabi, the *Revelations of the Hidden* of Hujwiri, the *Brilliant Flashes* of Iraqi and writings of Sijzi and Kubra. It is very likely that besides Hindawi, the local Indian dialect current at that time, he was familiar with Sanskrit. In his commentary on the Gītā, Abdur Rahman related the Vedas to the Quran, thereby lending Islamic authority to the Bhagavad Gītā and bringing it into the fold of the 'Celestial Books' and justifying, in the seventeenth century, its translation and study by Muslims.

[9] Gītā 18:61:

Sun Arjun, khuda hai, khuda har kaheen
Khudayee ke dil men khuda hai makeen
Woh sab hastiyon ko ghumaata rahe
Woh maya ka chakkar chalaata rahe.

[10] Ibn al Arabi was born in 1165 CE in Murcia in Spain, of Arab lineage. He became the spiritual apprentice of two great Sufis in his day, one of them a lady named Fathima. Of her he says, 'I served her for several years, she being ninety-five years of age . . . with my own hands I built a hut for her of reeds, as high as she was, in which she lived until she died. She used to say to me, "I am your spiritual mother and the light of your earthly mother."' Ibn al Arabi is rated as the most prolific writer of Sufi thought. Apart from his magnum opus, the *Meccan Illuminations*, and his equally famous *Bezels of Wisdom*, he is reported to have written over two hundred fifty books, most of them still in manuscript form and untranslated.

[11] Ibn al Arabi, *al-Futūḥāt al-Makkiah*, Ch. 48.

[12] Mihrab is a niche in the wall of a mosque or a room in the mosque that indicates the direction of Mecca.

[13] Quran 50:16.

[14] Quran 33:40.

[15] Quran 35:3.

[16] *Mathnavi e Ma'navi* Book II.

[17] Quran 2:164.

[18] Gītā 15:12:

Yeh suraj ki taabish mera noor hai
Jahaan jiske jalwon se mamoor hai
Rahe chaand rakshaan mere noor se
To aatish darakshaan mere noor se.
Jo har simt paata hai mera hi noor

Mujhi mein jo har shay ka dekhe zahoor
Kabhi mujh se munh mod saktaa nahin
Kabhi mein usey chhod sakta nahin

[19] Gītā 7:4:

Yeh miti yeh paani yeh aag aur hawa
Yeh aakash dunya peh chhaaya huwa
Yeh daanish yeh dil yeh khayaal-e khudi
Hai in aatth hisson mein fitrat meri.

[20] Gītā 10:20:

Sun Arjun mein hoon aatman bilyaqeen
Jo hai jaandaron ke dil mein makeen
Mein hun misl-e jaan ahle jaan me nihaan
Mein awwal mein aakhir mein hoon darmiyaan.

[21] Yasna 44, verses 3–5, 7.
[22] Quran 13:13.
[23] Quran 2:186.
[24] Gītā 4:6.
[25] Gītā 8:20.
[26] Gītā 13:12.
[27] Gītā 10:20.
[28] Gītā 9:18.
[29] Gītā 7:7.
[30] Gītā 8:20.
[31] Gītā 9:4.
[32] Gītā 7:8.
[33] Gītā 7:9.
[34] Gītā 7:11.
[35] Gītā 9:18.
[36] Gītā 9:19.
[37] Gītā 10:4–5.
[38] Gītā 10:20.
[39] Gītā 7:12.
[40] Gītā 9:11, 9:13.
[41] Gītā 9:14.
[42] Gītā 9:15.
[43] Quran 82:17–19.
[44] Quran 92:13.

[45] Quran 80:1.
[46] Quran 41:6.
[47] Quran 20:14.
[48] Quran 20:114, 18:44.
[49] Quran 73:9.
[50] Quran 112:1–4.
[51] Quran 20:111.
[52] Quran 2:255.
[53] Quran 31:30.
[54] Quran 76:30.
[55] Quran 24:35.
[56] Quran 85:8.
[57] Quran 25:59, 21:30, 7:54, 65:12.
[58] Quran 36:81.
[59] Quran 85:9.
[60] Quran 51:58.
[61] Quran 45:19.
[62] Quran 6:59.
[63] Quran 35:11.
[64] Quran 37:96.
[65] Quran 57:3.
[66] *The Confessions* of St Augustine.
[67] Blaise Pascal, *Pensees* (Thoughts).
[68] Gītā 12:1.
[69] Gītā 12:5.
[70] *Life of Khwaja Moinuddin Chishti Sanjari Ajmeri*, Jalal Lucknavi, Hasan Printing Press, Lucknow.
[71] Sharfuddin bin Yahya Maneri was born in the thirteenth century CE in Bihar and is well known in India by his nom de plume of Makhdum-ul-Mulk or simply as Makhdum Saheb. He is the best-known saint of Bihar. Early in his life, he went in search of a guide and even met the most famous Sufi of those times, viz., Nizamuddin Aulia. He ultimately found his guide in a little-known Sufi teacher, Najibuddin Firdausi. Sharfuddin Maneri spent the last forty years of his life in Bihar Sharif and is buried there. His mausoleum is the most frequented pilgrimage centre of eastern India.
[72] Sharfuddin bin Yahya Maneri, *Maktubat-e-Sadi* (*Hundred Letters*).

[73] Martin Lings (Trans. & comm.), 'Memories of Dr Marcel Carret', *A Sufi Saint of the Twentieth Century*.

[74] Quran 2:177.

[75] Hadith Qudsi 18.

[76] Gītā 17:20.

[77] Quran 9:60.

[78] Quran 13:22.

The Shell of Prayer

[1] *Mathnavi e Ma'navi* Book III, Story I.

[2] Gītā 5:10:
   Rahe be ta'alluq kare jab amal
   Khuda hi ki khaatir kare sab amal
   Khata se hamesha rahegaa bari
   Kanwal ke na patte pe tahre tari.

[3] Aurobindo Ghose, *The Message of Gita*.

[4] Quran 4:43.

[5] Imam al-Ghazali, *Ihya-ul-uloom-al-Din*.

[6] Jalaluddin Rumi, *Fihi ma Fihi*.

[7] Sahih Muslim.

[8] I called to mind what the poet Iqbal had written about such souls.
   Parindon ki dunya ka dervesh hun main
   Main shaheen banata nahin aashiyana
   I am the faqir of the avian world. I am a falcon (always in flight) who never builds a nest.

[9] Abdul Qadir al-Gilani, *Jala' al-Khawatir, The Removal of Cares*.

[10] Ibid.

[11] Gītā 7:25:
   Mein chasm-e jahaan se nihaan hoon nihaan
   Magar mujhko naadaan samajh le ayaan.

[12] Gītā 10:20.

[13] Gītā 10:34.

[14] Ibn al Arabi, *al-Futūḥāt al-Makkiah, The Meccan Illuminations*.

[15] *Javid Nama*, translated by A.J. Arberry.

[16] Gītā 11:8.

[17] Quran 7:143.

[18] C.W. Ernst (Trans.), *Rūzbihān Baqlī*.

[19] Nur ad-Din Abd ar-Rahman Jami, *Lawaih, Flashes of Light*.

[20] Quran 53:6–10.

[21] Quran 57:2.

[22] Gītā 11:31.

[23] Gītā 11:32.

A Glimpse of Eternity

[1] Quran 103:1–3.

[2] Quran 7:31.

[3] Abd al-Karim ibn Hawazin al-Qushayri, *Risala al-Qushayriya*, Epistle on Sufism.

[4] Quran 55:26–27.

[5] Gītā 8:20–21.

[6] Gītā 2:55:
  To bhagwaan bole jo ho mahv-e zaat
  Jo man se kar-e door sab khwahishaat
  Rah-e jis kaa dil rooh se mutmayin
  Usi fard ko qaim-al-aql gin.

[7] Gītā 2:56, 57, 58, 62.

[8] Gītā 2:63.

[9] Gītā 2:64:
  Jo insaan kare khwahishen dil se door
  Hawas ka na ho jiske dil me futoor
  Na usmein khudi ho na ho mer ter
  Sukoon usko haasil hai, dil uska ser

[10] Sri Ramakrishna, *The Gospel of Sri Ramakrishna*, Sri Ramakrishna Math, Chennai, 1942.

[11] Imam al-Ghazali, *Kimiya-e-Sa'adat, Alchemy of Happiness*.

[12] R.C. Zaehner, *Mysticism Sacred and Profane*, Oxford University Press, London, 1957.

[13] *Samyutta Nikaya*: V:421.

[14] *Digha Nikaya* 11:308.

[15] *Angutava Nikaya* 111:55.

[16] *Yogavāsishta and Its philosophy*, pp. 96 ff.

[17] Shaikh Fadhlalla Haeri, *Prophetic Traditions in Islam*, 1999.

[18] Quran 25:63.

[19] Gītā 13:8.

[20] Quran 20:81.

[21] M.K. Gandhi, *The Bhagavad Gītā*.

[22] Najmuddin Kubra, *al-Siyar al-Hayir, The Bewildered Traveller*.

[23] Isaiah 58:3–12.

[24] Jalaluddin Rumi, *Fihi ma Fihi*.

[25] Gītā 2:47:

Tujhe kaam karna hai o mard-e kaar
Naheen uske phal par tujhe ikhtiyaar
Kiye ja amal aur na dhoond uska phal
Amal kar amal kar na ho be amal.

[26] Marcus Aurelius, *Meditations*, Book VII (adapted and translated by George Long), Shambhala, Boston and London, 1993.

[27] Shaikh Mahmoud Shabistari, *Gulshan-e-Raz, The Secret Garden*.

[28] Chuang Tzu (or Zhuangzi), *The Zhuangzi*.

[29] Guru Tegh Bahadur, Adi Granth Sahib.

[30] Gītā 12:15:

Jo duniya ko aazaar deta naheen
Jo duniya se aazaar leta naheen
Bari bughz-o aish-o gham-o khauf se
Wahi hai mera bhakt pyara mujhe.

[31] *The Gospel of Sri Ramakrishna*.

[32] Gītā 3:8.

[33] Quran 4:77.

[34] Quran 3:104.

[35] Quran 2:217.

[36] Quran 6:59.

[37] Quran 2:255.

[38] Gītā 3:24.

[39] Gītā 3:26.

[40] Swami Vivekananda, *Karma Yoga*, Chapter VI.

Work Is Worship

[1] Gītā 3:21:

Koyee naamwar shaks karta hai kaam
To karte hain taqleed uski awaam
Bada aadmi jo banay-e usool
Wahi sari duniya karegi qubool.

2 Gītā 12:4.

3 Gītā 2:48.

4 Sri Ramakrishna, *The Gospel of Sri Ramakrishna.*

5 Gītā 2:50:

Lagi hai jis-e aql-e khaalis ki dhun
Yaheen chhod dega woh sab paap pun
Kama yog tan man mein bas jaaye yog
Amal mein hunar ho to kahlaaye yog.

6 There is an old Latin proverb 'Laborare est orare,' work is worship. And also there is the English adage 'Nothing is worth doing which is not worth doing well.'

7 Sufism which started as an individual effort to establish a link between Man and God over a period of time developed into a discipline. Every Sufi tried to establish his own pattern of excercises through dhikr, both individually and collectively, through meditation, prayers and later even through breath control and other yogic excersices. In the second stage of development Sufism got established in schools following a founder, either during his own lifetime or after his death. Such schools of Sufism followed the disciplinary guidelines taught by the founder-teacher and were generally known eponymously after the name of the founder. Hence orders like Qadariyaa, Chistiyyaa, Kubraviyya, Rifaiyya and so on. Some of these schools believed that the first stage of Sufism starts with the Shariah namely the orthodox beliefs and practices of Islam. For instance, only after establishing oneself in the discipline of Shariah was the devotee permitted to go to the next stage. These schools did not permit their devotees to give up or to deviate from the orthodox practices such as regular prayers five times a day, fasting both during the month of Ramadan as well as supererogatory fast, paying the charity tax (zakat) and going on pilgrimage to Mecca. However, along with these requirements of the Shariah, they were expected to follow the measures of austerity—dhikr—meditations and so on prescribed by the school the devotee belonged. These schools were known as the sober schools of Sufism.

There were yet other groups of Sufi schools which believed that having established direct relationship with God, it was not necessary to strictly adhere to the requirements of the Shariah. Some of them, while following the Shariah, practised rituals frowned upon by the jurists and the orthodox ulema. Devotees of this school indulged in dancing, music and sometimes even smoking opium and hasheesh to detach themselves from their surroundings, to establish direct linkage with God. Some even went to extremes and practised self-mortification, self-flagellations, using knives and pins to poke into their throat and eyes, eat live snakes and sometimes even to go naked publicly. These were known as the ecstatic schools of Sufism.

8 Gītā 16:12.

9 Gītā 16:13, 14, 15:
Woh kahta hai aaj aik paayee muraad
To kal doosri haath aayee muraad
Yeh daulat meri hai yeh dhan hai mera
Mere paas hi yeh rahenge sada.

Kiya aik dushman ko mein-e halaak
Karoonga mein auron ko ab zer-e khaak
Mein dhanwaan, mera gharaana shareef
Bhala kaun hota hai mera hareef

10 Gītā 16:16:
Khayaalon ke phandon mein jakde huwe
Tawahhum ke jaalon mein pakde huwe
Jo karte hain yag bhi to bahr-e namood
Naheen paa-e band-e rusoom-o quyood.

11 Gītā 16:4.

12 Farid al-Din Attar was a thirteenth-century Persian poet, born in Nishapur, Iran, who was one of the greatest Muslim mystics. He is known to have composed around 45,000 distichs or couplets and numerous brilliant prose works.

13 Shaikh Abu Bakr Shibli (861–946) was an important Sufi of Persian descent. Initally a high official of Baghdad, he later pursued spirituality as a a disciple of Junayd Baghdadi. Persian poets Attar, Rumi and Sanai mention him. He was also associated with Hallaj.

14 Farid al-Din Attar, *Tadhkirat al-Auliya'*, Memorial of the Saints.

15 Gītā 12:13.

[16] Thiruvalluvar, *Thirukkural*, translated by C. Rajagopalachari, Bhavans Book University.

[17] Gītā 3:6.

[18] Gītā 9:12.

[19] Gītā 16:7–8.

[20] Gītā 16:10,11,12.

[21] Gītā 16:14,15,16.

[22] Imam An-Nawawi, Ahadith Qudsi, edited by A.K. Kazi and Alan Day.

[23] Quran 4:61.

[24] Quran 4:140.

[25] Quran 8:49.

[26] Quran 9:67.

[27] Quran 33:60.

[28] Quran 63:4.

[29] Quran 102:1.

[30] Gītā 16:23–24.

[31] Gītā 6:16.

[32] Quran 31:19.

[33] Corinthians 10:51.

[34] Gītā 6:34–35.

[35] Gītā 16:8.

[36] Gītā 5:24.

[37] Quran 93:11.

[38] Gītā 6:5:
Munaasib naheen khud ko insaan giraaye
Woh khud ko ubhaar-e, woh khud ko uthaaye
Ki insaan khud apna hi ghamkhwaar hai
Woh khud apna badkhwaah-o ghaddaar hai

[39] Jalaluddin Rumi, *Mathnavi*.

[40] Gītā 6:6.

[41] Gītā 6:6, 7, 8, 9.

[42] Jalaluddin Rumi, *Diwan-i-Shams*.

[43] Gītā 14:13:
Tamogun jab insaan mein ho zor par
To ho moh ghaalib Kuru ke pisar
Andhera tabiyat pe chaa jayegaa
Jumood usko ghaafil bana jaayega.

    Tamogun se dhoka bhi ghaflat bhi ho
    Tabiyat pe ghaalib jahaalat bhi ho.

44 Gītā 6:34:
    Man insaan kaa chanchal hai aur beqaraar
    Rahe dodta bhaagta baar baar.

45 Gītā 16:21–22.

46 Quran 12:53.

47 Quran 79:40.

48 Quran 18:27.

49 Gītā 5:23:
    Na chhoda abhi jis ne tan ka qafas
    Magar kar liye zer taysh-o hawas
    Aseer-e badan rahki aazaad hai
    To insaan woh yogi hai, dil shaad hai.

50 Quran 18:28.

51 Gītā 14:17,18.

52 Gītā 6:18:
    agar usk-e qabu mein daim ho man
    faqat aātma hi mein qaim ho man
    rahe lazzat-e nafs se door door
    woh sarshaar hai yog mein bilzaroor.

53 As quoted in Frithjof Schuon's *Christianity/Islam*.

54 Imam al-Ghazali, *Ihya ul-uloom, Revival of Learning*.

55 Gītā 6:40.

56 Gītā 5:23:
    Woh yogi rahe jis ke man mein suroor
    Musarrat ho dil mein to seen-e mein noor
    Samaj lijiye haqse waasil us-e
    To ho brahma-nirvaan haasil us-e.

57 Shaikh Mahmoud Shabistari, *Gulshan-e-Raz*.

58 Gītā 6:30:
    Agar yog mein nafs sarshaar hai
    To phir yeh haqiqat namoodar hai
    Ki har shay mein hai aatman ki namood
    Ki har shay ka hai aatman mein wajood
    Jo har simt paata hai mera hi noor
    Mujhi mein jo har shay kaa dekhe zahoor

Prayer, Faith and Surrender

[1] Gītā 6:31:
Woh yogi rah-e go kisi dhang mein
Mujhi se ho wasil woh har rang mein.

[2] Quran 4:1.

[3] Quran 49:13.

[4] Quran 88:17–20.

[5] Gītā 6:30:
Jo har simt paata hai mera hi noor
Mujhi mein jo har shay ka dekh-e zahoor
Kabhi mujh se munh mod sakta naheen
Kabhi main us-e chod sakta naheen

[6] Shaikh Mahmoud Shabistari, *Gulshan-e-Raz*.

[7] Gītā 18:66:
Tu sab dharm chhod aur le meri rah
Tu maang aake daaman mein mere panaah
Tere paap sab door kardoonga mein
Na ghamgeen ho, masroor kardoonga mein.

[8] Gītā 9:29.

[9] Gītā 9:30.

[10] Gītā 18:67:
Yeh raaz us-se mat kah, jo zaahid na ho
Yeh raaz us-se mat kah, jo aabid na ho
Na us-se jo ho bad zabaan nukta cheen
Na us-se jo sunn-e ka khwahaan naheen.

[11] Gītā 3:26:
Agar moorakhon mein amal ka ho josh
Muzabzab na unko karen ahl-e hosh
Karen yog mein rakh ke khud karobaar
Yunhi unko rakkhen woh masroof-e kaar.

[12] Abul Kalam Azad, *Nasr-e-Abul Kalam Azad*, Haryana Urdu Academy.

The Secret of Unity

[1] Gītā 9:13, 14.

[2] Gītā 10:8, 9.

[3] Gītā 12:8.
[4] Gītā 17:1.
[5] Gītā 16:24.
[6] Gītā 17:28
[7] Nurcholish Madjid, *Worship as an Institution of Faith*, University of California Press, Berkeley, 2008.
[8] Quran 96:19.
[9] Frithjof Schuon, *Understanding Islam*.
[10] Gītā 9:27.
[11] Gītā 9:28.
[12] *Yogavāsishta* VI b 199:30.
[13] *Yogavāsishta* VI b 174:24.
[14] *Yogavāsishta* V 13:8.
[15] *Yogavāsishta* III 7:17.
[16] Farid al-Din Attar, *Tadhkirat al-Auliya'*, Memorial of the Saints.

The Madness of Love

[1] David R. Kinsley, *The Divine Player*, Motilal Banarasidas, 1979.
[2] A.L. Basham, *The Wonder That Was India*, Picador, 1967.
[3] A.K. Ramanujan, *Speaking of Siva*, Penguin Books India, 1973.
[4] Jayadeva is a twelfth-century Sanskrit poet born in Khurda district of present Orissa. His work *Geeta Govinda* is considered a key work in the tradition of Krishna Bhakti. It is written in the form of Ashtapadi or eight couplets. Their manner of rendition, especially in music and dance, has been highly influential in structuring many of the later classical art forms of India.
[5] Vishnu Puri is a mystic who is known to have lived either during the fifteenth or sixteenth century CE. The exact dates are unknown. He is often known to be Krishna Chaitanya's contemporary and to have composed *Bhakti-ratnavali* on his incitation.
[6] Margaret Smith, *Rābi'a the Mystic*, Cambridge University Press, 1996.
[7] Johann Christoph Burgel, *Rumi: Past and Present, East and West: The life, Teaching and Poetry of Jalâl al-Din Rumi*.
[8] Annemarie Schimmel, *Mystical Dimensions of Islam*.
[9] Baha al-Din Muhammad-i Walad, *Walad-nama*.
[10] David R. Kinsley, *The Divine Player*, Motilal Banarasidas, 1979.

[11] Ibid.

[12] Ibid.

[13] Richard Dawkins, *The God Delusion*, Bantam Press.

[14] Stephen Hawking, *The Grand Design*, Bantam Press.

[15] Proverbs 8:3.

[16] In this context, Rumi sings:

What is to be done, O Muslims, for I do not recognize myself,
I am neither a Christian, nor a Jew, nor a Zoroastrian nor a Muslim,
I am not of the East, nor of the West, nor of land, nor of sea;
I am not from nature's mine, nor from the circling Heavens.
I am not from India, nor of China, nor of Bulgaria nor of Saqsin;
I am not from Iraq, nor am I from Khorasan.
My place is Placeless, my trace is Traceless;
Am neither body, nor soul, for I belong to my Beloved's soul.
I have rejected duality, I have seen the two worlds as one.
I seek the One, I know the One, I see the One, I call the One.

[17] Gītā 4:35.

[18] Rabindranath Tagore (Trans.), *One Hundred Poems of Kabir*.

[19] Ibid.

[20] Gītā 4:11:

Mere paas jis raah se log aayen
Mein razi hoon Arjun muraad apni paayen
Udhar se chalen ya idhar se chalen
Mere sab hain raste jidhar se chalen.

What I Learnt

[1] Quran 49:13.

[2] Quran 10:19.

[3] Quran 2:213.

[4] Quran 16:36.

[5] Quran 40:78.

[6] Quran 14:4.

[7] Quran 21:25.

[8] Quran 3:84.

[9] Quran 3:199.

[10] *Yogavāsishta* III 96:51–53.

[11] Quran 2:111, 112.
[12] Quran 2:62.
[13] Quran 2:48.
[14] Quran 10:99.
[15] Quran 29:46.
[16] Quran 16:125.
[17] *Yogavāsishta* III 84:45–47.
[18] Quran 109:6.
[19] Quran 2:256.
[20] Abul Kalam Azad, *Nasr-e-Abul Kalam Azad*, Haryana Urdu Academy.
[21] Quran 22:67.
[22] Quran 2:148.
[23] Quran 2:177.
[24] Ibid.
[25] Gītā 9:16, 17, 18, 19.
[26] Gītā 9:30, 31, 32.

Bibliography

Abidi, Syed Taqi. (N.d.). *Kulliyat-e Ghalib (Farsi)*. New Delhi: Ghalib Institute.

Addas, C. (1993). *Quest for the Red Sulphur: The Life of Ibn Arabī*. (P. Kingsley, Trans.). Cambridge: The Islamic Texts Society.

Ahmed, H. (1975). *Srimad Bhagavath Gita*. Delhi: National Book Trust.

Ali, Mrs Meer Hassan. (1832). *Observations on the Mussalmauns of India* (Vols. 1–2). London: Parbury Allen and Co.

Ali, S.A. (1961). *A Short History of the Saracens*. London: Macmillan.

Andrews, C.F. (N.d.). 'A Pilgrim's Progress'. In Vergilius Ferm (Ed.), *Religion in Transition*. London: George Allen and Unwin.

Arabi, Muhyiddin Ibn. (1939). *al-Futūḥāt al-Makkiah*. Cairo.

Arabi, Muhyiddin Ibn. (1946). *Fusus al-Hikam*. Cairo.

Arabi, Muhyiddin Ibn. (1971). *Sufis of Andalusia: The Ruh al-quds nad al-durrat al-fakhirah*. (R.W.J. Austin, Trans.). London and New York: Routledge.

Arabi, Muhyiddin Ibn. (1980). *Bezels of Wisdom*. London: Paulist Press.

Arberry, A.J. (1935). *The Doctrine of the Sufis*. Cambridge: Cambridge University Press.

Arberry, A.J. (1942). *An Introduction to the History of Sufism*. London: Orient Longman.

Arberry, A.J. (1950). *Sufism: An Account of the Mystics of Islam*. USA: Dover Publications.

Arberry, A.J. (1958). *Classical Persian Literature*. Surrey: Curzon Press.

Arberry, A.J. (1963). *More Tales from the Mathnawi*. London: George Allen and Unwin.

Arberry, A.J. (1968). *A Sufi Martyr* (*A Translation of 'Aynu'l-Qudat's Apology*). London: George Allen and Unwin.

Arberry, A.J. (1968). *Mystical Poems of Rumi*. Chicago: University of Chicago Press.

Armstrong, K. (1992). *Muhammad: A Biography of the Prophet*. New York: HarperCollins.

Armstrong, K. (2007). *The Bible: A Biography*. Great Britan: Atlantic Books.

Armstrong, K. (2007). *Islam: A Short History*. New York: Random House.

Armstrong, K. (2011). *History of God*. New York: Random House.

Arnold, Edwin. (1879). *The Light of Asia*. London.

Asad, Muhammad (Trans.). (1980). *The Message of the Quran*. Gibraltar: Dar al-Andalus.

Assissi, St Francis. (N.d.). *Laudes*. In Lorna de' Lucchi (Trans. & Ed.), *An Anthology of Italian Poems: 13th-19th Century* (pp. 2–3, 347). New York: Alfred A. Knopf.

Attar, Farid al-Din. (1959). *Tadhkirat al-Auliya'*. R.A. Nicholson (Ed.). London: Luzac and Co.

Attar, Farid al-Din. (1964). *Muslim Saints and Mystics: Episodes from the Tadhkirat al-Auliya'*. (A.J. Arberry, Trans.). London: Penguin.

Attar, Farid al-Din. (1971.). *The Conference of the Birds*. (C.S. Noth, Trans.). Berkeley: University of California Press.

Augustine, St. (1952). *The City of God*. (G.G. Walsh, Trans.). N.p.: Catholic University Press of America.

Augustine, St. (1958). *Confessions*. New York: Pocket Books Inc.

Aurelius, M. (1969). *Meditations*. London: Penguin.

Azad, Maulana. (1937). *Tarjumanul Quran*. N.p.

Bacon, F. (1986). *The Essays*. London: Penguin.

Barnett, L.D. (1973). *Brahma-Knowledge, Philosophy of Vedanta*. New York: Gordon Press Publishers.

Bayan-ul-Quran. (N.d.). (A.A. Thanvi, Trans.). Karachi.

Beruni, al-. (1887). *Kitab al-Hind*. Eduard Sachau (Ed.). London: Kegan Paul, Trench Trubner & Co.Ltd.

Browne, E.G. (1928). *A Literary History of Persia* (Vols. 1–4). Cambridge: Cambridge University Press.

Browne, L. (1945). *The Wisom of Israel*. New York: Random House.

Buitenen, J.A. (1980). *The Mahabharata*. Chicago: University of Chicago Press.

Bukhari, al-. (1862–1908). *Kitab gami 'as-sahih* (Vols. 1–4). L. Krehl and W. Juynboll (Eds.). Leiden: BRILL.

Chidbhavananda. (1992). *Bhagavad Gita*. Tiruchirappalli: Ramakrishna Tapovanam.

Chinmayananda, Swami. (1989). *Bhagavat Gita*. Mumbai: Chinmaya Publications.

Chinmayananda, Swami. (2006). *The Upanishads*. Mumbai: Chinmaya Publications.

Chittick, W.C. (1989). *The Sufi Path of Knowledge: Ibn al-Arabi's Metaphysics of Imagination*. New York: State University of New York Press.

Confucius. (1910). *Analects*. (W. Soothill, Trans.). Yokohama: Fukuin Printing Co.

Cook, M.A. (1981). *Early Muslim Dogma*. Cambridge: Cambridge University Press.

Cragg, K. (1973). *The Mind of the Quran: Chapters in Reflection*. London: George Allen and Unwin.

Cragg, K. (1994). *The Event of the Qur'ān: Islam in Its Scripture*. Oxford: One World Publications.

Cragg, K. (2000). *The Call of the Minaret*. Oxford: One World Publications.

Daftary, F. (1990). *The Ismailis: Their History and Doctrines*. Cambridge: Cambridge University Press.

Dara Shukoh. (1929). *Majma-ul-bahrain Or The Mingling of the Two Oceans*. Kolkata: The Asiatic Society.

Dara Shukoh. (1961). *Sirr-I Akbar*. Tara Chand and M. Jalali Na'ini (Ed.). Tehran: Taban.

Davies, J. (1897, 2003). *Hindu Philosophy: The Bhagavad Gita*. Delhi: Rupa.

Din-natha. (1928). *Sri-Krishnavatara-Lila*. Kolkata: Asiatic Society, Bengal.

Eaton, Richard M. (1972). *Sufis of Bijapur: Some Social Roles of Medieval Muslim Saints*. Paper read at the conference of South East Asian Studies, 29 March 1972. New York.

Encyclopædia of Islam (Vols. 1–12) (2nd ed.). (1960–2005). Leiden: E.J. Brill.

Ernst, C.W. (1996). *Rūzbihān Baqlī: Mysticism and the Rhetoric of Sainthood in Persian Sufism*. Richmond, Surrey: Routledge.

Ezekiel, I.A. (1966). *Sarmad*. N.p.: Radhasoami Satsang Beas, Punjab.

Fakhry, M. (2004). *A History of Islamic Philosophy*. New York: Columbia University Press.

Farquhar, J. (1920). *Outline of the Religious Literature of India*. Delhi: Motilal Banarasidas.

Flood, G.D. (1996). *An Introduction to Hinduism*. Cambridge: Cambridge University Press.

Gandhi, M.K. (1927). *The Story of My Experiments with Truth*. Ahmedabad: Navajivan Pub. House.

Gandhi, M.K. (1980). *The Bhagavadgita*. New Delhi: Orient Paperbacks.

Ghalib, Mirza Asadullah Khan. (1987). *Dewan* (Urdu). Lahore: Majlis-e-Tariqi-e-Adib.

Ghazali, Abu Hamid al-. (1893). *Jawahar-al-Quran*. Lebanon: Dar al-Fikr.

Ghazali, Abu Hamid al-. (1924). *Mishkat-al-Anwaar* (*The Niche for Light*). (W.H. Gairdner, Trans.). Kolkata: Royal Asiatic Society.

Ghazali, Abu Hamid al-. (1934). *Munqidh-min-al-dhalal* (*Awakening from Darkness*). J. Saliba and K. Ayyad (Eds.). Damascus.

Ghazali, Abu Hamid al-. (1957). *Ihya-ul-uloom-al-Din* (*Revival of Learning*) (Vols. 1–4). Egypt: Dar Ihya al-Kutub al-Arabiyah.

Ghazali, Abu Hamid al-. (1961). *Maqasid-al-Falasifa*. Dunya (Ed.). Cairo: Matba'at as-Sa'ada.

Ghazali, Abu Hamid al-. (1963). *Tihafat-al-Falasifa* (*Incoherence of Philosophy*). (S.A. Kamali, Trans.). Lahore: Kazi Publications.

Ghazali, Abu Hamid al-. (1964). *Nasihat al-muluk* (*Book of Counsel for Kings*). (R.R.C. Bagley, Trans.). Oxford: Oxford University Press.

Ghazali, Abu Hamid al-. (1971). *Al-Maqsad al-asna' fi sharh ma'ani asma Allah al-Husna*. Fadlou Shehadi (Ed.). Beirut: Dar al-Mashriq.

Ghazali, Abu Hamid al-. (1980). *Qistas-al-Mustaqim* (*The Just Balance*). (Richard McCarthy, Trans.). Boston: Twayne Publishers.

Ghazali, Abu Hamid al-. (N.d.). *Kimiya-e-Sa'adat* (*Alchemy of Happiness*). (Claud Field, Trans.). Delhi: Renaissance Publishing House.

Gibb, Hamilton A.R. (1949). *Mohammedanism: A Historical Survey*. New York: Oxford University Press.

Gilani, Abdul Qadir. (1958). *futuh al-ghayab*. Lahore: Sh. Muhammad Ashraf.

Gilani, Abdul Qadir. (1960). *Al-fath ar-rabbani*. Cairo: Mataba'al at-Manar.

Gilani, Abdul Qadir. (1988). *Ghuniyat-al-Talibin*. Baghdad: Dar Al-Hurya.

Gilani, Abdul Qadir. (1993). *Fath-ar-Rabbani, The Sublime Revelations*. (Muhtar Holland, Trans.). Houston: Al-Baz Pub. Inc.

Goldziher, I. (1966). *Muslim Studies* (Vols. 1–2). (S.M. Stern, Trans.). London: George Allen and Unwin.

Growse, F.S. (Trans.). (1978). *The Ramayana of Tulasidasa*. Delhi: Motilal Banarasidas.

Grunebaum, Gustave E. von. (1953). *Medieval Islam*. Chicago: University of Chicago Press.

Guillaume, Alfred. (1955). *The Life of Muhammad: A Translation of Ibn Ishaq's Sirat Rasul Alla*. Oxford: Oxford University Press.

Hafiz: Fifty Poems. (1970). (A.J. Arberry, Trans. & Ed.). London: Cambridge University Press.

Hafiz: The Mystic Poets. (2004). (Gertrude Bell, Trans.). Woodstock: SkyLight Paths Publishing.

Hanbal, Ahmad ibn. (2001). *Musnad*. Beirut: Mu'assasat ar-Risala.

Hasrat, Bikrama Jit. (1953). *Dara Shikuh: Life and Works*. Calcutta: Munshiram Manoharlal.

Helmut Gatje. (1996). *The Qur'an and Its Exegesis*. London: One World Publications.

Hodgson, Marshall G.S. (1961). *The Venture of Islam* (Vols. 1–3). Chicago: University of Chicago Press.

Hourani, Albert. (2009). *Arabic Thought in the Liberal Age*. Cambridge: Cambridge University Press.

Hujwiri, Ali ibn Uthman. (1911). *Kashf al-mahjub*. (R.A. Nicholson, Trans.). London: Gibb Memorial Trust.

Husaini, Saiyid Abdul Qadir. (1970). *The Pantheistic Monism of Ibn al-Arabi*. Lahore: Sh. Muhammad Ashraf.

Ikram, Shaikh Muhammed. (1969). *Rud-I Kauthar*. Lahore: Ferozsons.

Iqbal, Muhammed. (1908). *The Development of Metaphysics in Persia*. London: Luzac & Co.

Iqbal, Muhammed. (1915). *Asrar-e-Khudi (Secrets of the Self)*. (Reynold A. Johnson, Trans.). London: Macmillan.

Iqbal, Muhammed. (1930). *The Reconstruction of Religious Thought in Islam*. Delhi: Adam Publishers.

Iqbal, Muhammed. (1932). *Jāwidnāme*. Lahore: Iqbal Academy.

Iqbal, Muhammed. (1966). *Javed Nama*. (A.J. Arberry, Trans.). Lahore: Iqbal Academy Pakistan.

Iqbal, Muhammed. (N.d.). *Kulliyat* (Urdu). Lahore: Iqbal Academy.

Jami. (2010). *Flashes of Light: A Treatise on Sufism*. N.p.: Golden Elixir Press.

Jeffery, A. (1938). *The Foreign Vocabulary of the Quran*. Baroda: Oriental Institute.

Judge, William Q. (1946). *The Bhagavad Gita: The Book of Devotion.* California: The Theosophical Society.

Kabir. (1915). *One Hundred Poems of Kabir.* (R. Tagore, Trans.). Shantiniketan: Shantiniketan Press, Visva-bharati.

Kathir Ibn. (2003). *Tafsir.* Riyadh: Maktaba Dar-us-Salam.

Keddie, Nikki R. (Ed.). (1972). *Scholars, Saints and Sufis: Muslim Religious Institutions since 1500.* Berkeley: University of California Press.

Keith, A.B. (1993). *A History of Sanskrit Literature.* Delhi: Motilal Banarasidas.

Khan, Khaja. (1923). *Studies in Tasawwuf.* Madras: The Theosophical Publishing House.

Khusrau, A. (1966). *Mathnawi Nuh Sipahr.* Lahore: Ishrat Publishing House.

Kiernan, V. (1947). *Poems from Iqbal.* Bombay: Kutub Publishers.

Kocchar, R. (2000). *The Vedic People.* Hyderabad: Orient Longman.

Krishnananda, Swami. (1997). *The Philosophy of Religion.* Rishikesh: Divine Life Society.

Kubra, Najmuddin. (N.d.). *Risala fi fadilat as-asalat.* Istanbul: İstanbul Üniversitesi Kütüphanesi.

Lewis, F.D. (2000). *Rumi: Past and Present, East and West: The Life, Teaching and Poetry of Jalâl al-Din Rumi.* Oxford: One World Publications.

Lewisohn, L. (1999–2000). *The Heritage of Sufism* (Vols. 1–3). Oxford: One World Publications.

Lings, M. (1971). *A Sufi Saint of the Twentieth Century.* Berkeley: University of California Press.

Lings, M. (1994). *Muhammad: His Life Based on the Earliest Sources.* Lahore: Suhail Academy.

Madelung, W. (1998). *The Succession to Muhammad: A Study of the Early Caliphate.* Cambridge: Cambridge University Press.

Madhvacharya. (2008). *Bramha Yoga Bhagavad Gita.* New York: Michael Beloved.

Madjid, N. (N.d.). *Worship as an Institution of Faith.* Michigan: University of Michigan Press.

Malik, Hafeez (Ed.). (1971). *Muhammad Iqbal: Poet-Philosopher of Pakistan.* New York: Columbia University Press.

Maneri, Sharfuddin bin Yahya. (1980). *Maktubat-e-Sadi (The Hundred Letters).* (Paul Jackson, Trans.). London: Paulist Press.

Massignon, Louis. (1982). *The Passion of al-Hallaj* (Vols. 1–4). (H. Mason, Trans.). New Jersey: Princeton Review Press.

Maududi, M. (1972). *Tafhim al Quran* (Vols. 1–6). New Delhi: Markazi Maktaba Islami Publishers.

Miller, B.S. (1984). *Gītagovinda of Jayadeva: Love Song of the Dark Lord.* New Delhi: Motilal Banarasidas.

Mishkat al-Masabih. (1970). (J. Robson, Trans.). Lahore: S.M. Ashraf.

Mohammed, Khwaja D. (1930). *Dil Ki Gita.* Lahore.

Mujeeb, M. (1967). *The Indian Muslims.* London: George Allen and Unwin.

Müller, Max F. (1884). *The Upanishads.* New York: Dover.

Murthy, Chidananda. (N.d.). *Basavanna.* Delhi: National Book Trust.

Nasr, Seyyed H. (1921). *Studies in Islamic Mysticism.* Cambridge: Cambridge University Press.

Nasr, Seyyed H. (1923). *The Idea of Personality in Sufism.* Cambridge: Cambridge University Press.

Nasr, Seyyed H. (1931). *Tales of Mystic Meaning.* London: One World Publications.

Nasr, Seyyed H. (1950). *Rumi: Poet and Mystic.* London: One World Publications.

Nasr, Seyyed H. (1961). *Selected Poems from the 'Divan-i Shams-I Tabriz'.* Cambridge: Cambridge University Press.

Nasr, Seyyed H. (1962). *The Mystics of Islam.* (Originally published in 1914). Chester Springs, Pa; London: Routledge Kegan Paul.

Nasr, Seyyed H. (1966). *Ideals and Realities of Islam.* London: George Allen and Unwin.

Nicholson, R. (1914). *The Mystics of Islam.* London: Routledge Kegan Paul.

Nicholson, R. (1925–29). *Mathnavi of Jalaluddin Rumi* (Vols. 4–6). J.W. Gibb Memorial Series, London.

Nizami, Khaliq Ahmad. (1953). *Tarikh-e masha'ikh-i Chisht.* Delhi: Al Indiya Baz-i Hanafi.

Nomani, S. (N.d.). *al Ghazali.* Kanpur: Narai Press.

O'Flaherty, W.D. (1970). *Hindu Myths.* London: Penguin.

O'Flaherty, W.D. (1981). *The Rig Veda.* London: Penguin.

Odes: From the Divan of Hafiz. (1904). (Richard Le Gallienne, Trans.). London: Duckworth & Co.

Olivelle, Patrick. (1996). *Upanishads.* Oxford: Oxford University Press.

Padwick, C.E. (1961). *Muslim Devotions: A Study of Prayer-Manuals in Common Use*. London: SPCK.

Pagels, E.H. (1979). *The Gnostic Gospels*. New York: Random House.

Palmer, E.H. (Trans.). (1880). *The Quran*. In Max Müller (Ed.) (1898), *Sacred Books of the East* (Vol. 9). London: Routledge.

Panikkar, R. (1977). *The Vedic Experience: Mantramañajari*. New Delhi: Motilal Banarasidas.

Pascal, Blaise. (1995). *Pensées*. (A.J. Krailsheimer, Trans.). Harmondsworth: Penguin.

Pickthall, M.M. (1938). *The Meaning of the Glorious Koran*. Hyderabad-Deccan: Government Central Press.

Prabhupādā, A.C. (1972). *Bhagavad-gītā as It Is*. Bangalore: Bhaktivedanta Book Trust.

Prasad, R.C. (Trans.). (1990). *Tulasidasa's Shriramacharitamanasa*. Delhi: Motilal Banarasidas.

Quran: A New Translation. (2004). (A. Haleem, Trans.). London: Oxford University Press.

Qushayri, Abu'l-Qasim al-. (1912). *Ar-risala fi'ilm at-tasawwuf*. Cairo.

Radhakrishnan, S. (Ed.). (1953). *The Cultural Heritage of India* (Vols. 1–4). Calcutta: The Ramakrishna Mission.

Radhakrishnan, S. (1994). *The Bhagavadgita: With an Introductory Essay, Sanskrit Text, English Translation, and Notes*. New Delhi: HarperCollins.

Ragozin, Z.A. (1961). *Vedic India*. New Delhi: Munshi Ram Manohar Lal.

Rahman, F. (1982). *Islam & Modernity: Transformation of an Intellectual Tradition*. Chicago: University of Chicago Press.

Rahman, F. (1989). *Major Themes of the Qur'ān*. Minneapolis: Bibliotheca Islamica.

Rai, Lakhpat. (1978). *Sarmad – His Life & Rubais*. Gorakhpur: Hanumanprasad Poddar Smarak Samit.

Rajaram, M. (2009). *Thirukkural*. Chennai: Rupa.

Ramanujacharya. (1922). *Introduction to Bhagvad Gita*. Madras: Theosophical Publication House.

Ranganathananda, S. (N.d.). *Message of the Upanishads*. Mumbai: Bharatiya Vidya Bhavan.

Renard, J. (2008). *Friends of God: Islamic Images of Piety, Commitment, and Servanthood*. Berkeley: University of California Press.

Rippin, A. (1988). *Approaches to the History of the Interpretation of the Qur'ān*. Michigan: University of Michigan Press.

Rolland, R. (1965). *The Life of Vivekananda and the Universal Gospel*. Calcutta: Advaita Ashrama.

Rumi, Maulana Jalaluddin. (1925–29). *Mathnavi* (Vols. 1–3). (R. Nicholson, Trans.). J.W. Gibb Memorial Series, London.

Rumi, Maulana Jalaluddin. (1928). *Fihi ma fihi*. Abdul Majid Daryabadi (Ed.). Azamgarh.

Rypka, Jan. (1968). *History of Iranian Literature*. Doedrecht: Springer.

Sale, G. (1882). *A Comprehensive Commentary on the Quran*. London: Routledge.

Sanā'i, Abu'l- Majd Majdud. (1908, reprint 1971). *The First Book of the Hadiqatu'l-Haqiqat or the Enclosed Garden of the Truth of the Hakim Sana'i of Ghazana*. (Major J. Stephenson, Ed. & Trans.). New York: Macmillan.

Sands, K.Z. (2006). *Ṣūfī Commentaries on the Qurān in Classical Islam*. London: Routledge.

Śaṅkarācārya. (1901). *The Bhagavad Gita: With the Commentary of Sri Sankaracharya*. Alladi Mahadeva Shastri (Ed. & comm.). Mysore: GTA Printing Works.

Saraswati, M. (1962). *Śrimad Bhagavadgita*. Varanasi: Chowkhamba Sanskrit Series Office.

Sardar, Z. (2011). *Reading the Qur'an*. Oxford: Oxford University Press.

Sarrāj, Abu Nasar as-. (1914). *Kitāb al-luma 'fi't- tasawwuf*. R.A. Nicholson (Ed.). Gibb Memorial Series no. 22, London and Leiden.

Schimmel, A. (1963). *Gabriel's Wing: A Study into the Religious Ideas of Sir Muhammad Iqbal*. Leiden: BRILL.

Schimmel, A. (1975). *Mystical Dimensions of Islam*. Chapel Hill: University of North Carolina Press.

Schimmel, A. (1978). *The Triumphal Sun*. London: Fine Books Ltd.

Schimmel, A. (1980). *Islam in the Indian Subcontinent*. Leiden: BRILL.

Schuon, F. (2008). *Christianity/Islam: Perspectives on Esoteric Ecumenism*. Indiana: World Wisdom.

Schuon, F. (2011). *Understanding Islam: A New Translation with Selected Letters*. Indiana: World Wisdom.

Shabistari, Mahmud. (1880). *Gulshan-e-Raz: The Rose-Garden of Mysteries*. (E.H. Whinfield, Ed. & Trans.). London: Octagon Press.

Shah, A. (1980). *The Assemblies of al-Hariri (Retold)*. London: Octagon Press.

Shah, Bullhe. (1960). *Diwan*. Faqir M. Faqir (Ed.). Lahore.

Shaw, B. (1942). *Plays: Pleasant and Unpleasant*. New York: Dodd Mead & Co.

Sivananda, Swami. (1968). *Bhagavad Gita: Text and Commentary*. Uttaranchal: The Divine Life Society Press.

Smith, Margaret. (1928). *Rābi'a the Mystic and Her Fellow-Saints in Islam*. Cambridge: Cambridge University Press.

Smith, Margaret. (1935). *An Early Mystic of Baghdad*. London.

Sri Aurobindo. (1946). *The Message of Gita*. Anilbaran Roy (Ed.). London: George Allen and Unwin.

Stephen, D. (1918). *Early Indian Thought*. Cambridge: Cambridge University Press.

Subramaniam, V.K. (2005). *Mystic Songs of Meera*. New Delhi: Abhinav Publications.

Sunan al-Muslim. (N.d.). (S. Muslim, Trans.). N.p.

Sunan al-Tirmidhi. (1990). New Delhi: Kitab Bhavan.

Suyuti, Jalaluddin. (2007). *Tafsir al-Jalalayn*. (J.a.-D Maḥallī, Trans.). London: Dar Al taqwa.

Syed, A.A. (2003). *The Spirit of Islam*. London: Methuen.

Tabassum, Sufi Ghulam Mustafa. (1981). *Sharh Ghazliyat-e Ghalib (Farsi)* (Vols. 1–2). Lahore: Packages Ltd.

Tao Te Ching. (1954). London: John Murray Publishers Ltd.

The Bible. (1937). Cambridge: Cambridge University Press.

The Bible. (1984). USA: Watch Tower Bible and Tract Society.

The Bible. (N.d.). India: The Gideons International in India.

The Dhammapada and Sutta-Nipata. (1895–1910). (Max Müller and V. Fausboll, Trans.). London: Routledge.

The Noble Quran. (1992). (M.M. Khan, Trans.) Lahore: Kazi Publishers.

Tilak, B.G. (1915). *Srimad Bhagavadgita Rahasya Or Karma-Yoga-Sastra*. Bombay: Vaibhav Press.

Valmiki. (1959). *Ramayana of Valmiki* (Vols. 1–3). London: Shanti Sadan.

Valmiki. (1981). *Ramayana*. (Kamala Subramanian, Trans.). Mumbai: Bharatiya Vidya Bhavan.

Vivekananda, S. (1970). *Karma Yoga*. Belur: Advaita Ashrama.

Vyasa. (1965). *Mahabharatha*. (Kamala Subramanian, Trans.). Mumbai: Bharatiya Vidya Bhavan.

Vyasa. (1978). *The Mahabharata* (Vols. 1–3). (J.A.B. van Buitenen, Trans. & Ed.). Chicago: University Press of Chicago.

Walad, Baha al-Din. (1941). *Divan-I Sultan Veled*. F. Nafiz Uzluz (Ed.). Istanbul: Uzluk Basımevi.

Walad, Baha al-Din. (1959). *Ma'arif*. Tehran: Majlis.

Walker, B. (1968). *The Hindu World: An Encyclopedic Survey of Hinduism* (Vols. 1–4). New York: Praeger.

Ward, W. (1996). *History, Literature and Mythology of the Hindoos*. (Originally published in 1822). London: Motilal UK Books of India.

Watt, W. Montgomery. (1953). *The Faith and Practice of Al-Ghazali*. London: George Allen and Unwin.

Watt, W. Montgomery. (1963). *Muslim Intellectual: A Study of Al-Ghazali*. Edinburgh: University Press.

Wensinck, A.J. (1940). *La pensée de. Ghazzali*. Paris: Librairie D'Amerique Et D'Orient.

Whinfield, E.H. (Trans.). (1887). *'Mathnavi-I Ma'navi': Spiritual Couplets*. London: Octagon Press.

Wilkins, W.J. (1887). *Modern Hinduism*. London: Unwin.

Woodroffe, J.G. (1997). *Introduction to Tantra Shastra*. Madras: Ganesh & Co.

Woodroffe, J.G. (N.d.). *The Principal of Tantra*. Madras: Ganesh & Co.

Woodward, F. (Reprint 2002). *Some Sayings of the Buddha*. New Delhi: Asian Educational Services.

Zaehner, R.C. (1960). *Hindu and Muslim Mysticism*. Berlin: Schocken Books.

Zaehner, R.C. (1969). *Mysticism, Sacred and Profane*. Oxford: Oxford University Press.

Zarathustra. (1887). *Avesta: Yasna*. (Lawrence Heyworth Mills, Trans.). In Max Müller (Ed.) (1898), *Sacred Books of the East* (Vol. 31). London: Routledge.